# HANDS-ON DATABASE

## AN INTRODUCTION TO DATABASE DESIGN AND DEVELOPMENT

### Steve Conger
*Seattle Central Community College*

**Prentice Hall**

Boston   Columbus   Indianapolis   New York   San Francisco   Upper Saddle River
Amsterdam   Cape Town   Dubai   London   Madrid   Milan   Munich   Paris   Montreal   Toronto
Delhi   Mexico City   Sao Paulo   Sydney   Hong Kong   Seoul   Singapore   Taipei   Tokyo

**Editorial Director:** Sally Yagan
**Editor in Chief:** Eric Svendsen
**Executive Editor:** Bob Horan
**Product Development Manager:** Ashley Santora
**Editorial Project Manager:** Kelly Loftus
**Editorial Assistant:** Jason Calcaño
**Director of Marketing:** Patrice Lumumba Jones
**Senior Marketing Manager:** Anne Fahlgren
**Marketing Assistant:** Melinda Jensen
**Production Project Manager:** Renata Butera
**Creative Art Director:** Jayne Conte
**Cover Designer:** Suzanne Behnke
**Cover Art:** Kheng Guan Toh/Fotolia, Inc
**Media Editor:** Denise Vaughn
**Media Project Manager:** Lisa Rinaldi
**Full-Service Project Management:** Chitra Sundarajan/Integra Software Services Pvt. Ltd.
**Printer/Binder:** Edwards Brothers
**Cover Printer:** Lehigh-Phoenix Color/Hagerstown
**Text Font:** Palatino

Microsoft® and Windows® are registered trademarks of the Microsoft Corporation in the U.S.A. and other countries. Screen shots and icons reprinted with permission from the Microsoft Corporation. This book is not sponsored or endorsed by or affiliated with the Microsoft Corporation.

Many of the designations by manufacturers and seller to distinguish their products are claimed as trademarks. Where those designations appear in this book, and the publisher was aware of a trademark claim, the designations have been printed in initial caps or all caps.

**Library of Congress Cataloging-in-Publication Data**
Conger, Steve.
    Hands-on database : an introduction to database design and development / Steve Conger.
      p. cm.
    Includes index.
    ISBN-13: 978-0-13-610827-6 (alk. paper)
    ISBN-10: 0-13-610827-X (alk. paper)
    1. Database design.   I. Title.
    QA76.9.D26C644 2012
    005.74'3—dc22
                                                                    2010032774

10 9 8 7 6 5 4 3 2 1

**Prentice Hall**
is an imprint of

www.pearsonhighered.com

ISBN 10:    0-13-610827-X
ISBN 13: 978-0-13-610827-6

*To Maureen, Bryan, and Chelsea*

# BRIEF CONTENTS

# CONTENTS

# PREFACE

Many students taking an introductory database course need hands-on experience. Typically, they are under pressure to finish quickly with a certificate or degree and get to work. They need to get actual practice in the process of designing and developing databases that they can apply in their future employment. They need to create tables, enter data, and run SQL queries.

This book is designed for them.

*Hands-on Database: An Introduction to Database Design and Development* focuses on the process of creating a database. It guides the students through the initial conception of the database. It covers gathering of requirements and business rules, the logical and physical design, and the testing of the database. It does this through a continuous narrative that follows a student, Sharon, as she designs and constructs a database to track the tutoring program at her school. It shows some of her missteps as well as her successes. Students get hands-on experience by doing practices and developing scenarios that parallel the narrative.

After completing this book, students will have a good sense of what is involved in developing and creating a database. Following is a list of the book outcomes. A student who has completed this book will be able to

- give a general definition of a relational database
- identify a variety of ways to gather database requirements
- define business rules for a database
- create an entity design for a database
- normalize a design up to Third Normal Form
- develop a database in a given DBMS
- run SQL queries against sample data to test requirements and business rules
- define the general security context of a database and its users
- document the process of database design and development

## THE SCENARIO APPROACH

The scenario approach is at the heart of the book. It informs both the narrative and the exercises. A scenario in its essence is a story problem. It provides a context from which to work. It is much easier for a student to understand database design if he or she sees it as a solution to a particular set of problems. There is an emphasis on defining business rules and then testing the database design against those rules. The scenarios also provide a sense of process. They give the student some guidance in how to go about defining and developing a database. I would argue that even computer science students could benefit from this approach. It would allow them to experience how the concepts they have learned can be applied to the actual development process.

The scenario that makes up the body of the book describes Sharon, a database student, in the process of creating a database to manage the school's tutoring program. She encounters several problems. The way the tutoring sessions are scheduled is awkward and inefficient. The reports that the manager of the program needs to make are difficult and time consuming to put together. It is also difficult, at times, to track the tutors' hours. Sharon sees a database as a solution to these problems and sets about defining its requirements, designing it, and building a prototype. She enters some sample data and then tests the database using SQL to enter and retrieve the information required. Finally, she looks carefully at the security issues inherent in the database.

At the end of each chapter, after the practices, there are four additional scenarios for the student to develop. The **Wild Wood Apartments** scenario involves creating a database to manage a chain of apartment buildings. **Vince's Vintage Vinyl Record Shop** offers a scenario of a small shop owner who needs a database to handle his inventory, sales, and purchases. **Grandfield College** leads students through the process of making a database to track what software the school owns, the licensing for that software, on what machines the software is installed, and what users have access to those machines. The **WestLake Research Hospital** scenario involves creating a database to track a double-blind drug study for a new antidepressant.

The scenarios are meant to be complex enough to keep the student involved but simple enough not to overwhelm the novice. Each scenario presents different challenges. Students could work on some or all the scenarios, or they could be broken into groups with each group assigned one of the scenarios. The scenarios are open ended, that is, they offer room for student creativity and innovation. The students and the instructor are free to define many of the parameters and business rules as they proceed. But each scenario, in each chapter, has specific deliverables that help keep the students on track.

## OTHER FEATURES

### Process Driven

The book models the process of developing a database from the beginning through the final stages. It provides students with tools and techniques for discovering requirements and business rules. It also provides them with suggestions for organizing and managing all the complex details that go into developing a database. The book emphasizes the need to understand the data and the relationships among the data. It shows them the value of carefully designing a database before actually implementing it. Then when the database is first developed, it emphasizes the need to test it, to make sure it meets the requirements and business rules before deploying the database. Finally, it emphasizes the need to secure a database against both accidental and intentional threats.

### Normalization

Normalization is an important but complex issue in database development. Anyone who works with databases is expected to have some knowledge of normalization. For this reason, I believed it important to introduce the students to the concepts and vocabulary of normalization. But, because this is an introductory book focused on the process of development and design, I discussed only the first three normal forms. I have found that most databases that achieve at least the Third Normal Form are functional, if not optimal, in design. That being said, I do believe anyone working in databases should become familiar with all the normal forms and principles of normalizations. In the "Things to Look Up" segment of Chapter 4, I direct students to look up the other normal forms and pick one of them to explain to other students. Also, in Appendix D, "Common Relational Patterns," the last example shows an ERD of a database that has been normalized beyond Third Normal Form.

### SQL

Chapter 7 in *Hands-on Database* contains an extensive introduction to SQL. It covers SELECT statements, of course, using a variety of criteria, as well as using scalar functions, especially date and time functions, and various aggregate functions. Inner and outer joins are discussed. INSERT, UPDATE, and DELETE statements are introduced. The chapter also illustrates the use of Views and provides an example of a stored procedure and a trigger. Chapter 8 looks at stored procedures in terms of how they can be used to protect data integrity and security. SQL commands related to Logins and permissions are also introduced.

Perhaps more important than the specific SQL commands presented is the context in which they are introduced. In the text, Sharon uses SQL to test the requirements and business rules of the Tutor Management database. In the scenarios, students use SQL to test the requirements and business rules of the databases they have created. In Chapter 8, they see SQL as a tool for securing a database. By presenting it in this way, students see SQL as a vital part of database development and not just an academic exercise.

## Security

Security issues are discussed at several points in the book. It is brought into consideration during the information-gathering phases in Chapters 2 and 3. But it is dealt with in detail in Chapter 8.

Chapter 8 attempts to show the student a structured approach to security. It looks at each user of the database and creates a table that delineates exactly what permissions that user needs on each object in the database. It applies a similar technique for analyzing threats to the database. Then it introduces the concept of roles as collections of permission. It shows how a developer could create an application layer of views and procedures and then assign roles and permissions to those objects rather than to the underlying tables.

Finally, the chapter discusses the importance of disaster management and of creating a set of policies and procedures for recovering from any conceivable disaster.

## Software Used by the Book

The book uses Microsoft SQL Express 2008 R2 for the database and Microsoft Visio 2010 for the database diagramming. The SQL Express software is offered free from Microsoft. At the time of writing this Introduction, SQL Express is available at http://www.microsoft.com/express/Database/. This is, of course, subject to change. But one can always go to the Microsoft site and type SQL Server Express in the Bing search box. This will list the current download URL.

I selected SQL Server Express because it is readily available and because it provides a more realistic and complete database management system experience than Microsoft Access, which is often used in classroom settings. SQL Server Express lets the students experience managing multiple databases in a single management environment. The SQL Express Management Studio also contains a query analyzer that allows students to easily run SQL queries and view the results. Unlike Access, SQL Server Express supports stored procedures and triggers. Finally, again unlike Access, SQL Express provides a rich set of security features that are more typical of commercial database management systems. If, however, an instructor prefers or must use Microsoft Access, Appendix A explains how to substitute it for SQL Server. The appendix notes the variations in practices and examples in each chapter required for the adaption.

Other database software such as MySQL or Oracle could also be adopted for use with the book. Although the book uses SQL Server Express, its focus is on the process of developing and designing a database. The principles of this process are applicable to any DBMS.

Microsoft Visio is readily available to students for schools that belong to the Microsoft Developers Network Academic Alliance (MSDNAA). It can also be purchased at a significant discount from places like the Academic Superstore and other academic outlets. Visio offers a range of tools and templates that help make diagramming and modifying diagrams easy and enjoyable for students. Appendix C offers additional instruction in how to use the Database Model template in Visio 2010. Of course, other modeling software could be easily substituted, or students could be asked to simply draw their models on graph paper. What is important are the concepts, not the particular tools.

## CHAPTER CONVENTIONS

Each chapter contains several elements other than the narrative about Sharon. These elements are meant to provide greater depth and to provoke the student to think about some of the broader implications of the material.

## Things You Should Know

These extended sections provide background and descriptions of various aspects of database development and design. In many ways, they function like the more traditional textbook. They provide definitions, explanations, and examples that provide a deeper, more comprehensive context to the things that Sharon is doing in the narrative.

### Things to Think About

These are sidebars that invite the student to consider questions about the processes or topics under discussion. The questions in these sections do not have definite answers. They are meant to encourage thought and discussion.

### Cautions

Cautions are found in the margins of the text. Their purpose is to warn the students about potential mistakes or common errors.

### Documentation

This section is found at the end of each chapter. It provides a summary of how a student would go about documenting the activities conducted during the chapter.

### Things to Look up

This section is also found at the end of each chapter. It guides students to other resources and topics not fully covered in the book.

### Vocabulary

Vocabulary is an important part of any discipline. Anyone who wants to work in the database field will be expected to know and understand certain terms.

Vocabulary words are highlighted in margins and are repeated in an exercise at the end of each chapter where the student is asked to match the word with the definition. SQL terms are listed in tables at the ends of Chapters 6 and 8. The terms are also defined in the Glossary at the end of the book.

### Practices

Practices are found at the end of each chapter. They are designed to give each student hands-on experience with the materials of the chapter. Most practices are self-contained, but some do build on each other. In particular, the practices for Chapter 5 and 6 are related. In Chapter 5, the students build a Pizza database, and in Chapter 6, they query that database with SQL.

### Scenarios

As mentioned earlier, Scenarios are the life of the book. There are four scenarios which students build on throughout the book. Their purpose is to provide students with the full experience of developing a database, from identifying the initial concept to testing the fully built database. For students, the most effective use of these scenarios would be to follow one or more of the scenarios throughout the entire term.

### Outline

The book contains eight chapters, four appendixes, and a glossary. It is meant to be just long enough to be covered fully in a single term. Following is an outline of the book with a summary of each chapter's narrative and a list of the outcomes for that chapter.

### Chapter 1: Who Needs a Database

**NARRATIVE** Sharon, a student at a community college, applies to become a tutor for database-related subjects at the school. She discovers they use spiral notebooks and spreadsheets to manage the tutoring information. She suggests to the supervisor that they could benefit from a database and offers to build it. The supervisor agrees to the project. Sharon interviews her and gets a sense of what the overall database will entail and drafts a statement of scope. She and the supervisor discuss the statement and make some modifications.

**OUTCOMES**

- Define relational databases
- Understand the position of relational databases in the history of databases
- Identify major relational database management systems
- Identify main characteristics of relational databases
- Understand SQL's role in relational database
- Recognize some indications of where a database could be useful
- Define a statement of scope for a given database scenario

## Chapter 2: Gathering Information

**NARRATIVE** Now that she has the scope of the database, Sharon begins to gather information about the data the database will need to capture and process. First, she looks at the spiral notebooks that have been used to schedule tutoring sessions. She also looks at the spreadsheets the supervisor develops for reports and other related documents. Then she arranges an interview with several of the tutors and an additional interview with the supervisor, and creates a questionnaire for students who use the tutoring services. Finally, she spends an afternoon in the computer lab, observing how students schedule tutoring and how the actual tutoring sessions go.

**OUTCOMES**

- Review documents to discover relevant entities and attributes for database
- Prepare interview questions and follow up
- Prepare questionnaires
- Observe work flow for process and exceptions

## Chapter 3: Requirements and Business Rules

**NARRATIVE** Having gathered all this information, Sharon must figure out what to do with it. She searches through her notes for nouns and lists them. Then she looks at the lists to see if there are additional topics, or subjects. Then she groups which nouns go with which topics. For each topic area, Sharon identifies some candidate keys. Next, she looks through her notes to determine what the business rules of the tutoring program are. She lists the rules and makes notes for further questions. The rules seem complex, and Sharon remembers something from a systems analysis class about UML diagrams called Use Case diagrams. She uses these diagrams to graphically show how each actor—tutor, student, and supervisor—interacts with the database.

**OUTCOMES**

- Use nouns from notes and observations to discover database elements
- Group elements into entities and attributes
- Define business rules
- Develop Use Case diagrams to model requirements

## Chapter 4: Database Design

**NARRATIVE** Sharon is ready to design the database. She looks at her topics lists and diagrams an initial set of entities, using Visio. She analyses the relationships among the entities, adding linking tables wherever she finds a many-to-many relation. Then she adds the other items from her list to the appropriate entities as attributes. For each attribute, she assigns a data type. She reviews the design to ensure that she has captured all the data and the business rules.

**OUTCOMES**

- Use the database modeling template in Microsoft Visio
- Create entities and add attributes
- Determine the appropriate relationship between entities
- Resolve many-to-many relationships with a linking table

## Chapter 5: Normalization and Design Review

**NARRATIVE** Now, with the help of an instructor, Sharon checks to make sure the database conforms to the rules of normalization. She reviews the database thus far with her supervisor.

**OUTCOMES**

- Evaluate entities against first three normal forms
- Adjust the relational diagram to reflect normalization

## Chapter 6: Physical Design

**NARRATIVE** Sharon builds a prototype of the database, creating all the tables and setting up the relationships. When she has it set up, she enters 5 or 10 rows of sample data so she can test the database.

**OUTCOMES**

- Implement a physical design of the database based on the logical ERDs
- Choose appropriate data types for columns
- Enter sample data into tables

## Chapter 7: SQL

**NARRATIVE** Sharon writes some SQL queries to see if she can get the needed information out of the database. She tests for database requirements.

**OUTCOMES**

- Name the main events in the development of SQL
- Run SELECT queries with a variety of criteria
- Join two or more tables in a query
- Use the aggregate functions COUNT, AVG, SUM, MIN, and MAX
- INSERT, UPDATE, and DELETE records
- Use SQL to test business rules

## Chapter 8: Is it Secure?

**NARRATIVE** In this chapter, Sharon looks at the security needs of the database. It is important to give everyone the access that they require to do the things they need to do. But it is also important to protect the database objects and data from either accidental or intentional damage. Sharon discovers that security is complex and requires careful planning.

**OUTCOMES**

- Analyze security needs and restrictions for users of the database
- Analyze threats to database integrity
- Understand the concepts of authentication and authorization
- Create logins and users
- Create roles

## Appendixes

**USING MICROSOFT ACCESS WITH THE BOOK** A quick overview of using Microsoft Access instead of SQL Server with the book. It looks at each chapter and shows how you would use Access and what adjustments you will need to make to the practices and scenarios.

**SQL SERVER EXPRESS** An overview of how to use the SQL Server Management Studio to create and access databases in SQL Server Express.

**VISIO** An overview of the Visio environment, with a special focus on the database templates.

**COMMON RELATIONAL PATTERNS** A review of some of the most common relational patterns students will encounter in database design such as the Master/Detail relation, weak entities, linking tables, and so on.

**GLOSSARY OF TERMS** Glossary of all vocabulary terms.

## SUPPLEMENTS

The following online resources are available to adopting instructors at www. pearsonhighered.com/irc:

*Instructor's Manual*—It contains a chapter outline and answers to all end-of-chapter questions for each chapter of the text.

*PowerPoint Presentations*—These feature lecture notes that highlight key text terms and concepts. Professors can customize the presentation by adding their own slides or by editing the existing ones.

*Test Item File*—An extensive set of multiple choice, true/false, and essay-type questions for each chapter of the text. Questions are ranked according to difficulty level and referenced with page numbers from the text. The Test Item file is available in Microsoft Word format and as the computerized Prentice Hall TestGen software, with WebCT, Blackboard, Angel, D2L, and Moodle-ready conversions.

*TestGen*—A comprehensive suite of tools for testing and assessment. It allows instructors to easily create and distribute tests for their courses, either by printing and distributing through traditional methods or by online delivery via a local area network (LAN) server. TestGen features Screen Wizards to assist you as you move through the program, and the software is backed with full technical support.

*Image Library*—A collection of the text art organized by chapter. This collection includes all of the figures, tables, and screenshots from the book. These images can be used to enhance class lectures and PowerPoint slides.

*CourseSmart eTextbooks Online*—**CourseSmart** (www.coursesmart.com) is an exciting new *choice* for students looking to save money. As an alternative to purchasing the print textbook, students can purchase an electronic version of the same content and save up to 50% off the suggested list price of the print text. With a CourseSmart etextbook, students can search the text, make notes online, print out reading assignments that incorporate lecture notes, and bookmark important passages for later review.

## ACKNOWLEDGMENTS

I would first of all like to acknowledge my patient and enthusiastic students who worked through draft versions of this text and provided invaluable feedback. I would also like to thank Pearson Prentice Hall and especially Bob Horan and Kelly Loftus, who provided support, encouragement, and advice throughout the lengthy process of completing this book. I also could not have written the book without the careful and diligent feedback from the reviewers:

Georgia Brown, *Northern Illinois University*
Geoffrey D. Decker, *Northern Illinois University*
George Federman, *Santa Barbara City College*
Jean Hendrix, *University of Arkansas at Monticello*
Stephen L. Hussey, *St. Louis University*
Chunming Gao, *Michigan Technological University*
David Law, *Alfred State College*
Seongbae Lim, *St. Mary's University*
Tina Ostrander, *Highline Community College*
Michele Parrish, *Durham Technical Community College*
Richard Scudder, *University of Denver*
Elliot B. Sloane, *Villanova University*
Lee Tangedahl, *University of Montana*

Finally, I would like to acknowledge my family, who showed enormous patience with the hours I spent at my computer.

# ABOUT THE AUTHOR

When he first started working on his English degree, a professor told Steve Conger that an English major can be used in a variety of ways. His subsequent career proved that. After graduation, he worked for over a year in the Coeur d'Alene Idaho school district, assisting children with learning disabilities. Then, for six years he worked for the U.S. Forest Service as a surveyor's assistant, while going to graduate school in the off-seasons. After graduating, he moved to western Washington, where he worked as a nurse's aide until he was hired to teach at Seattle Central Community College. As a part-time instructor who owned a computer, he realized early that he could teach more sections and earn more money teaching computer classes than he could teaching English composition. Despite this varied career path, Steve has never regretted his English degree or given up his love of writing.

Steve Conger has taught at Seattle Central Community College for over twenty years. He helped design the current successful Information Technology Program, and for the last several years, he has taught database and programming courses using Microsoft SQL Server and .Net programming languages. For several years, he has been a board member for the statewide Working Connections workshops, which offer affordable IT training to college instructors. Currently, Working Connections is sponsored by Bellevue College's Center for Excellence.

Steve Conger has a master's degree in English from the University of Idaho and a bachelor's degree in Literary Studies from Gonzaga University.

Currently, he lives in Eatonville, Washington, with his wife and two children. His two other children live in the area and have kindly provided him and his wife with three grandchildren.

## CHAPTER 1

# Who Needs a Database

## OVERVIEW OF RELATIONAL DATABASES AND THEIR USES

This chapter introduces Sharon, a college student who is working toward a degree in Database Development and Administration. She signs up to become a tutor and realizes that the tutoring program is in desperate need of a database to track tutoring sessions. She volunteers to develop it and after some discussions defines a statement of work for the database.

## CHAPTER OUTCOMES

**By the end of this chapter you will be able to:**

- Define relational databases
- Understand the position of relational databases in the history of databases
- Identify major relational database management systems
- Identify main characteristics of relational databases
- Understand SQL's role in relational database
- Recognize some indications of where a database could be useful
- Define a statement of work for a given database scenario

## THE SITUATION

Sharon is a student taking database classes. She is near the end of her program and has done quite well. Like any student, she could really use some extra money and has decided to inquire about tutoring. She has noticed that many students seem to struggle with relational database concepts, particularly in the early classes, and she is fairly sure there would be a demand for her services.

The administrator of the tutoring program at the college is named Terry Lee. Terry invites Sharon into her office and offers her a seat. She smiles.

"So you want to tutor?"

"Yes. I think I would be good at it."

"What subjects do you think you could tutor?"

"I was thinking especially of database-related topics. I can do relational design and SQL [Structured Query Language]. I think I can tutor Microsoft Access, SQL Server, and even other database management systems. I can also do some database programming."

Terry nods. "That's good. We do have some requests for tutoring in those areas, but so far no one to provide the tutoring. Before you can begin, you will need to get recommendations from two instructors who teach in the area you want to tutor. Also you will need to do a short training session."

Sharon smiles, "That's no problem."

"Good." Terry rises from her seat. "Let me show you how things work."

*RELATIONAL DATABASE*

A type of database that stores data in tables that are related to each other by means of repeated columns called keys.

*RELATIONAL DESIGN*

It involves organizing data into tables or entities and then determining the relationships among them. **SQL** is the language relational databases use to create their objects and to modify and retrieve data.

## Things You Should Know

### Databases

A database, at its simplest level, is a collection of related data. It doesn't have to be electronic. The card catalogs that libraries used to have were certainly databases. A scientist's spiral notebook where he or she keeps notes and observations could be considered a database, so too could a phone or address book. When we say "database," though, we usually mean electronic databases, databases that run on computers.

### Flat File Databases

The simplest form of an electronic database is the flat file database. Flat files usually consist of a file which stores data in a structured way. A common format for flat file databases is the delimited file. In a delimited file, each piece of data is separated from the next piece by some "delimiter," often a comma or a tab. The end of a row is marked by the new-line character (usually invisible). It is important, if the file is to be read correctly, that each row contain the same number of delimiters. Another kind of flat data file is the fixed-width data file. In such files, all the columns share a fixed width in characters. These flat files can be read by a computer program and manipulated in various ways, but they have almost no protections for data integrity, and they often contain many redundant elements.

Redundancy refers to repeating the same data more than once. It can occur in a number of ways. Data could be repeated over and over again in the same file. For instance, the following example shows an equipment checkout list.

Notice how in Table 1-1 Nancy Martin's name is repeated, and it would be repeated as many times as she checks out equipment. Another type of redundancy occurs when the same data is stored in different files. For instance, you might have a file of club members that stores Nancy's name and address, and then a separate file for fee payments that repeats her name and address. One problem with this system is that, other than having to type in everything several times, each time you reenter the same data, there is a greater chance of mistyping it or making a mistake of some kind. Another problem occurs when you need to change her address. Say Nancy moves and she notifies the person at the desk in the club about her change of address. The desk clerk changes the address in the membership file, but fails to change it, or to notify someone in billing to change it, in the fee payment file. Now when the club sends out a bill or statement of fees, it goes to the wrong address. It is always best to enter each piece of data in one and only one place.

Spreadsheets, such as Excel, can also be used as flat file databases. Spreadsheets offer a great deal more functionality than simple delimited files. Cells can be given a data type such as "numeric" or "date time." This helps ensure that all the entries in a given column are of the same type. You can also define valid ranges for data (e.g., you can stipulate that a valid term grade is between the numbers 0 and 4). Spreadsheets usually contain data tools that make it possible to sort and group data. Most spreadsheets also contain functions that allow the user to query the data. But despite these enhancements, spreadsheets still share many of the redundancy and data integrity problems of other flat file formats.

### Hierarchical Databases

The most common database model before the relational model was the hierarchical database. Hierarchical databases are organized in a tree-like structure. In such a database, one parent table can have many child tables, but no child table can have more than one parent.

This sounds abstract, and it is. One way to visualize it is to think of the Windows (or, for that matter, the Mac or Linux) file system. The file system has a hierarchical structure. You have a directory, under which there can be subdirectories, and in those subdirectories, there can be other subdirectories or files. You navigate through them by following a *path*.

```
C:\Users\ITStudent\Documents\myfile.txt
```

This tree-like organization is very logical and easy to navigate, but it does present some of the same problems of redundancy, data integrity, and comparability of data. It is not uncommon for

---

*DELIMITED FILES*

These have some sort of character separating columns of data. The delimiter is often a comma or tab, but can be any non-alphanumeric character. In **fixed length** files, the length in characters of each column is the same.

*DATA INTEGRITY*

It refers to the accuracy and the correctness of the data in the database.

*REDUNDANCY*

It refers to storing the same data in more than one place in the database.

**Table 1-1** Equipment Checkout

| Member ID | Member Name | Date | Time | Equipment No. |
|---|---|---|---|---|
| 23455 | Nancy Martin | 2/10/2010 | 4 PM | 2333 |
| 45737 | Taylor Smith | 2/10/2010 | 4:15 PM | 3331 |
| 23455 | Nancy Martin | 2/10/2010 | 4:45 PM | 2221 |

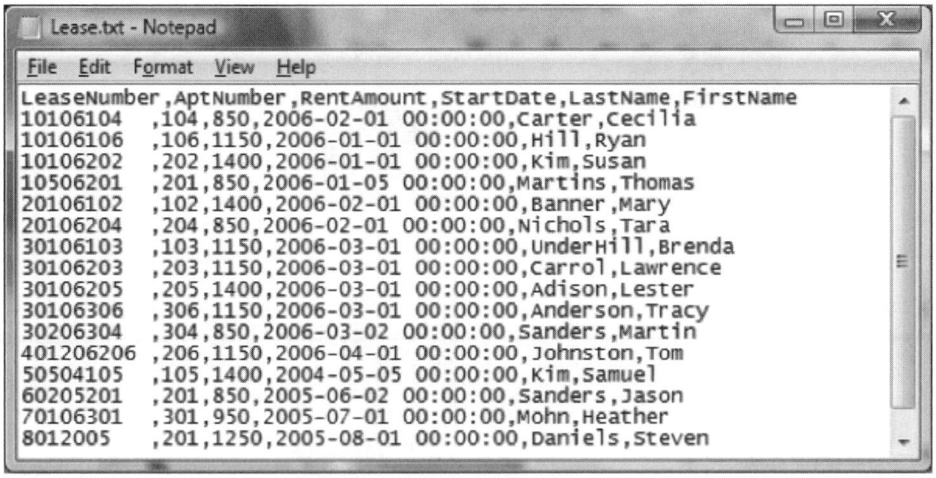

```
LeaseNumber,AptNumber,RentAmount,StartDate,LastName,FirstName
10106104    ,104,850,2006-02-01 00:00:00,Carter,Cecilia
10106106    ,106,1150,2006-01-01 00:00:00,Hill,Ryan
10106202    ,202,1400,2006-01-01 00:00:00,Kim,Susan
10506201    ,201,850,2006-01-05 00:00:00,Martins,Thomas
20106102    ,102,1400,2006-02-01 00:00:00,Banner,Mary
20106204    ,204,850,2006-02-01 00:00:00,Nichols,Tara
30106103    ,103,1150,2006-03-01 00:00:00,UnderHill,Brenda
30106203    ,203,1150,2006-03-01 00:00:00,Carrol,Lawrence
30106205    ,205,1400,2006-03-01 00:00:00,Adison,Lester
30106306    ,306,1150,2006-03-01 00:00:00,Anderson,Tracy
30206304    ,304,850,2006-03-02 00:00:00,Sanders,Martin
401206206   ,206,1150,2006-04-01 00:00:00,Johnston,Tom
50504105    ,105,1400,2004-05-05 00:00:00,Kim,Samuel
60205201    ,201,850,2005-06-02 00:00:00,Sanders,Jason
70106301    ,301,950,2005-07-01 00:00:00,Mohn,Heather
8012005     ,201,1250,2005-08-01 00:00:00,Daniels,Steven
```

**FIGURE 1-1** Delimited Text Example

the same data to be repeated in more than one place in the tree. Whenever data is repeated, there is a risk of error and inconsistency. It can also be very difficult to compare a piece of data from one branch of the database with a piece from an entirely different branch of the database.

---

## THINGS TO THINK ABOUT

*Hierarchical databases are still in use in many institutions. This is especially true of large institutions such as banks and insurance companies that adopted database technologies early.*

*These institutions invested heavily in the development of these databases and have committed decades of data to their files. Although database technologies have improved, they are reluctant to commit the time and money and to incur the risk of redeveloping their databases and translating their vast stores of existing data into new formats.*

*The basic philosophy is, if it still works, let well enough alone. Most companies are conservative about their databases, for understandable reasons.*

*What do you think companies like Microsoft or Oracle have to do to convince companies to upgrade to their newest database products?*

---

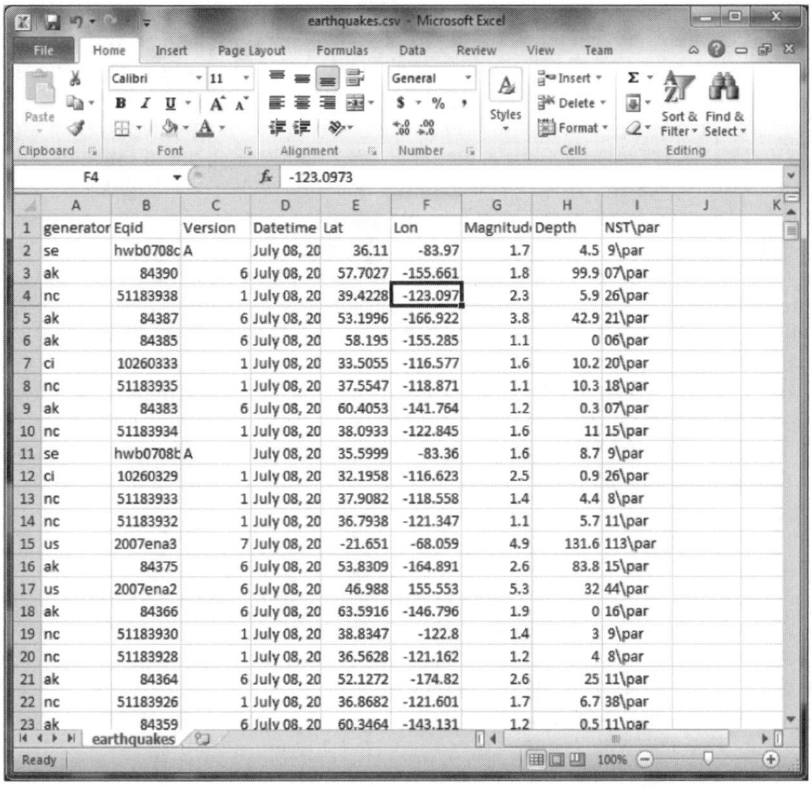

| | A | B | C | D | E | F | G | H | I |
|---|---|---|---|---|---|---|---|---|---|
| 1 | generator | Eqid | Version | Datetime | Lat | Lon | Magnitud | Depth | NST\par |
| 2 | se | hwb0708c | A | July 08, 20 | 36.11 | -83.97 | 1.7 | 4.5 | 9\par |
| 3 | ak | 84390 | 6 | July 08, 20 | 57.7027 | -155.661 | 1.8 | 99.9 | 07\par |
| 4 | nc | 51183938 | 1 | July 08, 20 | 39.4228 | -123.097 | 2.3 | 5.9 | 26\par |
| 5 | ak | 84387 | 6 | July 08, 20 | 53.1996 | -166.922 | 3.8 | 42.9 | 21\par |
| 6 | ak | 84385 | 6 | July 08, 20 | 58.195 | -155.285 | 1.1 | 0 | 06\par |
| 7 | ci | 10260333 | 1 | July 08, 20 | 33.5055 | -116.577 | 1.6 | 10.2 | 20\par |
| 8 | nc | 51183935 | 1 | July 08, 20 | 37.5547 | -118.871 | 1.1 | 10.3 | 18\par |
| 9 | ak | 84383 | 6 | July 08, 20 | 60.4053 | -141.764 | 1.2 | 0.3 | 07\par |
| 10 | nc | 51183934 | 1 | July 08, 20 | 38.0933 | -122.845 | 1.6 | 11 | 15\par |
| 11 | se | hwb0708b | A | July 08, 20 | 35.5999 | -83.36 | 1.6 | 8.7 | 9\par |
| 12 | ci | 10260329 | 1 | July 08, 20 | 32.1958 | -116.623 | 2.5 | 0.9 | 26\par |
| 13 | nc | 51183933 | 1 | July 08, 20 | 37.9082 | -118.558 | 1.4 | 4.4 | 8\par |
| 14 | nc | 51183932 | 1 | July 08, 20 | 36.7938 | -121.347 | 1.1 | 5.7 | 11\par |
| 15 | us | 2007ena3 | 7 | July 08, 20 | -21.651 | -68.059 | 4.9 | 131.6 | 113\par |
| 16 | ak | 84375 | 6 | July 08, 20 | 53.8309 | -164.891 | 2.6 | 83.8 | 15\par |
| 17 | us | 2007ena2 | 6 | July 08, 20 | 46.988 | 155.553 | 5.3 | 32 | 44\par |
| 18 | ak | 84366 | 6 | July 08, 20 | 63.5916 | -146.796 | 1.9 | 0 | 16\par |
| 19 | nc | 51183930 | 1 | July 08, 20 | 38.8347 | -122.8 | 1.4 | 3 | 9\par |
| 20 | nc | 51183928 | 1 | July 08, 20 | 36.5628 | -121.162 | 1.2 | 4 | 8\par |
| 21 | ak | 84364 | 6 | July 08, 20 | 52.1272 | -174.82 | 2.6 | 25 | 11\par |
| 22 | nc | 51183926 | 1 | July 08, 20 | 36.8682 | -121.601 | 1.7 | 6.7 | 38\par |
| 23 | ak | 84359 | 6 | July 08, 20 | 60.3464 | -143.131 | 1.2 | 0.5 | 11\par |

**FIGURE 1-2** Excel Spreadsheet

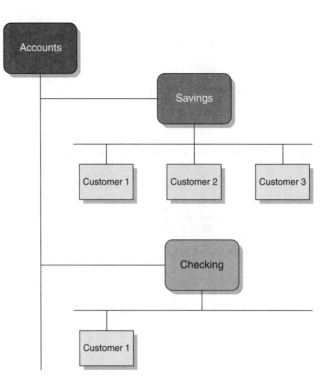

**FIGURE 1-3**   Hierarchical
Database Model

### Relational Databases

By far, the most popular type of database for at least the last 30 years is the relational database. The idea for relational databases came from a man named Edgar F. Codd in 1970. He worked for IBM, and he wrote a paper on, at that time, a new theoretical design for databases. This design would be based on the mathematics of set theory and predicate logic. He formulated the basics of the relational design in 12 rules. The first rule, called the "information rule," states, "All information in a relational database is represented explicitly at the logical level and in exactly one way—values in tables."

Briefly, in the relational model data would be organized into tables. Even the information about the tables themselves is stored in tables. These tables then define the relationships among themselves by means of repeating an attribute or column from one table in another table. These repeating columns would be called "keys." He also specified that the logical design of a database should be separate and independent of physical design considerations such as file types, data storage, and disk writing and reading functions. He specified that there should be a "data sublanguage" that can perform all data-related tasks. SQL has evolved into this language. We will discuss it more thoroughly in a later chapter. For a discussion of Codd's 12 rules, see Wikipedia at http://en.wikipedia.org/wiki/Codd's_12_rules.

This may sound complex, and it certainly can be, but it solved many of the problems that plagued the databases of the day. One of those problems was data redundancy. As mentioned earlier, redundancy refers to the need to store the same data in more than one place in the database.

In a relational database, the redundancy is minimized. A bank would enter the customer's data only once, in one place. Any changes would be made only in one place. The only redundancy allowed is the repetition of a key column (or columns) that is used to create relationships among the tables. This significantly reduces the chances of error and protects the integrity of the data in the database.

Another problem the relational design helped solve was that of relating data from different parts of the database. In many of the previous database designs, a programmer had to write a routine in a language like Fortran or Cobol to extract the data from various parts of the database and compare them. In a well-designed relational database, every piece of data can be compared or joined with any other piece of data. The relational design was a huge step forward in flexibility.

The chief drawback of a relational database is the inherent complexity of the design. It is fairly easy to design a bad database that will not do what a client needs it to do. In a bad database design, you may find that you cannot enter the data you need to enter. This is often the result of an error in how the relationship was created. It may also not be possible to retrieve the data

_KEYS_

In relational databases, each table usually has one column designated as a **primary key**. This key uniquely identifies each row in the table. This primary key becomes a **foreign key** when it is repeated in another table to create a link between the tables.

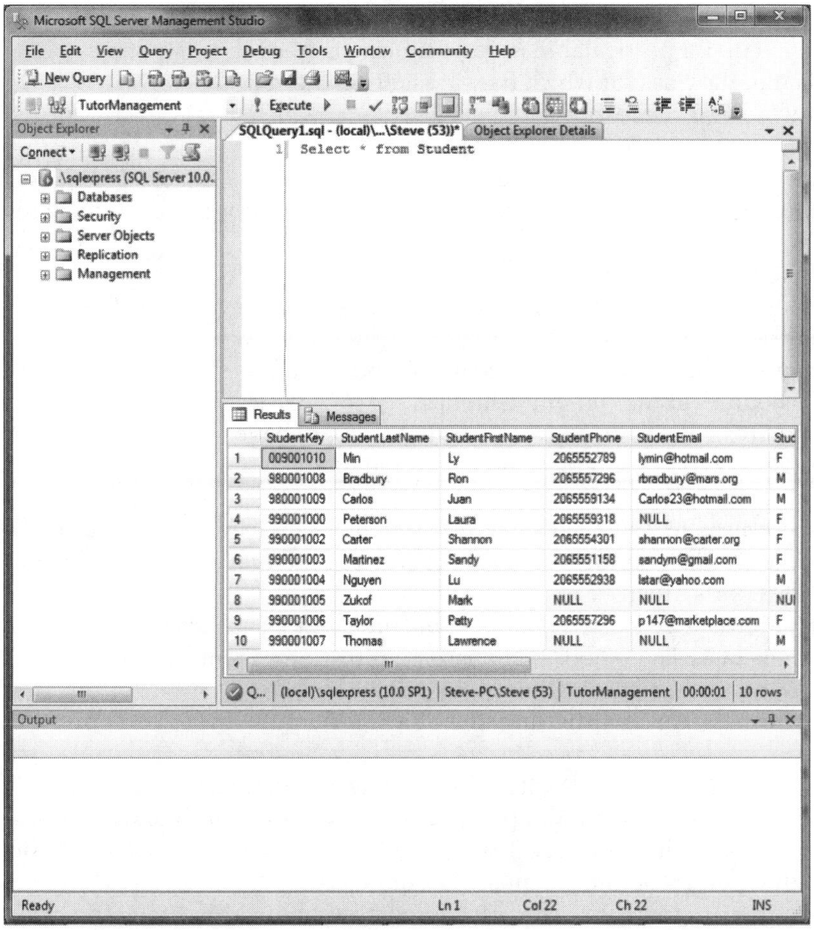

FIGURE 1-4  SQL Server Relational Database Manager Showing an SQL Query and Results

| Customer ID(PK) | Last Name | First Name | Address | City | State |
|---|---|---|---|---|---|
| C41098X3 | Carson | Lewis | 121 Center Street | Seattle | WA |
| CV1099B1 | Madison | Sarah | 1324 Broadway | Seattle | WA |
| D345XU24 | Brown | Lisa | 2201 Second Ave | Seattle | WA |

| Transaction ID | Transaction Type | Transaction Date | Customer ID(FK) | Amount |
|---|---|---|---|---|
| 10002345 | Deposit | 2009-2-12 10:25:06 | C41098X3 | 1245.76 |
| 10002346 | Deposit | 2009-2-12 10:27:13 | CV1099B1 | 500.00 |
| 10002347 | Withdrawal | 2009-2-13 14:45:57 | C41098X3 | 200.00 |

FIGURE 1-5  Primary Key and Foreign Key Relations Between a Customer Table and a Transaction Table

that you need. Because of the complexity of relational design, it is crucial that you follow a design process that clarifies both the nature of the data you wish to store and the structure of the database. That is what this book is designed to help you with.

The chief advantages in a well-designed relational database are data integrity and flexibility. These two advantages have made it the most commonly used database model for the past 30 years or so.

## THE OPPORTUNITY

They walk from Terry's office down the hall to the computer lab. Terry stops at the front desk. "The computer lab is one of our designated tutoring areas, and I suspect the one where most of your sessions would be scheduled." She picks up a clipboard containing several pieces of paper. "We have 2 pages for each week—an AM one and a PM one. At the beginning of the month, tutors enter their availability for each day, the durations for which they are available that day, and the courses they can tutor for. Students sign up for particular sessions. Tutoring is free for the students as long as they are enrolled in the class for which they are getting tutored."

"How do you check that?"

"Right now, it is mostly a matter of trust."

"How long is each tutoring session?"

"Tutoring sessions are for 30 minutes each, and a tutor can only do 30 sessions or 15 hours a week."

"What if you set up a time slot and nobody signs up?"

"As long as you show up when scheduled, we will pay you for the time. The pay, by the way, is $10.50 an hour."

"Thanks." Sharon looks over the notebook. "Just out of curiosity, what do you do with the schedules at the end of the month?"

"Actually, I take them back to my office every two weeks and type them into various spreadsheets to make reports to the people who pay for the tutoring and to determine the pay for the tutors themselves."

Sharon turns to Terry and says, "You know, you could really use a database. It would make it much simpler to track schedules and availability, and it could make doing your reports much easier."

Terry sighs. "I've known that for some time, but we just can't find anyone willing to take on the task. The school's database administrator is much too busy, and no one else feels competent or has the time to take on the task."

Sharon hesitates a little and then says, "I might be able to put a database together."

Terry looks hopeful. "Really? That would be wonderful. We even have some money in our budget so we could pay you something for your work."

"I am still learning database," Sharon cautions, "but I am pretty sure I could make you something that would meet most of your needs."

"Good, why don't you come by tomorrow about this time, and we will talk about it."

"I will be there."

---

## THINGS TO THINK ABOUT

*There are many situations that could be improved with the addition of a database. Whenever there is a large amount of complex data to handle, a database is likely to provide the best solution.*

*There are times, however, when the data involved is modest in scope and complexity that a relational database may be an overkill.*

*Relational databases are complex to develop and maintain.*

*The benefits when dealing with large amounts of data are worth the costs in development time and maintenance. But, sometimes, the best solution is simply a spreadsheet such as Excel.*

---

 ## Things You Should Know

### RDBMS

A relational database management system (RDBMS) is, as its name suggests, a system for managing relational databases. As a minimum, an RDBMS needs to allow a user to create one or more databases and the objects associated with that database such as tables, relationships, views, and queries. It also needs to support basic maintenance such as backing up the database and restoring it from a backup file. Moreover, it needs to support security, making sure that users and groups have access only to the databases and data that they are authorized to use.

Most commercial RDBMSs offer many features beyond these basic ones. Most include tools for monitoring and optimizing the performance of their databases. Many include reporting services to

| Table 1-2 | Some Relational Database Management Systems | |
|---|---|---|
| **RDBMS** | **Comments** | **URL** |
| ORACLE | The biggest and the first commercial RDBMS. Powers many of the world's largest companies | http://www.Oracle.com |
| SQL Server | Microsoft's RDMS product. Ships in many versions designed for different company needs. Also powers many large enterprises | http://www.microsoft.com/sql/default.mspx |
| DB2 | IBM's RDBMS | http://www306.ibm.com/software/data/db2/9/ |
| MySQL | The most popular open source RDBMS, currently owned by SUN | http://www.MySql.com |
| PostGres SQL | Another free, open source RDBMS. It is older and some would say more powerful than MySQL | http://www.postgresql.org/ |
| ACCESS | Microsoft's desktop database | http://office.microsoft.com/en-us/access/default.aspx?ofcresset=1 |

format and present the results of queries. Some even include complex business intelligence packages for analyzing business trends and patterns. Table 1-2 describes the most common RDBMSs, with a link to their home Web sites.

## GETTING THE SCOPE

After Sharon leaves Terry's office, she goes to one of the instructors, a professor named Bill Collins, from whom she hopes to get a recommendation. He is sitting in his office and smiles when he opens the door for her. "Come on in. How can I help you today?" She tells about her plan to tutor and asks for a recommendation. He says he will be happy to provide one. Then Sharon tells him about the possibility of making a database.

She says, "I've got a thousand ideas about how the database should look and what should be in it."

Bill cautions her, "Be careful not to get ahead of yourself. You need to remember you are not making this database for yourself. You are making it for a client. You need to listen carefully to what Terry and the other people who will use the database say about what they need and not get trapped by preconceived notions. The first thing you need to do is get as clear an idea as possible about what the database is intended to do."

"A statement of scope?"

"Yes, that would be a good place to start, but I would go farther and make a complete statement of work. That would include the scope, but it would also contain some discussion of the background, the objectives of the project, and a tentative timeline. I have some samples I can share with you. Listen, if you need any help or advice on this project, feel free to ask me."

"Thank you. Thank you very much."

 *Caution*
*It is easy to get carried away with your own excitement about a database project. You may be able to see several possible solutions and want to start designing right away. But it is critically important that you delay designing until you have a clear idea of what the client wants and needs. Patience and the ability to listen are among the most important skills of a database developer.*

*STATEMENT OF SCOPE*

A **statement of scope** is a short statement of one or more paragraphs that says in clear, but general, terms what the project will do. A **statement of work** is a more complete statement about the objectives and timeline of the project.

## Things You Should Know

### Statement of Work

A statement of work is a preliminary document that describes, in general, the work that needs to be done on a project. Often this is prepared by the people who want the work to be done and offered to contractors for bidding. But sometimes, as in this case, it can be used as an initial clarification of the task at hand.

It is important to have something like a statement of work for any major project so that everyone knows what is expected. Without it, people often find, sometimes late in the process, that different individuals have very different expectations about what the project should contain. A statement of work is also a good reference throughout the project to keep everyone on track and focused. The statement is preliminary and can be altered as the needs of the project change or grow. But, by

| Table 1-3 | Statement of Work Elements |
|---|---|
| **Element** | **Description** |
| History | Describes the reason for the project, usually a problem with the current system or an opportunity to provide new services. May describe the various steps and efforts that led to the current state of the project |
| Scope | Provides a general statement of the requirements and expectations of the project. It states only the high-level requirements and does not get into specifics. It does not go into detail about how things are to be done. It may include some general constraints such as time or budget limits |
| Objectives | The things the project is intended to achieve. Objectives aren't about creating specific elements of the database, for instance, but about what the database is supposed to achieve, that is, why the client wants the database in the first place |
| Tasks and Deliverables | Breaks the project into discrete tasks. Each task should have an estimated duration and concrete deliverables |

referring to the statement of work, you can guarantee that any changes or additions are a matter of discussion and not just assumed by one of the parties.

Table 1-3 delineates a few of the elements that can appear in a statement of work.

## THE FIRST INTERVIEW

The next day Sharon sits in Terry's office. She has brought a notebook in which she has written down some of the key questions she knows she will need to ask. Sharon knows it is important to be prepared and focused for any interview. She has also brought a diagram of a database she created for a nonprofit to show Terry as an example of the work she has done on database creation.

Terry says, "Thanks for coming in. You have no idea how long and how much we've wanted a database for the tutoring program. We have to generate several reports each term to justify our funding. It has gotten so that creating reports takes most of my time. It keeps us from doing things to improve the program. We also really need to be able to track what works and what doesn't better."

Sharon nods, "I really hope I can help. I've brought an example of a database I made for Capital Charities to show that I do have some experience creating databases. We did this as part of a project for a Database class."

Terry looks at the diagram as Sharon explains it.

"Capital Charities provides funds for basic utilities, food, and occasional repairs for poor families on a one-time, emergency basis. They needed to be able to track their contributors and their contributions. That was one part of the database. That data is stored in the contributor and contribution tables. That line between them indicates a one-to-many relationship. It uses what is called "crow's feet" notation. It shows that each contributor has contributed at least once and may have contributed many times. The crow's foot, those three lines, points to the many sides of the relationship. The other part of the database tracks the types and amounts of assistance given to each client. The client information is entered into the Client table."

She points to the ClientNotes entity, "There can be 0 or many notes about any client. Each client receives assistance at least once. That was a business rule of the charity. They only wanted to list as clients those they had actually given assistance to. Each act of assistance is associated with a particular councilor and can involve several different types of assistance. That is the reason for the AssistanceDetail table."

"It looks complex."

"It is a little. But I also built some forms and reports that made it such that the Capital Charities staff didn't have to navigate the database directly. It made it a lot easier to use."

*CROW'S FEET NOTATION*

A type of entity relation diagram where the relationships are depicted using lines and 0s. These are more descriptive of relationships than the diagrams using simple arrows.

Capital Charities:

Providing the basic necessities for those in need

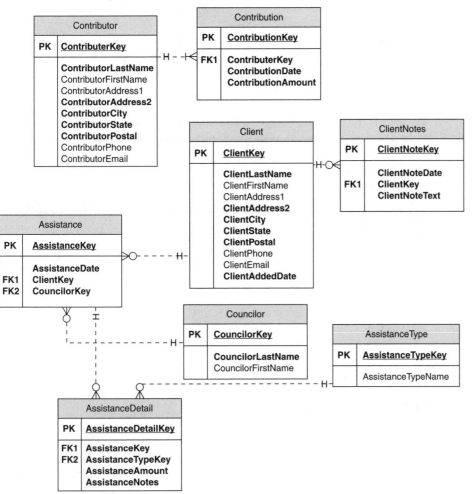

**FIGURE 1-6** Sample Entity Diagram for a Nonprofit

"Well, it certainly looks like you should be capable of doing this for us. What do you need from me?"

"You have already started suggesting some of the things I want to talk about today—things you want the database to do. What I need to get from you today is a clear sense of what you want the database to do for you. I don't need the specifics yet, just general statements of what you want to see and what the database needs to do to be useful to you."

Terry hesitates, "OK . . . Where do I start?"

"You already suggested a couple of things. You need to track what works and what doesn't. How would you determine that something is working or not working?"

## Things You Should Know

You should always go to an interview prepared. In this initial interview, you should be prepared to help the client get started on the right track and have questions that help focus them on the important aspects of the database. But you don't want to guide them toward some preconceived notion of what the database should be. Rather, your questions should help them guide you to a clearer understanding of what they need out of a database.

"Well, part of it is how many students are using the tutoring services. What courses are they taking tutoring for, and how the tutoring they receive helps them succeed in their courses? Do they get better grades? Does tutoring stop them from dropping the class? I know these are a bit vague and difficult to track."

"That's OK. What about scheduling tutors and students. What do you need to track to do that?"

"Well, we need to track tutors, of course, and what classes they can tutor for. We need to track their schedules so we know what times they are available. We need to know which students sign up for each session, and ideally we should be able to check that they are actually taking the course for which they are getting tutoring."

"Do you need to track demographic information for students?"

"If we could, that would be great. It would make our reporting much easier. Several of our grants are targeted at particular groups of students. We would have to guarantee that such information would remain private."

"What other reports do you need to make?"

"I need to know how many hours each tutor worked in a pay period. I need to know how many students each tutor saw. I also need to know how many unduplicated students were seen each term."

"Unduplicated?"

"Yes, individual students. A single student could get several sessions of tutoring. For some reports, we need to know how many individual students we are serving—not just how many sessions we have scheduled."

"Can you think of anything else?"

"We really need to know if a student actually got the tutoring they signed up for. Sometimes a student will sign up and then not show up for the actual session. It might also be good to know what courses students want tutoring in where we are not offering it. Maybe you could provide a way for students to request tutoring for courses or subjects."

"Anything else?"

"Nothing I can think of right now."

"OK. What I am going to do is take this and write up a statement of work describing the database, the objectives, and a tentative timeline. Then we can look at it and see if it really describes the database you need. If it doesn't, we can adjust it. When it does, we can use it to refer back to keep us on track so that we don't get lost in the details later."

"Thanks," Terry stands up. "I actually think we can do this. You really seem to know what you are doing. I am looking forward to it."

Sharon smiles, though she doesn't feel nearly as confident in her abilities. "I am looking forward to it too."

## IDENTIFYING THE BIG TOPICS

Sharon goes to the school cafeteria and gets a cup of coffee. She sits down to go over her notes. She knows it is important to review them while the interview is still fresh in her mind. The first thing she needs to do is to identify the big topics. What is the database about? What are the major components going to be? "Well, tutoring," she says to herself, "that is the big topic." But what does tutoring include? She takes out a pencil and starts a list, "Tutors, of course, and students and the tutoring schedule." She writes them in the list:

> tutors
>
> students
>
> tutoring schedule

"Is there anything else? Anything I am missing?" She frowns as she concentrates for a moment. "Courses! Tutors tutor for specific courses, and students are supposed to be registered in those courses in order to get tutoring." She adds it to the list. Students also should be able to request tutoring for specific courses. She adds *requests* to the list.

> tutors
>
> students

*ENTITIES*

An entity is something that the database is concerned with, about which data can be stored, and which can have relationships with other entities.

tutoring schedule

courses

requests

She thinks a bit longer. "We need to track whether students attended the sessions they scheduled. That is important, but is it a new topic? It could be part of scheduling." Terry wanted one more thing, she remembers. She wanted to track student success. To Sharon that seems like a different topic entirely. She recalls that Bill Collins in his class always insisted that a good database like a good table should be focused on a single topic. She decides to leave the list as it is.

*ATTRIBUTES*

These define entities. (The entity *customer* has attributes like name and address).

---

### Things You Should Know

Identifying the major topics of a database is an important exercise. It helps provide a clearer sense of just what the database is about. It is also the first step toward identifying the "entities" that will be used in the database design.

One way to begin identifying the major themes is to look at the nouns in your notes. See if they cluster together around certain themes. These themes are most likely the major topics of your database. We will look at this technique more closely later when we talk about defining entities and attributes.

It is important to note that a database may contain several themes, but all those themes should relate to a single overarching topic like tutoring. If there is more than one overarching topic, it may indicate that you should develop additional databases.

---

## WRITING THE STATEMENT OF WORK

Now that she has the big topics in mind, she begins to compose the statement of work. She begins with the history. The history is a statement of the problem. It can narrate how the current situation came to be the way it is. Sharon thinks about the things she saw and the things that Terry told her.

> For a long time the tutoring program has used a paper schedule to sign students up for tutoring. Tutors identify their schedule for a two-week period, and then a schedule is printed and placed in the computer lab. Students look through the schedule for sessions that match courses they are taking and the times they have available. This system has worked and continues to work, but it has several significant problems. For one, it can be difficult for students to find appropriate tutoring sessions. The paper forms are difficult to navigate and understand. Additionally, it is very difficult for the tutoring program to track the students using the tutoring. It is difficult or impossible to track demographic information. It is also difficult to assure that students are enrolled in the courses they receive tutoring in. Even tracking tutors' hours can be difficult.
>
> A database with a client application could significantly improve the situation, by providing a flexible, searchable schedule for students; better tracking of demographics and eligibility; and better tracking of hours tutored.

She pauses. That was hard to get going, but once she got started, it flowed pretty well.

> The tutoring database will be designed to manage the tutoring program at the college.

She isn't real happy with that as an opening sentence. She modifies it a little and forges ahead. It proves to be a lot harder than she imagined. The statement has to include all the general points but still be concise enough to give a clear indication of the purpose and functions of the database. After a lot of effort, she had this preliminary statement:

> The tutoring database will manage data for the tutoring program at the college. It will track available tutors and the courses they can tutor. It will also track each tutor's tutoring schedule. The database will store demographic

information for students who register for tutoring. This information will be private and used only to generate general reports which include no personal information. Students, who have registered, will be able to sign up for available tutoring sessions for courses in which they are enrolled. The database will track whether students attended their scheduled sessions.

Sharon looks it over carefully. What about the data about student success? Should that be a part of this database, or should that be a separate project? She decides to set it aside until she has talked with Terry.

She also wonders if she should state some of the things the database *won't* do. Things such as the following:

The database can be used to get the hours worked for each tutor, but it will not process pay or provide any payroll information.

The database will not validate student information against the school's registration database.

*CONSTRAINTS*

These are limits on what the database will do. Later we will see that you can also set constraints on the types and range of data that can be entered into a column in a table.

For the moment, she can't think of any other *constraints*.

She consults an example her instructor gave her to look at. The next step is to set out the objectives for the database. She spends some time thinking about this. Most of the objectives are spelled out in the scope. She pulls out some of the main points and makes a list.

- Streamline the process by which tutors enter their schedules and students sign up for them.
- Improve tracking of demographic data of students using the tutoring program.
- Improve tracking of tutors' hours and students' use of tutoring sessions

Next she needs to add tasks and a timeline. She jots down some notes on a paper. The first thing she will have to do is to gather information. She needs to know all the relevant data and processes. How long will that take? She makes a rough guess of two to three weeks. Then she will have to evaluate all the information she has gathered and use it to start developing a list of business rules and the first rough model of the data. That could take another couple weeks. Next she will have to refine and normalize the model. Sharon thinks she can do this in two or three days. Then she needs to actually make the database. That won't take long. She can probably do that part in a couple of hours. What then? Sharon muses for a while. The last part may take a fair amount of time. She will need to test the database and make sure that it meets all of Terry's needs. She will also have to test for security issues and privacy. That could take two or more weeks of intense work. Where does that put her? Sharon calculates and taking the longer times in each case comes up with nine or ten weeks. None of this is counting the fact that it will take a completely different development project to create a client application for Terry, the tutors, and students to interact with the database. But, Sharon says to herself, one project at a time.

Sharon almost has everything she needs for the statement of work, but there is still something missing. After a while it occurs to her: Every task should also have a deliverable, something concrete she can show Terry to let her know that the database is on track.

Sharon spends the next couple of hours completing her statement of work.

---

## THINGS TO THINK ABOUT

### Estimating Times

*One of the most difficult things for anyone who is new to developing databases is estimating the time it will take to complete the various tasks. Experience will help, but before you have enough experience how do you even begin to guess an appropriate time?*

*There are some techniques that can help. One is to make a weighted average. To do this, write down your most optimistic time estimate—*

*your best guess at the probable time it will take if everything goes perfect—and your most pessimistic time estimate—if everything goes wrong. Add them all together, but multiply your most probable estimate by 3, then divide the sum by five.*

$$(0 + Pt \times 3 + p)/5$$

*What other ways can you think of to help your time estimates be more accurate?*

## REVIEWING THE STATEMENT OF WORK

The following afternoon Sharon returns to Terry's office and shows her the statement. As Terry looks it over, Sharon says, "It is important that we both are clear about what we are working on. I don't want to go off and make a database and then find out it is not what you had in mind at all."

"No, I can see that is a really good idea." She sets the paper down. "What about the surveys of student success?"

"I thought about that, and I am not sure. Sometimes I think that does belong in this project, and other times, I think that it is a separate project on its own. I am not sure how we could get objective data on their success, but we could include evaluations by students or a quarterly survey. If we build the database as I have described it, we should be able to add the success-tracking features later or we could look at adding a second database devoted to tracking student success."

"OK, I can live with that. It would be nice if you could validate student information."

"Yes, but I don't really know how to do that. I also think it unlikely that I would be granted the permissions I would need on the school's registration database. You might be able to get the school's developers to look at that piece later."

"Fair enough. One other thing you don't have here, and I am not sure we talked about it, but it would be nice if students could request tutoring in courses that we don't currently have tutors for. It would help us know where the need is and where we need to try to recruit new tutors."

"That shouldn't be a problem. I can add that."

"Good. What do you need to proceed?"

"Well, let's go over the tasks and timeline. First, I am going to need to gather some information. I am going to need to see how you have been doing things. I will need to talk to some tutors, and maybe some students, and I probably need to see the reports you make to ensure that the database contains all the information you require. Then I will need to analyze all the information I get and begin to make a data model. After all that, I can actually make the database and test it."

Terry studies the timeline. "This is very clear and well done. How realistic do you think this timeline is?"

Sharon smiled. "It represents my very best guess. It could go faster if everything works out well, but it could also go slower if I encounter problems. I tried to be very conservative on the times, so I think there is a good chance it can be completed on schedule."

"Good, it would be ideal if the database could be in place by the beginning of next term."

Sharon warns, "There is another piece to all this. A client application needs to be developed so you, the students, and tutors can interact safely and easily with the database. But that is really a separate project."

Terry smiles. "You're right. We can tackle that when we have finished with the database."

"Tell you what, I will come by tomorrow with a revised version of this statement, and I will give you a preliminary plan of where we go next."

Terry stood up and put out her hand to shake. "Sounds good. I look forward to working with you on this."

## THE STATEMENT OF WORK

Home, later. Sharon revised the statement of work to include student requests. Here is her completed statement of work:

### STATEMENT OF WORK: TUTORING DATABASE PROJECT

#### History

For a long time the tutoring program has used a paper schedule to sign students up for tutoring. Tutors identify their schedule for a two-week period, and then a schedule is printed and placed in the computer lab. Students look through the schedule for sessions that match courses they are taking and the times they have available. This system has worked and continues to work, but it has several significant problems. For one, it can be difficult for students to find appropriate tutoring sessions. The paper forms are difficult to navigate and understand. Additionally, it is very difficult for the tutoring program to track the students using the tutoring. It is difficult or impossible to track demographic information. It is also difficult to assure that students are enrolled in the courses they receive tutoring in. Even tracking tutors' hours can be difficult.

A database with a client application could significantly improve the situation, by providing a flexible, searchable schedule for students; better tracking of demographics and eligibility; and better tracking of hours tutored.

### Scope

The tutoring database will manage data for the tutoring program at the college. It will track available tutors and the courses they can tutor. It will also track each tutor's tutoring schedule. The database will store demographic information for students who register for tutoring. This information will be private and used only to generate general reports which include no personal information. Students who have registered will be able to sign up for available tutoring sessions for courses in which they are enrolled. The database will track whether students attended their scheduled sessions. It will also track student requests for tutoring in additional courses and subjects.

### Constraints

The database can be used to get the hours worked for each tutor, but it will not process pay or provide any payroll information. The database will not validate student information against the school's registration database.

### Objectives

- Streamline the process by which the tutors enter their schedules and students sign up for them.
- Improve tracking of demographic data of students using the tutoring program.
- Improve tracking of tutors' hours and students' use of tutoring sessions.
- Track student requests for additional tutoring.

### Tasks and Timeline

1. **Gathering Data:** This task will consist in a number of interviews, questionnaires, and observations. Time allotted: 3 weeks.

   **Deliverable:** A list of scheduled interviews and observations and text of the questionnaires.

2. **Analyzing Data:** The data gathered will be analyzed to determine business rules and preliminary data modeling. Time allotted: 2 weeks.

   **Deliverable:** List of business rules—their basic entities and attributes—to be reviewed.

3. **Normalization:** The data model will be completed with entities and relationships normalized. Time allotted: 1 week.

   **Deliverables**: Entity relation diagram for review.

4. **Building the physical database:** The data model will be translated to the RDBMS. Tables containing columns with specific data types and relational and other constraints created. Time allotted: 3 days.

   **Deliverables:** The schema of the database for review.

5. **Testing and Security:** Sample data will be entered, and each of the business rules and requirements will be tested. General database security and security related to business rules will also be tested. Time allotted: 3 weeks.

**Deliverables**: Documented test results.

6. **Database Completion and installation:** Final changes and corrections are made. Sample data will be removed, and the database installed on a server. Final testing for server access and connections. Time allotted: 2 weeks.

**Deliverables:** The working database.

Total time between beginning of project and end: 11 weeks, 3 days.

## DOCUMENTATION

Documentation is a lot like flossing: Nobody likes to do it, and far more claim to do it than actually do. Developers want to work on their plan. The last thing they want to do, generally, is to take time out and describe what they are developing and how they are going about it. And yet, like flossing, few things are as important to a healthy database enterprise.

Imagine you have been hired to work as a data administrator for some company. They have a large and complex database, but the former administrator, who was also the developer, left no documentation. To do your job properly, you need to understand what each object in the database is meant to do. You also need to know what it is supposed to do and how data is processed. Managers expect you to be able to provide them with the data they need when they need it. Some pieces probably make sense right away, but several pieces remain obscure. You try to ask people about them, but managers are not database designers and, generally, they don't have a clue. Many of the people who were involved in the creation of the database have moved on, and it is difficult to get a clear sense of the original intentions or purpose of the database. Eventually you may solve the problems, but you will have spent countless hours in investigation, hours that could have been saved by a little documentation.

Documentation is one of the most important and one of the most neglected aspects of any database project. When you look at a database built by someone else, or even one that you may have made some time ago, it is often difficult to see why certain decisions were made, why the tables are the way they are, and why certain columns were included or left out. Without documentation, it can take a great deal of research and guesswork to understand the database. You may never understand all of its original logic.

So what does it mean to document a database? There are really two main aspects that need to be documented: the structure of the database itself and the process by which the database was developed.

Documenting the existing structure of the database includes describing the tables, the columns and their data types, and the relations between tables and any other database objects and constraints. This kind of documentation is often called a "data dictionary." Anyone can use this dictionary to look up any table and find out what columns it contains and what key fields it contains. He or she can also look up a column and determine its data type and what constraints, if any, were placed on the column. This is important information for anyone who needs to maintain the database or for application developers who wish to build software based on the database.

Documenting the process of developing the database should include recording the original intent of the database, the problems that it was meant to solve, the business rules to which it must conform, and important decisions that were made throughout the process. This information is essential to anyone who needs to maintain or modify the database. Such an individual needs to first understand why the database is as it is.

Then he or she needs to understand how his or her changes will affect the original purposes of the database.

As part of the development process, you should keep one or more notebooks in which you put all the documents and notes related to the project. The first thing you should add is the statement of work. The statement of work is one of the first and most important pieces of documentation. The history section captures the original reasons for developing the database. The scope and objectives provide insight into the specific tasks the database was intended to perform.

In the following scenario sections and in the rest of the book, there will be "to do" items that are labeled "Documentation" to help you record your development process.

## Things We Have Done

*In this chapter we have*

- identified a situation in which a database could prove valuable
- reviewed briefly the history of databases
- identified some of the components of relational databases such as entities and key fields
- observed an interview to gather general information about a database
- broke the general information into major topics
- used the major topics to develop a statement of work for the database

## Vocabulary

*Match the definitions to the vocabulary words:*

1. Attribute
2. Foreign key
3. Statement of work
4. Primary key

5. Data integrity
6. Redundancy
7. Delimited files
8. Relational database
9. Entity
10. Relational design

11. SQL
12. Constraints
13. Fixed width files

— a. A type of database that uses "relations," tables, to store and relate tables.
— b. The process of organizing data into tables or entities and then determining the relations among them.
— c. The language relational databases use to create their objects and to modify and retrieve data.
— d. These files have some sort of character separating columns of data. The delimiter is often a comma or tab, but it can be any non-alphanumeric character.
— e. Files where the length in characters of each column is the same.
— f. Refers to the accuracy and the correctness of the data in the database.
— g. Refers to storing the same data in more than one place in the database.
— h. This key uniquely identifies each row in the table.
— i. This key is the primary key repeated in another table to create a link between the tables.
— j. A short statement of one or more paragraphs that says in clear, but general, terms what the project will do.
— k. Something that the database is concerned with, about which data can be stored.
— l. Things that define aspects of entities.
—m. Limits on what the database will do.
— n. A document including the scope, objectives, and timeline for a given project.

## Things to Look Up

1. Look up Codd's twelve rules. Choose one of the rules to explain to your fellow students.
2. Look up the history of SQL. How many revisions of the standard have there been? What was added in the most recent one?
3. Use the Internet to look up database-related jobs. Make a brief report summarizing what you find.
4. A recent trend for major commercial database developers is to offer free "Express" versions of their databases. Microsoft has *SQL Express*, Oracle has *Oracle Express*, and DB2 has *DB2 Express*. Go to the company Web sites, and look up these Express editions. What features does each one have? What limits do they have? How do they compare to each other?
5. For some time, there have been attempts to move beyond relational databases, to find some new data model. One direction has been to move toward *object-oriented databases*. Another area of research is into XML-based databases. Choose one of these to look up, and write a brief summary of what the model entails and what is the current status of the model.
6. Look up statements of work. What are some additional elements that can be included?

## Practices

1. Think about keeping a home budget. Would it be better to keep the budget in spreadsheets or to create a budget database? Write a couple of paragraphs that describe your choice and at least three reasons to justify it.

2. Think of a small business or nonprofit that you know that could use a database. Explain why you think a database would help the business. List the benefits the business or nonprofit would gain from a database.

3. An *entity* is something the database is concerned with. For instance, a movie rental business would probably have an entity called DVD. *Attributes* are things that describe the entity. Make a list of possible attributes for a DVD entity.

4. You are going to interview a small business owner about creating a database for his sandwich shop and bakery. Make a list of questions for this initial interview. Remember at this point you just want the big picture and major requirements. Don't get too deep into the details.

5. Think about the sandwich shop and bakery in Question 4. List what you think the major topics would be.

6. A dentist office wants a database to track its appointments. The specifics of what they want to track are as follows:

    a. All customers of the dental office
    b. Customer appointments
    c. Which dentist serves each customer at the appointment
    d. Which assistants assist each dentist
    e. In brief what services were provided at the appointment

    The database will not track bills and payments (they have a separate software for this purpose).

    Write a statement of scope for the dental office database.

7. List the major themes for the dentist office database in Practice 6.

8. How long do you think it would take to gather the information needed to make the dentist office database in Practice 6? Discuss what steps you think would be involved and how long it might take you to build the database.

9. Look around the school or think of some businesses or nonprofits with whom you are familiar. Identify at least one situation in which a database could be of help.

    a. Describe why a database would improve the situation.
    b. Describe what the major topics of this database would be.
    c. Write a statement of work for this database.

10. An instructor has been keeping all his grade books in Excel for years. He has a separate spreadsheet for every course. In the spreadsheet, he tracks the scores for every assignment and test and then assigns term grades based on the overall averages. Whenever a former student contacts him requesting a letter of recommendation or whenever the administration requests information concerning a student in a previous term, he has to open and search several spreadsheets to get the student's information.

    a. What are some of the advantages a database would have over the current system for this instructor?
    b. What would be some of the major topics for the database?
    c. Write a statement of work for the preceding database.

## Scenarios

These scenarios are designed to give you the opportunity to experience database development from beginning to end. Each has its own unique challenges. The scenarios can be pursued individually or in small groups. I would suggest choosing one scenario that interests you to follow throughout the term. Later, if you are so inclined, you can return and work through some of the others.

### WILD WOOD APARTMENTS

Wild Wood Apartments owns 20 different apartment complexes in Washington, Oregon, California, and Idaho. Each apartment complex contains anywhere from 10 to 60 separate apartments, of varying sizes. All apartments are leased with a six-month or yearlong lease.

It is the company's practice to hire one of the tenants to manage each apartment complex. As manager, he or she needs to admit new tenants to the building, collect rents from existing tenants, and close out leases. The manager also needs to maintain the apartments by conducting any repairs, replacements, or renovations. These can be billed back to the parent company. For acting as manager, the tenant gets free rent and a stipend. The stipend varies depending on the size of the apartment building.

Each manager is expected to send a report to the Wild Wood Apartments company headquarters in San Francisco every quarter. This report summarizes the occupancy rate, the total revenues in rent, the total expenses in maintenance and repairs, and so on. Currently, managers fill out a paper form and mail it back to headquarters. Many apartment managers have complained that preparing this report is a very difficult and time-consuming process. Also, the managers at corporate headquarters have expressed concerns about the accuracy and verifiability of the reports.

To allay these concerns and to improve the ease and efficiency with which the apartment managers conduct their daily business, the company is proposing to develop a centralized database that can be used by the managers to track the daily business of their apartment building and to prepare their reports.

### To do

1. List the major topics for this database
2. Write a draft statement of work. Include a brief history, a statement of scope, objectives, and a preliminary timeline.
3. **Documentation:** Start a notebook, either electronically or physically, to record your progress with the scenario database. Add the statement of work and any notes to the notebook.

### VINCE'S VINYL

Vince Roberts runs a vintage record shop in the University district. His shop sells 45's, LPs, and even old 76 RPM records.

Most of his stock is used—he buys used vinyl from customers or finds them at yard sales and discount stores—but he does sell new albums that are released on vinyl. For a couple of years, he has kept most of his inventory either in his head or in a spiral notebook he keeps behind the sale counter. But his inventory and his business have grown to where that is far from sufficient.

Vince is looking for someone to make him a database. He knows he needs to get a better handle on several aspects of his business: He needs to know the extent and condition of his inventory. He needs to know the relative value of his inventory—some records are worth a fortune; some are nearly worthless. He also needs to track where, from whom, and for how much he purchased his stock. He needs to track his sales. He often is not entirely sure how much money he has spent or how much money he has earned.

In addition he would like to allow customers to make specific requests and notify them if a requested item comes in. More generally he would like to make an e-mail list of interested customers in order to let them know about new items of interest.

Someday, he would like to expand his business online. But he knows he needs to have everything under control before then.

**To do**

1. List the major topics for this database.
2. Write a draft statement of work. Include a brief history, a statement of scope, objectives, and a preliminary timeline.
3. **Documentation:** Start a notebook, either electronically or physically, to record your progress with the scenario database. Add the statement of work and any notes to the notebook.

## GRANDFIELD COLLEGE

The law requires that any business, including a school, track its software. It is important to know what software the school owns, in what versions, and what the license agreement for that software is. There are several different licensing schemes. The least restrictive is a "site" license which allows an institution to have a copy of the software on any machine on the business property. Other licenses specify a certain number of active copies for an institution but don't worry about which machine or user has the copy. The more restrictive licenses do specify one copy per specific machine or user.

Whatever the license agreement for particular software, it is essential for the institution to know which software is installed on which machine, where that machine is located, and which users have access to that machine. It is also important to track when the software is uninstalled from a machine and when a machine is retired.

An additional useful feature of any software-tracking database would be to track software requests from users to determine (1) if a copy of the software is available and (2) if it is something that should be purchased. All installations are reviewed and must be approved.

For now the school just wants the database to track faculty and staff computers and software. Software for student machines is a separate and complex issue and will be treated as a separate project at a later time.

**To do**

1. List the major topics for this database.
2. Write a draft statement of work. Include a brief history, a statement of scope, objectives, and a preliminary timeline.
3. **Documentation:** Start a notebook, either electronically or physically, to record your progress with the scenario database. Add the statement of work and any notes to the notebook.

## WESTLAKE RESEARCH HOSPITAL

A hospital is conducting a double blind test of a new depression drug. It will involve about 20 doctors and about 400 patients. Half of the patients will get the new drug, and half will get traditional Prozac. Neither the doctors nor the patients will know who is getting which drug. Only two test supervisors will know who is getting what. The test will last about 18 months. Each doctor will see 20 patients initially, though it is expected some patients will drop out over time. Each patient will be coming in twice a month for a checkup and interviews with their doctor. The drugs will be dispersed in a generic bottle by the two supervisors, one of whom is a pharmacist.

To track this study, the hospital will need a database. It will need to track patients' information from their first screening through each of their interviews. In particular, they are looking at whether the patient seems more depressed or less, what their appetite is like, are they sleeping, and what kind of activities they are engaged in, if any. Also, they will be looking for specific physical side effects such as rashes, high blood pressure, irregular heart rhythms, or liver or kidney problems.

Doctors need to be able to see their own patient's information, but not that of any other doctor's patients. They also need to be able to enter blood pressures, blood test results, the depression indicators, their own notes, and so on for each session.

Patients should be able to see their own medical profile, the doctor's notes, and nothing else.

Only the two researchers should be able to see everything: all patient information, all doctors' notes, and which drug each patient is being given.

There is always some danger of spying by other companies interested in similar drugs, so in addition to the security of the blind test, the database needs to be secured against outside intrusion as well.

**To do**

1. List the major topics for this database.
2. Write a draft statement of work. Include a brief history, a statement of scope, objectives, and a preliminary timeline.
3. **Documentation:** Start a notebook, either electronically or physically, to record your progress with the scenario database. Add the statement of work and any notes to the notebook.

## SUGGESTIONS FOR SCENARIOS

Scan the scenario descriptions and list the nouns. Identify the important nouns, the ones that describe features of the potential database. These should be your major topics. Each scenario should have at least four major themes. Some have more.

All of what you need for the history and statement of scope is present in the scenario descriptions. You are not expected to invent anything new at this stage, even though you might have ideas about other things the database could do.

At this point, the timeline is pure guesswork. Just give it your best guess. Think about what the deliverables will be, even though a lot of them involve things you haven't worked with yet. Use the statement of work in the chapter as a guide.

## CHAPTER 2

# Gathering Information

## INTERVIEWS, OBSERVATIONS, AND REVIEWING DOCUMENTS

Now that she has the scope of the database, Sharon begins to gather information about the data the database will need to capture and process. First, she looks at the sheets that have been used to schedule tutoring sessions. She also looks at the spreadsheets the supervisor develops for reports and other related documents. Then she arranges an interview with several of the tutors and a couple of students. As a follow-up, she creates a questionnaire for students who use the tutoring services. Finally, she spends an afternoon in the computer lab, observing how students schedule tutoring and how the actual tutoring sessions go.

## CHAPTER OUTCOMES

**By the end of this chapter you will be able to:**

- Review documents to discover relevant entities and attributes for database
- Prepare interview questions and follow up
- Prepare questionnaires
- Observe work flow for process and exceptions

## LOOKING AT THE DOCUMENTS

Sharon has arranged to meet with Terry early in the morning. She arrives on time, and Terry greets her. "Let's go look at how students sign up for tutoring now."

Sharon follows Terry to the lab. On the counter of the service station at the front of the lab, there is a clipboard with sign-in sheets for tutoring. Each sheet is for one week. Across the top are the days of the week. Down the left margin are times. Tutors mark the times they are available and what topics they are tutoring by listing their name and the class they are tutoring for in a time slot. Students sign up for a time slot.

Sharon looks at the sheets. "I presume TT stands for tutor and CL for class and ST for student. Is that correct?"

Tracy nods, "Yes that is correct."

"Is this all the information you have about the tutoring sessions? How do you know if the student showed up or not?"

**Tutoring for the Week of 4/12 to 4/16/2009**

| | Monday | Tuesday | Wednesday | Thursday | Friday |
|---|---|---|---|---|---|
| **9:00 AM** | TT:<br>CL:<br>ST: | TT:<br>CL:<br>ST: | TT:<br>CL:<br>ST: | TT:Aimes<br>CL:(Math 290)<br>ST:Laura Jones | TT:<br>CL:<br>ST: |
| | TT:<br>CL:<br>ST: | TT:<br>CL:<br>ST: | TT:<br>CL:<br>ST: | TT:Carson<br>CL: (ITC 110)<br>ST: | TT:<br>CL:<br>ST: |
| | TT:<br>CL:<br>ST: | TT:<br>CL:<br>ST: | TT:<br>CL:<br>ST: | Johnson<br>(ITC 224)<br>Shanna Taylor | TT:<br>CL:<br>ST: |
| **9:30 Am** | TT:Johnson<br>CL:(ITC224)<br>ST: | TT:<br>CL:<br>ST: | TT:Carson<br>CL: (ITC 110)<br>ST:Peter Laws | TT:<br>CL:<br>ST: | TT:Johnson<br>CL:(ITC 224)<br>ST:Bob Green |
| | TT:<br>CL:<br>ST: | TT:<br>CL:<br>ST: | TT:Johnson<br>CL: (ITC 224)<br>ST:Sara Lewis | TT:<br>CL:<br>ST: | TT:<br>CL:<br>ST: |
| | TT:<br>CL:<br>ST: | TT:<br>CL:<br>ST: | TT:<br>CL:<br>ST: | TT:<br>CL:<br>ST: | TT:<br>CL:<br>ST: |
| **10:00 AM** | TT:<br>CL:<br>ST: | TT:<br>CL:<br>ST: | TT:<br>CL:<br>ST: | TT:<br>CL:<br>ST: | TT:Stevens<br>C:(Math 100)<br>ST:Thomas Seth |
| | TT:<br>CL:<br>ST: | TT:<br>CL:<br>ST: | TT:<br>CL:<br>ST: | TT:<br>CL:<br>ST: | TT:<br>CL:<br>ST: |
| | TT:<br>CL:<br>ST: | TT:<br>CL:<br>ST: | TT:<br>CL:<br>ST: | TT:<br>CL:<br>ST: | TT:<br>CL:<br>ST: |
| **10:30 AM** | TT:<br>CL:<br>ST: | TT:Mary L<br>CL:(ENG 101)<br>ST:Ly Poon | TT:<br>CL:<br>ST: | TT:Mary L<br>CL:(ENG 101)<br>ST: | TT:Stevens<br>CL:(Math 100)<br>ST:Thomas |
| | TT:<br>CL:<br>ST: | TT:Sanderson<br>CL:(ITC 110)<br>ST: Anderson | TT:<br>CL:<br>ST: | TT:<br>CL:<br>ST: | TT:<br>CL:<br>ST: |
| | TT:<br>CL:<br>ST: | TT:<br>CL:<br>ST: | TT:<br>CL:<br>ST: | TT:<br>CL:<br>ST: | TT:<br>CL:<br>ST: |
| **11:00 AM** | TT:<br>CL:<br>ST: | TT:Mary<br>L CL:(ENG 101)<br>ST: Snodgrass | TT:<br>CL:<br>ST: | TT:Mary<br>L CL:(ENG 101)<br>ST:Martin Yang | TT:Stevens<br>CL:(Math 100)<br>ST:Brown |
| | TT:<br>CL:<br>ST: | TT:<br>CL:<br>ST: | TT:<br>CL:<br>ST: | TT:<br>CL:<br>ST: | TT:<br>CL:<br>ST: |
| | TT:<br>CL:<br>ST: | TT:<br>CL:<br>ST: | TT:<br>CL:<br>ST: | TT:<br>CL:<br>ST: | TT:<br>CL:<br>ST: |

**FIGURE 2-1**  Morning Tutoring Appointments

|          | Monday | Tuesday | Wednesday | Thursday | Friday |
|----------|--------|---------|-----------|----------|--------|
| 11:30 AM | TT:<br>CL:<br>ST: | TT:Mary L<br>CL:(ENG 101)<br>ST: | TT:<br>CL:<br>ST: | TT:Mary L<br>CL:(ENG 101)<br>ST: | TT:<br>CL:<br>ST: |
|          | TT:<br>CL:<br>ST: | TT:<br>CL:<br>ST: | TT:<br>CL:<br>ST: | TT:<br>CL:<br>ST: | TT:<br>CL:<br>ST: |
|          | TT:<br>CL:<br>ST: | TT:<br>CL:<br>ST: | TT:<br>CL:<br>ST: | TT:<br>CL:<br>ST: | TT:<br>CL:<br>ST: |

**FIGURE 2-1**    Continued

## Things You Should Know

### Gathering Information

Before you can actually begin designing a database, you must understand what data the database needs to store and how that data will be used. It is tempting to think you understand the gist of what is going on and start sketching out tables and columns, but it is always better to wait. Gather information. Make sure that you understand exactly what the customer needs to store in the database and why.

Gathering information is a complex task. Most projects have many facets that need to be accounted for. It can be quite daunting, but there are some basic steps to help you proceed.

- Initial interviews with the chief stakeholders (the managers or executives initiating the database project)
- Review of business documents to identify data elements
- Interviews with stakeholders
- Questionnaires
- Work shadowing (observing the flow of information)

The initial interview should provide the overview of the database. In it, you define the domain of the database, that is, what business tasks and information the database is meant to handle. You may get a few specific requirements in this initial interview, but the primary goal should be to get a clear picture of why the database is needed and what, in general, it is meant to do.

One of the first tasks should be to review any business documents. Business documents consist of forms and reports related to the data, but they can also include things like memos, organizational charts, mission statements, company goals, plans, and so on. Reviewing documents allows you to begin to make a list of what kind of content your database will have. It is important to ask about any abbreviation or item you don't understand.

Next, you should identify the chief stakeholders. A stakeholder is anyone who will interact with the database directly or indirectly. A stakeholder is anyone who has a "stake" in the results. Stakeholders include the managers and the employees who will work with the database. They probably also include IT staff who will develop, maintain, and support the database. They may also include direct customers and business partners.

Once you have identified stakeholders, you should arrange interviews with each group or possibly with all the stakeholders together. The purpose of the interviews is to get each stakeholder's perspective on what data the database needs to store for their use and how they will need to process that data.

Questionnaires may be more efficient to gather some types of information. Through this method, you can often get responses from more people than in an interview. Questionnaires are best for technical information and closed-ended questions that require simple, straightforward answers.

Finally, it is extremely valuable to watch how people work with the system they currently have. You can observe the "flow" of the data, how it is captured, and how it is used. It is also a valuable way to discover exceptions to the rule: "Oh, we always give Mr. Johnson a discount, he has been such a good customer" or "Sometimes we waive the fee. It is up to the clerk." If your database doesn't allow for common exceptions, it may prove too rigid to be useful.

*REQUIREMENT*

This is something a database must do. For instance, it must keep track of tutors and the classes for which they can tutor.

*WORK SHADOWING*

It means following and observing persons as they go through their work routine.

*DOMAIN*

This is the focus of the database. If the database is about the tutoring program, its domain is "tutoring."

*STAKEHOLDER*

Anyone with a "stake" in the final product. Anyone who will use or be affected by the database.

*EXCEPTION*

A variation in how things are done or recorded, an alternate process.

"I use these sheets but I also have the tutor's reports. Each tutor is supposed to fill out a short report form for each session time they sign up. In fact, the reports are my primary source of data. The sign-up sheets are just a check to make sure that I have all the report forms. Some tutors are a little lax about turning them in."

"Do you have any of those forms that I could look at?"

Terry smiles, "Of course." She walks behind the desk. "We keep the forms here for the tutors."

Sharon takes one of the forms and looks at it briefly. "It seems simple enough."

Terry nods. "It is quite simple. We wanted the tutors to focus on tutoring, not on paper work."

| Tutor Session Report Form | |
|---|---|
| Tutor Name | |
| Session Date | |
| Session Time | |
| Student ID | |
| Student Name (NA if no student signed up) | |
| Materials covered (NS if no show) | |

**FIGURE 2-2**  Tutor Session Report Form

Sharon asks, "Does it give you the information you need to make your reports."

Terry smiles wryly. "That's difficult to say. I use them, but it's certainly not easy to make my reports from them."

Sharon says, "Maybe you can show me some of the reports you need to make and explain what you have to do to complete them."

"No problem, let's go back to my office.

*Caution*
*Make sure you understand all the terms and abbreviations on the forms and reports you review.*

## Things You Should Know

### Reviewing Business Documents

The forms and reports a business uses to gather and disseminate information are an invaluable source for understanding several aspects of a business' data needs. For one thing, they provide clear insights into the daily business processes. They show how information is gathered about various transactions and then how that information is passed to other people and departments. Studying business documents can reveal not only what information is needed but also when and in what sequence. Second, carefully scanning the forms and reports will reveal many, perhaps most, of the individual pieces of data the database will need to contain. Business documents can reveal how the data will be used, that is, how it will be summarized, analyzed, and presented.

There are several kinds of basic business documents that can be relevant. Two of the most important documents are forms and reports. Forms are documents, either on paper or on the computer, that businesses use to capture data. They are used to "input" things like new customer information, sale details, or an employee's hours. Reports are documents that present "output" from the system. They summarize and analyze the data that was collected through forms and other means or the current status of inventory.

Several other types of documents can also be useful when trying to get a picture of the data that a database needs to process. Manuals and procedures can give you a sense of how things are processed, or, at least, how they are supposed to be processed. Memos and letters can provide some insight into issues that can arise in the system and also provide a sense of how the information moves through an organization and who is responsible for what parts of the information. Annual reports offer insights into the state of the organization and into what function the proposed database might serve within the broader business context. Even mission statements and goals can be useful. A database should be supportive of the mission and contribute to one or more of the stated goals.

*FORM*

A document, paper or electronic, that is used to gather data.

*REPORT*

A document, paper or electronic, used to display summarized or formatted data.

*PROCEDURES*

Documents that describe the approved steps for completing some business process. For example, a "How to" document.

In her office, Terry logs into her computer and brings up Excel. She opens a spreadsheet. "Here is an example of a simple time sheet."

**Tutor Pay**

| | For weeks beginning 4/6/2009 and 4/16/2009 | | | | |
|---|---|---|---|---|---|
| **Tutor** | **Week1** | **Week2** | **Total Hours** | **Wage** | **Gross Pay** |
| Aimes, Tabatha | 0.5 | 2 | 2.5 | $  10.50 | $  26.25 |
| Carson, Karen | 8 | 10 | 18 | $  10.50 | $  189.00 |
| Johnson, Luke | 3 | 4.5 | 7.5 | $  10.50 | $  78.75 |
| Lewis, Mary | 1 | 3.5 | 4.5 | $  10.50 | $  47.25 |
| Sanderson, Nathan | 3 | 3 | 6 | $  10.50 | $  63.00 |
| Stevens, Robert | 4 | 5.5 | 9.5 | $  10.50 | $  99.75 |
| **Totals** | **19.5** | **28.5** | **48** | | **$  504.00** |

**FIGURE 2-3**  Tutor Pay Spreadsheet 1

Sharon looks over the spreadsheet. "You get the hours for each tutor by going over those sign-up sheets and the report forms?"

"Yes."

"I imagine that can be labor intensive and error prone."

"You can only imagine. I used to assign this task to work-study students. But, no matter how good they were or how much I trusted them, I never felt confident until I had rechecked all the materials. So now I just do the payroll report myself."

"I think we can make this task a lot easier with a database and a lot more accurate. What other reports do you have to make?"

"Well, one important report is total student usage. For this, I report the total of all sessions attended by students in a term and then the unduplicated count of students."

"Unduplicated means you only count each individual student once. Is that correct?"

"Yes. We need to know how many total tutoring sessions are attended, but we also need to know how many individual students are taking advantage of the tutoring."

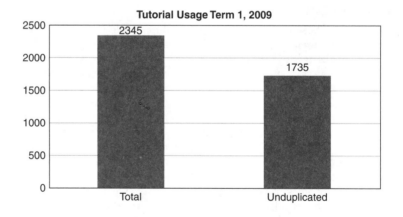

**FIGURE 2-4**  Total and Unduplicated Total

"Here are three other important reports. The first two charts cover demographics and the third those topics that are most sought after."

Sharon looks at the charts carefully for a moment and then asks a question: "How do you get the demographic information?"

Terry sighs, "It's not always easy. As long as the tutors remember to put in the students' ID numbers, I can locate the students on the school's Enrollment database. I can get their gender and ethnicity information there. If there is no student number for a particular student on any of the forms turned in, I can usually locate the student on the school's Enrollment database by searching for his or her last name and comparing that with the classes he or she is enrolled in and the topics he or she is seeking tutoring in. The hardest part is actually the unduplicated counts. I have to manually eliminate duplicates."

**Unduplicated Student Count by Gender**

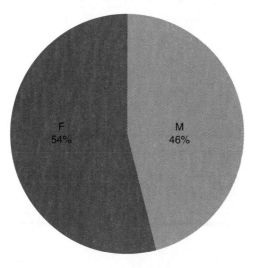

**FIGURE 2-5**   Unduplicated
Count by Gender

**Unduplicated Student Count By Ethnicity**

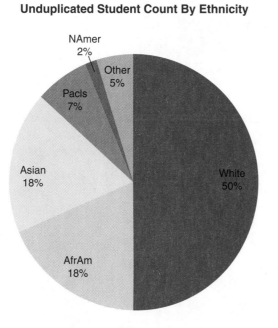

**FIGURE 2-6**   Unduplicated
Ethnicities

**Unduplicated Students by Subject Area**

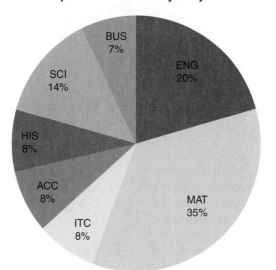

**FIGURE 2-7**   Unduplicated
Subjects

---

## THINGS TO THINK ABOUT

*Are there other forms you would have asked to look at, if you were Sharon?*

*What other kinds of forms could be relevant to the Tutor database?*

---

"That sounds like way too much work."

"Believe me it is. But many of our grants depend on ethnicity reports. We must show that we are serving a diverse population. Here is the actual spreadsheet I use to create the charts."

| Report Statistics | | | | |
|---|---|---|---|---|
| Fall Term 2010 | | | | |
| | | **Students** | | |
| **Total Usage** | | 2345 | **Workforce Retraining** | 247 |
| **Unduplicated Usage** | | 1735 | | |
| *Difference* | | *610* | | |
| | Unduplicated Demographics | | | |
| **Male** | | 937 | | |
| **Female** | | 798 | | |
| *Total* | | *1735* | | |
| | Ethnicity | | | |
| **White** | | 868 | | |
| **AfAm** | | 312 | | |
| **Asian** | | 312 | | |
| **PacIs** | | 121 | | |
| **NAmer** | | 35 | | |
| **Other** | | 87 | | |
| *Total* | | *1735* | | |
| | By Subject Area | | | |
| **ACC** | | 139 | | |
| **BUS** | | 121 | | |
| **ENG** | | 347 | | |
| **HIS** | | 139 | | |
| **ITC** | | 139 | | |
| **MAT** | | 607 | | |
| **SCI** | | 243 | | |
| *Total* | | *1735* | | |

**FIGURE 2-8** Report Statistics 1

Sharon looked over the spreadsheet. "You have to gather all that information by hand? I have just a couple of questions about some of the abbreviations. Does 'PacIs' mean 'Pacific Islanders'?"

"Yes."

"Also what does 'Workforce Retraining' refer to?"

"Several students received are identified as workforce retraining. Usually they are students who have lost their jobs and have been given government grants to return to school. Workforce retraining will pay for tutoring for those students."

"How are other students covered?"

"We get some money from different federal grants. Often these are tied to the diversity of the students we serve. Some are paid from funds at the college."

"Does the database need to track which students qualify for which funding?"

"No, I can handle that. If I can just get the basic counts and statistics easily, it will make my life a hundred percent better."

## Things You Should Know

### Types of Database

Relational databases can serve different needs for different users. These different needs can require different setups and structures.

One common usage of a relational database is as a Transaction database. A Transaction database, as its name suggests, records the data from immediate transactions such as sales or orders in real time, as they happen. These databases can be attached to a point of sale at a cash register, or they can be behind Web forms such as at Amazon.com or eBay. Transaction databases are optimized for speed and efficiency. Nobody wants a long wait while his or her order is being processed. Also, given the global nature of business, it is essential that many of these databases be as available as possible, preferably 24 hours a day seven days a week.

Another common use for a database is as a management information system (MIS). The purpose of an MIS is to use the data to provide data managers the information they need to manage an organization. An MIS focuses on data analysis. It is used to query data to return reports on things like total monthly sales, number of products sold, total shipping costs, and so on.

The MIS bases its reports on the data gathered by the Transaction database. In a simple situation like the tutoring program, where the number of users is relatively small, the Transaction database and the MIS database may be the same physical database. But in enterprise organizations, they are usually separated. The types of queries that an MIS runs to retrieve the data for reports would slow down the performance of the Transaction database more than is acceptable. So, typically, the data are periodically copied or shipped from the Transaction database to the MIS.

Increasingly, DBMS software is including tools for business intelligence. Business intelligence moves beyond management systems. Business intelligence systems mine data for patterns and trends that might help a business improve its offerings or services. A company, for instance, might analyze its customer data to find the ages and incomes of the customers who buy a particular product. They might look out for what other products those customers have purchased in a six-month period before or after the purchase of a particular product. They might look for a trend related to current advertising or a current event.

Data mining, exploring data sets looking for useful trends, is related to the idea of maintaining data warehouses. The concept of a data warehouse is to bring together all the data that an organization generates, not just the transactions that are recorded in formal databases, but also the memos, letters, minutes from meetings, and other documents any organization generates. The data warehouse brings them all together in a way in which and a place where data can be extracted and compared.

*TRANSACTION DATABASE*

A database that is optimized to keep track of transactions such as sales or purchases in real time.

*MANAGEMENT INFORMATION SYSTEM*

A database optimized for queries that return summary information about transactions.

*BUSINESS INTELLIGENCE*

A set of tools for analyzing trends and patterns in business data.

*DATA MINING*

Using business intelligence techniques on a variety of data sources brought together in a data warehouse.

---

## THINGS TO THINK ABOUT

*Why do you think the idea of data warehouses and data mining hold such an attraction to organizations? What are some of the benefits an organization could get from using business intelligence tools?*

---

The concept of the data warehouse is obviously very attractive, but it has proven very difficult to bring about in practice. New RDBMSs have included tools to incorporate more heterogeneous data such as documents, but it is still difficult to compare data from the different sources. One development that holds the promise of making data warehousing a reality is XML. XML is a set of technologies based on Unicode. XML is marked up text that follows a few simple rules. Ideally, an XML document is self-describing, that is, the markup tags tell a user what the text between consists of. Increasingly, business documents are saved as XML. (It is now the default format for Microsoft documents.) Tools have been developed for querying XML, allowing a user to extract and compare pieces of documents. RDBMS systems have also added data types and tools to store and manipulate XML documents. These developments may make data warehousing a fully realized business tool.

*XML*

Marked up Unicode text that follows a few strict rules—increasingly used as a file format for documents and data transferal.

## THINGS TO THINK ABOUT

*The confidentiality of data in a database is a major issue for many companies. The database may contain private information about employees or clients, or it may contain data that competitors could use to gain a competitive edge. Can you think of some ways that you could assure a client that you will keep all their data confidential?*

Sharon stands up. "Thank you. Looking at these reports will help me a lot. They give me a much better idea of what kind of data the database needs to track and store. Do you think I could get some copies to look at? I think I would also like to see examples of reports you have to make to your funding sources."

Terry hesitates for a moment, "I think I can do that—but some samples might have confidential information on them."

"I understand. You can give me blank ones, or you can black out private information. I promise not to divulge any information that could even remotely be considered private. I'll even sign something to that effect if you want."

"That shouldn't be necessary. I will get copies of the things I showed you and the other reports and get them to you tomorrow. What's next?"

"Thanks. The next thing I really need to do is interview some of the tutors and, if possible, a student or two to get their perspective. It is a good idea to have some representation of all the stakeholders. Is there a good time to do that?"

Terry thinks for a minute. "We have a tutor's meeting once a month. The next one is the day after tomorrow at 9:00 AM in Room 301. Would that work?"

"Yes that would work just fine, thank you."

"I'll ask the tutors if they know of any students willing to attend."

Sharon pauses a moment, thinking, and then asks, "How long do these meetings last?"

Terry says, "About an hour."

"And how many minutes can I use of it?"

Terry thinks for a minute. "I think we can give you 45 minutes of it."

"Thank you. I will see you then."

## Things You Should Know

### Interviews

Interviews can be an excellent way of gathering information. They are especially good for asking "open-ended questions." Open-ended questions are questions that don't have a definite answer. You can ask questions such as, "What is the best thing about the current system?" or "What would you most like to see out of a new system?" You can also ask questions such as, "describe what a typical sale is like" or "walk me through the process of registering a new customer."

There are several things to think about when conducting interviews:

You need to make sure you capture the points of view of every stakeholder group. It is not enough to get the manager's perspective on what a database should contain and do. You also need to get the perspective of the people who are going to work with the data every day. You need to get the opinions and needs of the IT people who will have to support and maintain the system. It is also likely that you will want to get some reaction and ideas from customers who will also be affected by the new system.

Often it is a good idea to get these opinions in separate interviews. You don't want those who work with the system to be intimidated or influenced by their managers. But if you can't conduct the interviews separately, try to get as many different groups of stakeholders together as you can and, if possible, arrange an outside facilitator—someone with no stake in the system, whose whole purpose is to make sure the process unfolds as fairly and completely as possible.

If you are conducting the interviews, it is absolutely vital that you be prepared. Know what questions you want to ask ahead of time. Know how much time you want to devote to each question. Also know how much time you can allot for follow-up questions or clarifications. Lay out the rules and timelines at the beginning of the interview so that everyone understands the process. During the interview, you must act as a facilitator. As such, your chief responsibilities will be to ask the questions and make sure everyone has a chance to respond. It is important to keep people on track and to politely cut them off if they veer too far from the subject or if their response is too long for the time allotted and will prevent others from having their turn. It is a delicate process, because you want as full an answer as possible.

Because facilitating is such a complex task, you should not complicate it further by also being the note taker. If you attempt to take notes, you will find either that you have to pause the interview while you record the responses or that you will continue with the interview and your notes will be incomplete. Neither is optimal. Assign this task to someone else, or use a recording device.

## PREPARING FOR THE INTERVIEW

That evening Sharon makes some notes for questions to ask during the interview. It is important that she ask the right questions. She jots down a few questions for the tutors.

- How do you set your schedule?
- How does a typical tutoring session go?
- What do you enter into the "topics covered" section of the report?
- How do you cancel a session?

Next she thinks of some questions to ask the students.

- How do you figure out what tutoring is available?
- How do you sign up for a session?
- Would you be willing to enter demographic information to get tutoring?

Sharon takes out her laptop and works out an interview plan.

*Caution*
*Always prepare for an interview. Conducting an interview without planning, at best, will result in an interview that is less focused than it could be and, at worst, could result in an awkward disaster that could erode confidence in you and the database project.*

| Tutor Interview | **Total time:** 45 minutes.<br>Allow 5 minutes for introductions. | |
|---|---|---|
| **Question** | **For** | **Time Allotted** |
| How do you set your schedule? | Tutors | 5 minutes |
| How do you sign up for a tutoring session? What would make the process easier? | Students | 3 minutes |
| What do you typically put in the section of the tutor report labeled "Materials Covered"? | Tutors | 2 minutes |
| How do you check to see if a student is in the class he or she is to be tutored for? | Tutors | 3 minutes |
| Why do you sometimes not get the students' ID number? | Tutors | 2 minutes |
| How do you cancel a session? | Tutors, students | 5 minutes |
| Would you be willing to enter your demographic information to get tutoring? | Students | 2 minutes |
| What is the number one thing you would like to see changed in the current system? | Tutors, students | 8 minutes |
| What part of the current system do you like? | Tutors, students | 5 minutes |
| Time for follow-up questions | Tutors, students | 5 minutes |

**FIGURE 2-9** Tutor Interview Plan

Sharon looks over the plan. It looks good on paper, but it is a pretty tight schedule. She is going to have to keep close track of the time. She is also worried about keeping notes. It will be almost impossible to both keep notes and facilitate the session. Then she remembers a digital recorder she had bought to record class lectures. She hadn't used it much because she found she preferred to type the lecture notes directly into her laptop, but for this interview, it would be perfect. Now she felt ready and could relax.

## THE INTERVIEW

Sharon arrives a few minutes early for the monthly tutors' meeting. She waits for a moment at the door of Room 301, reviewing the questions and the timing in her mind. She had to make sure the answers were concise, which could be difficult. People tended to want to talk and go off on tangents and accounts of personal experience. Shortly after Sharon arrives, Terry walked up and opened the room. "Good Morning," she said. Over the next five minutes, several people arrived and took seats. When it is time for the meeting to start, Terry stands in front of the classroom and introduces Sharon.

Sharon stands and smiles, "Good morning. I think the first thing we should do is introduction. Most of you probably know each other, but I would like to know you better. Just tell your name and what you tutor, or, if you are a student, give me your name and what subject you are getting tutoring for. We can start with you." She points to a young man sitting in the back corner of the room.

Sharon listens as the people in the room introduce themselves. She jots down their first names as they do the introduction. There are nine tutors and two students. Sharon is surprised to learn during that one of the tutors is not a student at the school. He is in fact an MBA student from another school. Terry explains, "Not all our tutors are our students. We utilize people from the community and other schools who want to participate in our tutoring program." A tenth tutor arrives late. Sharon smiles as he enters and asks him to introduce himself. Then, with a glance at the clock, Sharon begins: "As Terry said, I am working on building a database to help keep track of tutoring. I hope it will make all your lives a little easier. To build it, I need to understand what you do better, and what you would like to see, so I am going to ask you some questions. We don't have much time this morning, only about 30 minutes, so we are going to have to keep the answers pretty short. I will leave you with my email so you can let me know of things that you forgot about or didn't have a chance to tell me or any questions you might have. Also, I am going to record your answers on my digital recorder, if no one objects. It will help me to focus on your answers."

Sharon asks her first question. One tutor explains how she figures out her schedule. The hours she is in class are obviously unavailable. But she also looks at the meeting times for the classes she is tutoring. It doesn't make much sense to schedule tutoring sessions for when the students would be in class. Then she decides how many hours she can devote based on her own class work and other activities. The other tutors nod in agreement. "That's pretty well how we do it too."

Terry chimes in: "Tutors can work any number of hours up to the maximum of 15 a week."

Sharon looks at the students. "Jason, Sandy, how do you sign up for a session, and what would make the process easier?"

Jason looks at Sandy. She nods, so he answers first. "I go into the computer lab and look at the sign-up sheets. First, I see what time slots are available, and then I look at who the tutor is. If I can, I choose a tutor I know and like. It can be really hard sometimes to see what is available. The sheets can get pretty messy, and it can be really hard to read some tutors' handwriting."

Sandy adds. "It would be nice if there were some easy way to search for all the sessions that go with a class and see the time and tutors. It would be really nice if you could look ahead too. I would love to schedule a series of sessions for a month or more, but the sheets don't go out that far."

"The next question is for the tutors, and it is pretty specific. I've seen the report forms you are supposed to fill out for each session, and I was wondering what exactly you put in the box labeled 'Materials covered.'"

A female tutor, Sharon glanced at the list to recall her name—Ann, replies: "It varies, sometimes I put a subject in like 'quadratic equations,' or 'ratios'; sometimes I put in a specific lesson number." Another tutor replies, "I teach English. I usually put down things like 'paragraphing,' or 'agreement' or 'sentence fragments.' We don't put down everything in detail, just the gist of what we covered."

*Caution*
*If possible, use a recorder or have someone else take notes. It is almost impossible to facilitate a meeting and take notes too.*

Sharon thinks of a quick follow-up question for Terry. "Is that enough? Do you get the information you need?"

Terry nods, "Yes, I really only need a general sense of what was covered."

Sharon looks at her list of questions. "This one is for the tutors again. How do you check to see if a student is registered in the class he or she is requesting tutoring in? How about you, Nathan?"

She has noticed that Nathan, one of the tutors, seems to be a bit reluctant. He is sitting with his arms crossed in a protective stance, and his expression is not as friendly as most of the others. He takes a few seconds before he answers. "I usually don't check. I generally trust the students. We really don't have a good way to check anyway. We don't have rosters for the classes, and we can't really look it up." He pauses again for a moment and then adds, "I like the current system. It's flexible and easy to understand. Everybody is familiar with it. I am afraid that changing things will just make it all more complicated."

---

### THINGS TO THINK ABOUT

*Change, such as creating a new database, affect people's lives at work. It means a change in the way they have always done things.*

*Some people anticipate change with excitement, looking forward to a new and hopefully better way to do things. Others are less enthusiastic. Some are actually resentful or see it as a threat.*

*Don't be too quick to dismiss the negative attitudes. They may well have valid reasons for feeling as they do.*

*What would be the best way to handle such resistance in an interview? Do you think it would help to try to anticipate some of the objections beforehand?*

---

Sharon smiles and says, "That's good to know. I really hope that, in the end, this database will make everyone's life easier, but you can help keep me honest. If something makes things more complicated as we develop this, let me know, and we will see if we can fix it."

Sharon proceeds with the rest of the interview questions. She finds out that student IDs are missed because the form is filled out after the session and sometimes the tutor forgets to ask for it before the student leaves. Also, Mary tells her that the forms can be turned in a couple of different ways. They can be left after each session at the desk for Terry to pick up. They also can be kept by the tutor and turned in directly to Terry at the end of the pay period. Sharon also realizes, hearing the discussion, that canceling sessions was going to be a complicated matter, one that she was going to have to follow up on. The two students present are willing to enter their demographic information and don't have any concerns, but Sharon isn't sure everyone will feel the same. The one thing everyone would like to see changed is the scheduling process. And, the one thing everyone likes about the current system is its flexibility.

When the interview is over, Sharon glances at the clock. Three minutes to spare. She thanks everyone for their participation and turns off her digital recorder. Before she leaves the meeting to Terry, she asks if any of the tutors would be willing to let her shadow them as they go through a couple of tutoring sessions. Mary Lewis said that would be fine. "When would you like to do it?"

"When is your next session?"

"Tomorrow at 11:00 A.M. in the computer lab."

"OK, I'll meet you there."

*Caution*
*Go over your notes or recording within twenty-four hours. It is important to review them while the memory of the interview is still fresh.*

## THE QUESTIONNAIRE

Sharon still has some questions about how the students who use the tutoring services will interact with the database. She suspects it will be very hard to get an interview set up with enough students to constitute a representative sample, so she decides to create a simple questionnaire that the tutors can give their students after a session.

### Tutoring Services Questionnaire

1. Would you be willing to enter demographic information such as gender and ethnicity to sign up for tutoring?
   a. Yes
   b. No
2. Would you be willing to list the classes in which you are currently enrolled?
   a. Yes
   b. No
3. Which is the most important factor when you are looking for a tutoring session to sign up for?
   a. The particular tutor
   b. The time slot
   c. Neither of the above
4. When you can't make a tutoring session, which do you do most often?
   a. Leave a note on the schedule
   b. Contact the tutor by email or phone
   c. Contact the tutoring office
   d. Simply not show for the session
5. Which of the following best describes the process of finding a session and signing up?
   a. Difficult and confusing
   b. Not as easy as it should be
   c. Not too difficult
   d. Easy
6. If you could sign up online, which layouts would you prefer. Rank them in order of preference
   a. __View all available tutoring sessions for all classes
   b. __View all available tutoring sessions for a specific class
   c. __View all available tutoring sessions for a given date
   d. __View all available sessions for a specific tutor

*Caution*
*Make sure your questions are clear and not ambiguous. If possible, have two or three other people review your questions to make sure they are asking what you meant to ask.*

She prints it out. She will show it to Terry after her session with the tutor tomorrow.

## Things You Should Know

### Questionnaires

**CLOSED-ENDED QUESTIONS**

Multiple-choice, true and false, and ranked-value questions—questions with a definite answer.

Questionnaires are best for "closed-ended" questions. Closed-ended questions are questions that can be answered with a yes or no, by multiple choice, or by ranking a set of values. They are good for quick assessments of processes or attitudes toward a system.

Questionnaires have some advantages over interviews. They can be quicker and easier to arrange than interviews. They can also be less expensive because they take less of the stakeholder's time. With interviews, you can get responses from a wider number of stakeholders. Questionnaires can be easier to summarize and evaluate than interviews.

But they also have some disadvantages. For one thing, it is harder to evaluate the accuracy or honesty of the response. In an interview, you have all the nonverbal clues to guide you, and you have the ability to ask an immediate follow-up question. With the questionnaire, you have only what is on paper. Also questionnaires are not good for open-ended and complex questions. Generally, people don't want to write long blocks of text in response to a question.

Interviews and questionnaires are, of course, not exclusive. Both can be useful. If you use a questionnaire, there are a couple of things of which you have to be careful. First, make sure your questions are not ambiguous. Words can often be taken to mean two or more entirely different things. You know what you mean, but with a questionnaire, you won't be there to clarify. It is always a good idea to have two or three people read your questions and make sure that they are indeed asking what you meant them to ask. Second, make sure you get a representative response. That is, make sure that your questionnaire is given to enough people in enough different situations in order to get the fairest and most accurate response.

---

**THINGS TO THINK ABOUT**

*Consider the following questions:*

> *What are the top 5 things you do at work each day?*
> *Would this work better as a question in an interview or on a questionnaire? Why?*

---

## TUTORS AT WORK

The next day at 10:55 A.M. Sharon shows up at the computer lab. Mary Lewis arrives at the same time. They greet each other, and Mary begins explaining the process. She walks over toward the clipboard. "The first thing I do is look at the schedule here to see if anyone is signed up. I also look to see if I know the student. If I've worked with them before, it helps me have some idea of what they need."

Sharon thinks about that a second. "That's got to be hard. English is a big subject. How do you know or have any idea what a student is going to need?"

Mary laughs, "It's not really that bad. Tutoring is always tied to a specific class. So, I know what the instructor covers in that class and have a pretty good idea of what most students have trouble with."

They have to wait for a moment because a student is rummaging through the papers. He looks a little frustrated. Mary offers, "Can I help?"

He looks up. "I am looking for a math tutor."

"What class is that?"

"Math 110."

"I think John tutors for that class. Let me look." She scans the sheets. "Yes. He has two sessions this afternoon and two tomorrow afternoon. Here." She points out the sessions on the paper. He signs his name under the first one.

"Thanks. They should make it easier to find what you need. Thanks again."

"Now I can see what we have going today." She glances at the paper. "Looks like I have a new student today, a Mark somebody—I can't really read the last name."

Mary goes to the desk and gets one of the Tutor Session Report forms. "I always fill this out first thing. Some tutors don't bother to fill them out until they are due for payroll. That's hard. It is almost impossible to remember everything." She enters her name, the date, and the time. As she finishes, she glances at her watch. "Looks like Mark is running late."

Sharon asks, "Does that mess up the rest of your schedule?"

"No, if I have another session immediately after, I will just cut this short. If I don't have one right after, I might go a bit long."

"So you may be working more than you're getting paid for?"

Mary smiles, "It balances out."

Mark shows up and apologizes for being late. Mary asks him to spell his last name so she can put it on the form. Then she introduces Sharon. "She's watching me today to get some ideas for a database, if that is alright with you."

"Sure, no problem."

"What can I help you with today?"

Mark is having a problem with the bibliography for his research paper. Mary leads him over to a computer reserved for tutors and begins to show him how to cite different types of sources. When the session is finished, she says, "Well, Mark, I hope that helps."

Mark replies, "Thanks, yes that does help very much."

---

**THINGS TO THINK ABOUT**

*Can you think of some other insights you can gain by observing people actually working with the data?*

*Business managers may actually want some common exceptions to the process to be eliminated, for business reasons. But, how do you think workers would react to a database application that enforces strict procedural rules without any room for exception?*

---

After he leaves, Mary enters the materials covered in the Tutor Report Form.

Sharon asks, "What do you do with the report form when you are done with it?"

"That's a good question. You can give it to the people at the desk to pass on to Terry, but nobody does that. The desk workers are busy, and it's easy for them to mislay a piece of paper. So generally we just keep them ourselves until they're due."

"It must be pretty easy to lose them that way too."

"It can be if you aren't organized—and some of the tutors aren't. They can have troubles sometimes."

"Do you have another session today?"

Mary nods. "Yes, in a couple of hours. I have class in between. Let's take a look."

Mary goes back to the clipboard and searches through the papers. "Looks like nobody is signed up yet."

"You get paid anyway, right?"

"Yes," Mary says, "but the problem is, if over half your sessions go unfilled for a month, Terry will reduce the number of sessions you can offer."

"I didn't know that. Is that a rule that always applies?"

"Yeah, it's a rule, though Terry might let it slide for an extra month if you think you can get business to pick up."

Mary reaches into her notebook and pulls out a sheet of paper. "Here, Terry gives this to all the tutors. It states some of the basic rules. I am surprised she didn't give it to you."

Sharon glances at the paper:

## YOUR RESPONSIBILITY AS A TUTOR

- *Schedule your availability every two weeks.*
- *You can tutor a maximum of 15 hours in a week.*
- *Show up for every session even if no students are scheduled and stay the length of the session.*
- *Fill out a session form for every session.*
- *Turn in all session forms on the 10th and 20th of each month.*

*Never do a student's homework for them.*

*You are there to help them understand how to do their homework: If it comes to my attention that you have been doing students' homework, you could lose your tutoring privileges.*

*If you have fewer than half of your sessions filled in a 4-week period, you will be asked to reduce the number of sessions you offer.*

"Thanks, this is really helpful. I will meet you back here for the next appointment. Just out of curiosity, what do you do if no one shows up?"

"Usually, I just work on my own homework."

### Things You Should Know

### Work Shadowing

It is important to see how the data that your database is going to store are actually used in day-to-day business processes. You can ask people to describe what they do, and you can review the procedure manuals, but there is no substitute for actually watching people at work.

There are several insights you can gain from this: One is to see the actual flow of data, how it is captured, how it is transmitted to the next stage, and how it is transformed or changed in the process. It also lets you observe how frequently something is used and its relative importance. Perhaps the most important thing work observations can provide you is information about exceptions and undocumented processes. When people describe their jobs, they tend to describe the main activities they are supposed to do, the ones that match their job description. They tend to forget all the little things they do that are not part of the job description, shortcuts, or exceptions. "Well, I am supposed to give this to Jill and then she gives it to John, but Jill is very busy, so I usually give it directly to John." "Oh, we never charge Mr. Clemson a late fee. He has a hard time getting around since his stroke and we know he is always good for the payment, so we just waive the fee." If your database rules are too strict to allow some of these kinds of exceptions, it may prove too rigid to actually use.

## DOCUMENTATION

It is important to keep a record of your information-gathering process. A list of the business documents you looked at, along with your questions and answers about each, can prove invaluable later when you are reviewing your database for completeness. Summaries of interviews and questionnaire results are also important. All these documents should be kept in a project notebook.

## Things We Have Done

*In this chapter we have*

- looked over documents and reports to gather information about the data the database will need to store
- prepared an interview

- conducted the interview
- prepared a questionnaire
- followed a tutor to observe the actual work process

## Vocabulary

*Match the definitions to the vocabulary words:*

1. Closed-ended question
2. Domain
3. Business intelligence
4. Exception
5. Form

6. Transaction database
7. Open-ended question
8. Procedure
9. Data mining
10. Report
11. XML
12. Management information system
13. Requirement
14. Data warehouse
15. Stakeholder
16. Work shadowing

— a. Anyone who has a stake in the process
— b. A document for gathering data input
— c. A document for displaying summarized data
— d. A question that has no set answer
— e. A collection of all the various types of business information including databases and documents
— f. A multiple-choice question
— g. A set of tools for analyzing business trends
— h. Something the database needs to do to be successful
— i. An alternate way of doing a process
— j. Marked up Unicode text that follows a set of a few strict rules
— k. A database optimized for queries that summarize transaction data
— l. The official steps and rules for completing some process
— m. The purpose or subject of a database
— n. Combining data in a variety of formats for trends and patterns
— o. Observing workers handling data on the job
— p. A database optimized for storing and processing real-time transactions

## Things to Look Up

1. Information gathering is often presented as a part of Systems Design and Analysis. Look up "Systems Analysis and Design Life Cycle." What are the parts of this life cycle? How do you think this relates to database development?
2. Look up "Joint Application Development" or JAD. Briefly describe the process. Do you think this would work with database development?

3. Search for an article on database design. Does it have any discussion of information gathering? If so, what steps does it suggest?
4. What does the term "business intelligence" mean? What tools does the Microsoft business intelligence suite that ships with SQL Server contain?
5. Look up "Management Information Systems." What are some of the features that are associated with such systems?

## Practices

1. Look at any common receipt from a grocery store or a restaurant. List all the potential data elements on the receipt. What abbreviations of terms you don't understand? Make a list of questions you would ask someone if you were going to make a database to store this data.
2. Here is a report from a college help desk database. List the stakeholders who should be interviewed.

3. Using the form from Practice 2, see what abbreviations or terms you don't understand. Make a list of questions you would ask if you were going to make a database to store this data.
4. Create a questionnaire for the users of the form in Practice 2 with 4 or 5 questions. Your goal should be to understand how and when they use the form.

| R#: 44331 | | | | Status: In Process | | |
|---|---|---|---|---|---|---|
| **User:** Michael Lawrence | | **C#:** NA | | **Rm:** 2176B | | **P#:** NA |
| **Date Entered** | | 8/19/2010 6:00 PM | | | | |
| **Assigned to:** | | David Betting | | | | |
| **Assigned On:** | | 8/20/2010 11:00 AM | | | | |
| **Description:** Please quickly install a computer from order 317026 (faculty ones in 3157) before Michael gets here to start work next week. Standard staff office setup, and we'll add his special needs after he's here. I think his old dead computer is there, but he might want something from it. Ticket is a level 1. | | | | | | |
| **T Notes:** New computer is in place. Old computer is at my office. – D. Betting | | | | | | |

**FIGURE 2-10** Help Desk Report

5. Here is a form to create a new account at a Web-based company:

| | |
|---|---|
| *Email Address | |
| *Last Name | |
| First Name | |
| Address | |
| City | |
| State | |
| *Home Phone | |
| *Zip Code | |
| *Enter a Password | |
| *Confirm Password | |
| *Enter a Password Hint | |

You have an interview with a manager at the company. List at least 3 questions you would ask him about this form.

6. You are going to create a database to track clubs and activities on campus. Make a list of some of the types of documents you would like to look at.

7. Tomorrow you are going to interview several students who belong to various clubs aforementioned in Practice 6 and their faculty advisors. You will have one hour to conduct the interview. Think about what questions you might ask, and make a plan like the one Sharon made on page 20 for the interview.
8. Create a questionnaire to follow up on the interview in Question 7. It will be distributed in each of the next campus club meetings.
9. Think about some job that you have held. Can you list two or three exceptions—that is, things you did that were different than the standard procedures, such as shortcuts or one-time variations? (If you can't think of a job, think of your classroom experience. Have you ever seen an instructor make an exception for a class or a student?) List the rules and the exceptions, and briefly comment on why a database should or should not allow for each of them.
10. Think of a job you held, or, if you haven't held a job, think of yourself as a student. What would somebody doing a job shadow on your day observe?

## Scenarios

Each of the scenarios has different requirements. Each is documented differently.

### WILD WOOD APARTMENTS

As a follow-up on your initial interview with the project coordinators, Wild Wood Apartments has agreed to show you some samples of various forms and reports. The first example is of a spreadsheet to keep track of leases at one apartment complex:

| Apartment Number | Lease Number | Lessee Name | Start Date | End Date | Rent Amount ($) | Deposit ($) | Current |
|---|---|---|---|---|---|---|---|
| 201 | 201050109 | Charles Summers | 5/1/2009 | 5/1/2010 | 1,500.00 | 3,500.00 | 1 |
| 110 | 110060109 | Marilyn Newton | 6/1/2009 | 12/1/2009 | 1,200.00 | 2,900.00 | 1 |
| 306 | 306060109 | Janice Lewis | 6/1/2009 | 6/1/2010 | 1,250.00 | 3,000.00 | 1 |
| 102 | 102060109 | Larry Thomas | 6/1/2009 | 6/1/2010 | 1,250.00 | 3,000.00 | 1 |
| 209 | 209060109 | Mark Patterson | 6/1/2009 | 12/1/2009 | 1,450.00 | 3,400.00 | 1 |

The second example is of a spreadsheet used to track rent payments.

| Date | Name | Apartment | Lease Number | Amount paid ($) | Late |
|------|------|-----------|--------------|-----------------|------|
| 7/1/2009 | Martin Scheller | 203 | 203011208 | 1,200.00 | |
| 7/1/2009 | Roberta Louise | 311 | 311060108 | 1,400.00 | |
| 7/1/2009 | Sue Tam | 111 | | 1,400.00 | |
| 7/1/2009 | Laura Henderson | 207 | 207020209 | 1,350.00 | |
| 7/1/2009 | Thomas Jones | 110 | 110010109 | 1,200.00 | |
| 7/2/2009 | Shannon Hall | 205 | 205010109 | 1,350.00 | |
| 7/2/2009 | Bob Newton | 104 | 104030209 | 1,250.00 | |
| 7/9/2009 | Dennis Smith | 209 | | 1,400.00 | X |

The third is an example of tracking maintenance requests and responses.

| Apartment Number | Date | Problem | Type | Resolution | Resolution Date | B Expense ($) | T expense ($) |
|------------------|------|---------|------|------------|-----------------|---------------|---------------|
| 303 | 7/5/2009 | Left burner out on range | electrical | Electriction rewired | 7/10/2009 | 150.00 | – |
| 201 | 7/5/2009 | Water wastage from overflowing bathtub | floor | Replaced flooring with new tile | 7/21/2009 | 200.00 | 350.00 |
| 101 | 7/6/2009 | Dishwasher backing up | plumbing | Filter clogged; cleared it | 7/6/2009 | 35.00 | – |
| 207 | 7/15/2009 | Hole in plaster | walls | Patched hole | 7/17/2008 | – | 250.00 |
| 113 | 7/15/2009 | Refrigerator failed | utilities | New refrigerator | 7/20/2009 | 690.00 | – |

Finally, here is an example of the report that each apartment manager must turn in to the main office quarterly.

| **Wild Wood Apartments** | | | | |
|---|---|---|---|---|
| **Quarterly Report** | | | | |
| **Building #** | #12 | | | |
| **Address** | 1321 EastLake, Seattle, WA. 98123 | | | |
| **Quarter** | Spring | | **Year** | 2009 |
| **Total Apartments** | **Currently Occupied** | | **Percent** | **No. changing tenants** |
| 45 | 40 | | 89% | 13 |
| **Revenues** | | | | |
| **Total Rent Revenue** | 175,500.00 | | | |
| **Expenses** | | | | |
| **Utilities** | 2,450.00 | | | |
| **Maintenance** | 11,298.00 | | | |
| **Repairs** | 9,790.00 | | | |
| **Insurance** | 5,340.00 | | | |
| **New Tenant Cleaning** | 10,400.00 | | | |
| **Wages** | 19,200.00 | | | |
| **Total Expenses** | 58,478.00 | | | |
| **Unrecovered Rents** | 3,200.00 | | | |
| **Total Profit/Loss** | 113,822.00 | | | |

**FIGURE 2-11**  Wild Wood Quarterly Report

## Job Shadow Report

I followed apartment manager for the Eastlake Apartments, Joe Kindel, for four hours on March 1, 2010. It was the day the rents were due. Joe's apartment is also his office. The first thing he did after he opened up and let me in was to pick up a locked box that was chained to the floor just outside his apartment door. "The tenants can drop in their rents here," he told me.

Joe took the box inside, unlocked it, and pulled out the checks while his computer started up. When it was ready, he began entering the renters' names, apartment numbers, and payment amounts into a spreadsheet. While he was working, a tenant came in and handed him a check. He thanked him and added it to the pile. When he had finished, he checked his list against a list of tenants. He told me that three had not paid their rent yet.

He called each of the three. The first did not answer, so he left a message. "I am not too worried about him," Joe told me. "He isn't always on time, but he always pays within the 5-day grace period."

I asked about the grace period. Joe answered me, "The company allows a renter to be up to 5 days late without a penalty. If you pay after that, there is a $100.00 penalty tacked on to the rent."

He called the second renter. She was at home and asked if he could wait until the 10th. Joe said, "OK" and then explained to me, "She's an older woman and dependent on social security and retirement checks. I give her a little more leeway. The company lets me because she has lived here forever and has always been a good tenant. This last one though is just no good." He picked up the phone and called. He got no answer, and there was no answering machine. Joe told me that he was about ready to evict this last tenant. He is habitually late, and he is actually two months behind in his rent. Joe tells me how difficult it is to actually evict someone.

While he is telling me stories about past evictions, the phone rang. A woman in apartment 211 told him that her stove wasn't working. Joe opened a second spreadsheet and entered some of

the details. He also wrote some notes on a pad of paper. He reassured the woman that he would deal with it quickly and promised to come by in the afternoon.

After four hours, I thanked Joe for his time and left him to his lunch.

**To do**

1. Make a list of questions that you would ask about these forms and reports.
2. Identify the stakeholders for Wild Wood Apartments.
3. Create a plan for an hour-long interview with representatives of these stakeholders. Then meet with the instructor to discuss possible answers to the questions.
4. Create a questionnaire of at least 5 questions for the managers of the 20 apartment buildings.
5. Look at the Job Shadow Report. Do you see any exceptions to the general rules? Do you see any new business rules uncovered? What additional questions arise from the report?

## VINCE'S VINYL

Vince hasn't kept very complex records, but he does have a few things he can show you. The first thing he has is an example of the notes he takes when he purchases an album from a customer.

| Date | 5/14/2009 | | | | |
|---|---|---|---|---|---|
| Seller's Name | Seller's Phone Number | Album | Notes | Condition | Paid ($) |
| John Raymond | 206.555.2352 | Rubber Soul | Amer. Not British vers. 2nd edition, good Sleeve | fair | 4 |
| Marylin Tayler | 206.555.0945 | Led Zepplin IV | Not orig. Sleeve damaged, vinyl good | good | 4.75 |
| Jennifer Louis | 206.555.4545 | Gift of the flower to the Garder | Rare Donovan, box set, box cond. poor, but vinyl excellent | excellent | 12.25 |
| Laura Hall | 206.555.2080 | Dark Side of the Moon | | good | 4.45 |

Here is an example of a sale to a customer:

| Date | 5/12/2009 | | | |
|---|---|---|---|---|
| Customer | Album | Price ($) | Tax ($) | Total ($) |
| John Larson | Dylan, Blond on Blond | 19.95 | 1.65 | 21.60 |
| Tabitha Snyder | America | 5.95 | | |
| | Joni Mitchell, Blue | 6.25 | | |
| | Joan Baez, Ballads | 4.20 | 1.36 | 17.76 |
| Brad Johnson | McCartney, Venus and Mars | 5.00 | 0.42 | 5.42 |
| Maureen Carlson | Decemberists, The Crane wife | 15.50 | | |
| | Muddy Waters | 7.75 | 1.92975 | 25.18 |

## Job Shadow Report

I sat with Vince for a full day of work. The morning was quiet, and Vince spent the time sorting through a stack of albums that he had purchased earlier in the week. He took each one out of the sleeve and inspected it carefully. "Sometimes I catch things

that I didn't see when I actually purchased it," he explained to me. "It is too late now, of course, to do anything about it, but I want to be fair to the people I sell it to." He put a sticker on the cover and put "good" and a price of $6.50. I asked him about how he classified and priced things. He told me he had four levels: mint, good, fair, and poor. *Mint* was only for things that were nearly perfect. *Good* meant there were no scratches and the vinyl was not warped and not too worn. *Fair* meant the vinyl was a bit more worn and might have a light scratch or two. *Poor* meant the vinyl was scratched and probably warped. He didn't buy poor vinyl unless it was an extremely rare album. Prices were based on what he thought the album would bring. He based it mostly on experience.

After a while, a customer came in. He asked if Vince had seen a copy of an old album. He commented that he didn't think it had ever made the transition to CD. Vince said he had seen it, but he didn't have a copy currently, but if the customer wanted he would take his name and number and let him know when he next got a copy. The customer agreed and then, after looking around for about 20 minutes, returned to the counter with 5 albums. Vince wrote down each album title and the price and then added the prices on a hand calculator. The total came to $35.50. Vince said, "Make it thirty, and we'll call it good." Vince explained that it was good for business. It made the customer feel good, and they were more likely to come back. Several more customers came in, and their transactions followed a similar pattern.

In the afternoon, a customer came in with a stack of albums he wanted to sell to Vince. Vince went through the albums, taking each one out of its sleeve and inspecting it. In the end, he split the albums into two piles. He told the customer he was interested in the first pile of about 12 albums and would offer him $20.00 for them. The customer pulled one album out of the pile Vince had selected and said, "I thought this one might be worth a little more. It is a first print." Vince looked at it again. "Yes it is, but it is scratched and only in fair condition. Still, I'll make it $25 if that makes it seem more fair to you." The customer agreed. Vince told him he wasn't really interested in the second pile of albums. The customer could either take them back or Vince would put them on his 5-for-a-dollar pile. The customer chose to leave them.

Vince put the albums in a pile by his desk. Several more customers came and went. Vince chatted pleasantly with all of them. Several purchased an album or two. At about four, Vince turned the open sign in his window to closed, and I thanked him for his time and left.

### To do

1. Study Vince's sample notebook entries. Make a list of questions you would ask about the data in them.
2. Identity the stakeholders in Vince's record store.

3. Prepare an interview with Vince and two of his best customers: one who both sells albums to Vince and buys and one who mostly just buys. Then meet with the instructor to discuss possible answers to the questions.
4. Create a questionnaire for those who sell albums to Vince about changes they would like to see in the process.
5. Look at the Job Shadow Report for Vince. Do you see any exceptions? What additional business rules do you see? What additional questions does the report raise?

### GRANFIELD COLLEGE

The software management team has several spreadsheets to keep track of software. They show you several samples. The first is just a listing of software:

| Software | Version | Company | License Type |
|---|---|---|---|
| Windows Vista | Business, Service Pack 2 | Microsoft | MS Site |
| MS Office | 2007 | Microsoft | MS Site |
| Visual Studio | Professional 2008 | Microsoft | MS Instuctional |
| PhotoShop | CSS3 | Adobe | Adobe1 |
| FileZilla | 5 | FileZilla | Open Source |
| German | 2.5 | LanguageSoft | LanguageSoft1 |

The second is a key to the different licensing agreements and types:

| Licence Type | Start Date | End Date | Terms | Pricing | Pricing Unit |
|---|---|---|---|---|---|
| MS Site | 7/1/2005 | 7/1/2010 | Can install as many copies as needed on campus and on laptops controlled by the school. Includes all service patches, updates, and version changes | 12,500 | 5 years |
| Ms Instructional | 7/1/2005 | 7/1/2010 | Used for instructional purposes only. Cannot be used for school development projects | 3,000 | 5 years |
| Adobe1 | 7/1/2009 | 7/1/2010 | Reduced price per installed copy, max of 25 active copies | 450 | Per active copy |
| Open Source | 7/1/2009 | 7/1/2020 | Free for use as long as registered | 0 | |
| LanguageSoft1 | 7/1/2009 | 7/1/2010 | 25 copies | 5,200 | For 25 copies |

Here is an example of the list of who has what software

| CCS Number | Location | Assigned User |
|---|---|---|
| 3214 | Rm214 | Cardwell |

| Software | Install date | Rmv Date |
|---|---|---|
| Vista Business | 5/3/2008 | |
| Ms Office | 5/3/2008 | |
| PhotoShop | 6/4/2008 | |
| DreamWeaver | 6/4/2008 | |

| CCS Number | Location | Assigned User |
|---|---|---|
| 3114 | Rm212 | Larson |

| Software | Install Date | Rmv Date |
|---|---|---|
| Vista Business | 4/15/2008 | |
| MsOffice | 4/15/2008 | |
| Visual Studio Pro | 6/12/2009 | |
| DreamWeaver | 6/14/2009 | 7/12/2009 |

And, finally here is sample of a request for new software:

## Requests

| CCS Number | User | Request Date | Software | Reason | Response | Response Date | Status |
|---|---|---|---|---|---|---|---|
| 2123 | Johnson | 5/20/2009 | Camtasia | I am conducting several online classes. I need to be able to create visual demos to post to the class Web site | We don't currently have a license for Camtasia but will explore acquiring one | 5/24/2009 | Pending |

## Job Shadow Report

I spent the day on 4/12/2010 following Sheri, a member of the software management team at Grandfield College. The first thing she did after settling into her office was check a spreadsheet that listed pending installations. She showed me the list and told me that she had about six installations to do that morning. She also noted that it was the most boring part of her job. "Nothing like watching the progress bar on the monitor for hours at a time," she said. Next, she checked her emails. There were three requests for additional software. She opened a spreadsheet and entered the request information. She told me that she would check later to see if the school had the software or if it was something they would have to purchase. If it was a purchase, she would have to get permission. She replied to each of the emails to acknowledge their request.

After noting the requests, she looked again at the installation to be done. She went to a cupboard and pulled out some disks. She told me that some software can be installed from a network drive, but for some she has to bring the media. She also grabbed a notebook. We went to the first office. She spoke for a few moments with the woman who occupied the office. They laughed at a few things. Sheri said that with luck the installations should take no more than 30 minutes. The woman left the office to let Sheri work. Sheri logged into the computer as administrator and slipped in a DVD. She started the install.

I asked her about the notebook. Sheri told me that she carried it for two reasons. If there were any problems with the install that she couldn't solve, she would write down the error messages and take them to the other techs to resolve. She also would note in the book whether the installation was a success or not. She didn't put it in the spreadsheet until the installation was complete and successful.

The rest of the morning, Sheri moved from office to office installing software. On that day, at least, there were no major installation issues. While we waited, she told me about other days that didn't go so easily. She told me about how difficult it could be to troubleshoot a bad install, and how obscure and undocumented settings could require hours of research before they were discovered and resolved.

The installations were finished by lunch. After lunch, Sheri checked with the department receiving new software and packages. There were several that had arrived. Sheri carefully unpackaged each arrival and noted each in a spreadsheet. Then she checked the licensing agreements. Some she knew, others she had to check, often looking up the licensing agreement online. "Everybody is different," she told me. "Some let you install the software anywhere on-site. Some will only allow a certain number of copies. Some can be placed on a server, while some only allow client installations. Some are tied to a particular user. It would make my life easier if things were consistent."

Late in the afternoon, Sheri received a call for an instructor requesting disks for a piece of software. She told him "sure," if he would come up and get it. He arrived at the door shortly afterward. She gave him the disks and made him sign for them in a notebook. "I'll have them back to you tomorrow morning," he said. Sheri explained, "There are two or three instructors who have administrative privileges on their machines. They do their own installations and their own support." I asked if they track the software on those instructors' machines. Sheri told me that they do as best as they can, but the instructors can do pretty much as they want. To get the admin privileges, they have to sign a release saying they won't violate any licensing agreements and that they accept the fact that the school IT staff will not support their computers.

Following this, it was time to quit. Sheri shut down her computer. I thanked her for allowing me to follow her and wished her "good evening."

## To Do

1. Study the samples given earlier. Make a list of questions you would ask about the data in them.
2. Identify the stakeholders in the software-tracking system.
3. Prepare a plan for a one-hour interview with representatives of the stakeholders listed earlier. Then meet with the instructor to discuss possible answers to the questions.
4. Create a questionnaire for faculty and staff about changes they would like to see in the request process.
5. Review the job shadowing report. Do you see any exceptions? Do you see any additional business rules? What additional questions does the report raise?

## WESTLAKE RESEARCH HOSPITAL

The drug study is unique in many ways. For one, the forms and the type of information they capture are more complex. For another, privacy rules make it difficult to shadow doctors or researchers. But, still, if you are going to create a database, you must begin to gather the requirements and figure out what data are needed to be tracked.

Here is the Initial Medical History Form that each patient is asked to fill out:

## Initial Medical History Form

Name _____ Date_____

Birth Date _____

Address_____

City_____ State_____ Zip_____

Phone_____ Email_____

Group no.:_____ Nervous disorder ☐ yes ☐ no

Agreement no.:_____ Any form of cancer ☐ yes ☐ no

List any prescription or nonprescription medicines you are currently taking.

_____

_____

List any known allergies to medicines.

_____

_____

Have you ever been told you had one of the following?

_____ Lung disorder ☐ yes ☐ no

_____ High blood pressure ☐ yes ☐ no

Heart trouble ☐ yes ☐ no

Disease or disorder of the digestive tract ☐ yes ☐ no

Disease of the kidney ☐ yes ☐ no

Diabetes ☐ yes ☐ no

Arthritis ☐ yes ☐ no

Hepatitis ☐ yes ☐ no

Malaria ☐ yes ☐ no

Disease or disorder of the blood? (describe)_____

Any physical defect or deformity? (describe)_____

Any vision or hearing disorders? (describe)_____

Any life-threatening conditions? (describe)_____

Any contagious disorders? (describe)_____

How would you describe your depression?

   a. Severe and continuous

   b. Severe but intermittent

   c. Moderate and continuous

   d. Moderate but intermittent

When did your depression first begin? _____

Which of the following symptoms have you experienced

   ☐ Sleep difficulties

   ☐ Loss of appetite

   ☐ Loss of libido

   ☐ Inability to leave house

   ☐ Anxiety in social situations

   ☐ Thoughts of suicide

Briefly describe your history of depression. Include any earlier attempts at treatment.

_____

_____

_____

(continued)

Is there a history of depression in your family?

☐ Yes

☐ No

If yes, explain -

_____

The next form is the form the doctor would fill out for each patient visit.

## Patient Visit Form

### Vitals

Blood Pressure _____

Weight _____

Pulse _____

Does the patient believe his/her depression

☐ Has increased

☐ Decreased

☐ Remained the same

Check all symptoms the patient has experienced.

☐ Sleep difficulties

☐ Loss of appetite

☐ Loss of libido

☐ Inability to leave house

☐ Anxiety in social situations

☐ Thoughts of suicide

List any additional symptoms or side effects

_____

_____

Doctor's Notes

Recommendation:

☐ Continue with study

☐ Drop from study

If drop, explain -

_____

## Job Shadow Report

The doctors and the directors of the study were reluctant to allow me to observe them with an actual patient, but one of the doctors, Dr. Lewis, did agree to sit with me and walk me through the process of a patient visit.

"The first thing I do in the morning," he told me, "is review the day's appointments." He turned on the computer and showed me the way it is currently done. The secretary sends an email with a table of the patients and times of the appointments. He prints out the list and then goes to his cabinet to pull out the files of the individual patients for review. He reviews their initial medical history and the notes of previous visits. He makes some notes on a notepad for each patient.

When the first patient arrives, he greets them and asks how they are doing. He told me he keeps it casual, but he notes any complaints or signs of deepening depression. Then he goes through the parts of the Patient Visit Form. The nurse has already taken the patients' blood pressure, heart rate, and weight. He looks at them, and if the blood pressure is high, or if there has been a dramatic change in one of the measures since the last visit, he asks the patient about it. The he asks about their depression. He doesn't necessarily use the exact words of the form or follow it in order, but he makes sure he covers all of it. He records a few notes in a notebook while the patient talks but waits until the patient leaves to write most of the summary. He also waits until the end to make his recommendation to continue or to drop the patient from the study.

I asked Dr. Lewis how he makes that determination. He told me that it is a judgment call. Most of the time it's in the patient's interest to continue with the study, but if the patient is showing signs of significant side effects or if the patient seems in eminent danger of doing harm to himself or herself, he would recommend the patient be dropped and given alternative or more aggressive treatment. I asked if there were any other reasons for dropping a patient. He said that some patients were dropped from the study because of lack of participation, because they didn't show up for appointments, or were inconsistent in taking their medications. He also noted he always worried that such patients were possibly the most depressed and needed the most help.

### To do

1. Study the forms given earlier. Make a list of questions you would ask about the data in them.
2. Identify the stakeholders in the drug study.
3. Prepare for a one-hour interview with representatives of the stakeholders listed earlier. Then meet with the instructor to discuss possible answers to the interview questions.
4. Create a questionnaire for doctors about what they think would help improve the process.
5. Review the Job Shadow Report. Do you see any exceptions? Do you find any additional business rules in the account? What additional questions does the report raise?

## Suggestions for Scenarios

It is obvious these scenarios don't have all the information that you need. Focus your questions on making sure you understand all the bits of data you will need to make your database. You, your team, if you are working with a group, and your instructor can decide on the answers to these questions. As you discuss possible answers, several real-world issues may arise that add a great deal of complexity to the database design. Handling some of these complexities can be a good exercise, but students and instructors should feel free to simplify where needed. Too much complexity can be overwhelming to someone just beginning to develop databases.

## CHAPTER 3

# Requirements and Business Rules

Having gathered all the information about the database she can, Sharon must figure out what to do with it. She decides to review her notes to identify all the issues with the current system. First, she looks again at the issues with the current database. This helps her refocus on the purpose of the database. Then she lists the requirements for the database. Next, she clarifies the business rules that define how the data are gathered and used. With all this analysis done, she begins to identify the specific attributes the database must contain. She reviews the materials including the forms and reports and identifies the key nouns. Then she begins to organize them into entities and attributes. Finally, she identifies some candidate keys for the entities.

**CHAPTER OUTCOMES**

**By the end of this chapter you will be able to:**

- Identify the issues with the current database
- Define and list requirements
- Define business rules
- Search materials for nouns to define entities and attributes
- Identify candidate keys for entities

## GETTING STARTED

Sharon feels a bit overwhelmed by all the information she has gathered. How is she going to organize it in a way that makes sense and helps her determine the structure and design of the database? She pulls out a notebook and tries to sketch a plan of action. It is not easy. She decides to give her instructor, Bill, a call. Luckily, he is in the office and picks up the phone. She explains her dilemma, "I need a plan, some way to make sense of all this material."

Bill thinks for a moment and then says, "Here is what I usually do: I go through the materials and identify all the issues with the current system. That helps me get the purpose of the database back in focus. Usually the reason for developing a database is to fix those issues. Next, I look at all the requirements. What exactly does the database need to do? Remember to look at it from each user's perspective. Then I would go through the materials and identify all the business rules. The rules can give you clues as to what data must be included and how people will use them. Some of it can be incorporated into the database, and some will have to be implemented in the client application that will need to be developed at some point. Does that help?"

Sharon replies, "Enormously, I don't know how to thank you enough."

Bill laughs, "No problem. Just make a good database."

## Things You Should Know

### Client/Server Relations

A server is a program that makes a "service" or resource available for a "client" that requests it. For instance, a Web server makes a Web page available to a browser that requests the page to view.

Some computers are called "servers." Generally, this means that they are optimized to run server software. They often have more processing power and memory than other computers. They also often run an operating system that has tools to monitor and balance service requests such as Windows Server 2008.

Most database management programs also act as servers. They make database resources such as data available to the programs that request them. The requesting program is called a client. The client could be a Web page or a windows program or even another database requesting data.

It is important to note that what makes a server or a client so is the relationship between them: A server provides services requested by a client. The server and client can be on the same physical machine, or they can be on separate machines in different parts of the world.

*SERVER*

A program that offers services to requesting programs.

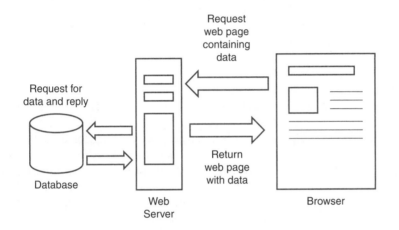

**FIGURE 3-1**   Client Server

Typically users access the database through a client application such as a Windows program or a Web page. Most users do not have the skills or the patience to navigate a relational database to find the data they need. They require an application to query the database, to return and organize the data in ways that they can use. In addition, giving users direct access to the database poses numerous security risks and issues.

Database design is one major task. Designing the client application or applications for the database is another major task. In Chapter 8, we will briefly explore some of the tools and processes involved in creating a simple client application for the Tutor database.

## REVIEW OF THE ISSUES

Sharon pulls out her notes. She looks at the notes from her first discussion with Terry. Terry had mentioned a couple of issues with the current system. For one, she found it difficult to determine student demographics for her reports. For another, Terry noted that sometimes it was difficult to determine even how many hours an individual tutor worked in a given time period.

The interview had revealed additional issues. Tutors sometimes found it difficult to keep track of report sheets. They didn't fill them out on time, lost the papers before the turn-in date, or turned them in late. Students found it difficult to locate the right tutor for their class on the sign-up sheet.

Next, Sharon reviewed the results of her questionnaire. She had received about 80 responses, which was quite good. She had spent some time and summarized the results. She looked at that summary sheet now.

*CLIENT*

A program that requests a service from a server.

- About 80% would be willing to enter demographic information including ethnicity.
- 95% would be willing to enter their current classes.

- About 70% said the time slot was the most important factor; 25% said the tutor, and 5% said neither of the above.
- Of students who canceled a tutoring session, 30% said they left a note on the schedule form. About 12% said they called the desk, and about 5% said they called the tutoring office. About 15% said they simply didn't show up. A total of 28 of the students put an NA, and several of them also noted they had never canceled a session.
- For question 5 on the difficulty of signing up, 40% found it confusing, 30% found it not as easy as it should be, 23% said not too difficult, and 7% said easy.
- The consensus on ways to look for sessions was b, c, d, a.

The questionnaire reinforced the idea that locating an appropriate session and signing up are important issues.

---

### THINGS TO THINK ABOUT

*It is always good to review what you have already done. Database development is an iterative process. You have to constantly go back and refine what you have already done.*

*What do you think would be some of the dangers of just forging ahead in a purely linear way?*

---

Finally, Sharon reviews her notes from her observation of tutoring sessions. The issue of the difficulties students experience signing up recurred again, plus the occasional difficulty of reading a student's name from the schedule. A couple of additional issues were uncovered. Tutoring times can overlap, run long, or be cut short. Sharon wonders if this is just inevitable or if some mechanism can be built into the scheduling to help fix it. The last issue she notes is that Mary said there were different ways to turn in the tutoring report. Either the tutor could turn in the report at the computer lab desk, or the tutor could hold the reports and turn them in to Terry on the due date. Sharon believes having two ways to turn in the reports contributes to the issue of lost or late reports.

Sharon sits down and jots down the issues she has uncovered:

- It is difficult to get and track demographic information.
- It is difficult to summarize and confirm individual tutors' tutoring hours.
- A related issue: getting the tutoring session reports filled out and turned in on time.
- It can be difficult to find an appropriate tutoring session in the paper schedule.
- It can be difficult to read the schedule.
- Times can overlap, run long, or be cut short.

Sharon sits back. These are the issues her database will be designed to solve. Just to be sure, Sharon reviews the original statement of work again. In the History section, it says the following:

> This system has worked and continues to work, but it has several significant problems. For one, it can be difficult for students to find appropriate tutoring sessions. The paper forms are difficult to navigate and understand. Additionally, it is very difficult for the tutoring program to track the students using the tutoring. It is difficult or impossible to track demographic information. It is also difficult to assure that students are enrolled in the courses they receive tutoring in. Even tracking tutors' hours can be difficult.

*PROBLEM DOMAIN*

The business problem the database is meant to address.

Her review has revealed the same issues that were identified in the original statement of work. So now that she is confident she understands the problem domain, she is ready to move on.

## REQUIREMENTS

The next thing Bill said to do was to go through her notes again and identify all the requirements, the things the database must do. Once again Sharon returns to the statement of work. The Scope section lays out the general requirements clearly:

> The Tutoring database will manage data for the tutoring program at the college. It will track available tutors and the courses they can tutor. It will also track each tutor's tutoring schedule. The database will store demographic information for students who register for tutoring. This information will be private and used only generate general reports which include no personal information. Students, who have registered, will be able to sign up for available tutoring sessions for courses in which they are enrolled. The database will track whether students attended their scheduled sessions. It will also track student requests for tutoring in additional course and subjects.

He also noted that she should look at it from different users' points of view. What does the database need to do for the tutor? What does it need to do for Terry? What does it need to do for the student? The next step is to work these requirements out in greater detail.

---

## Things You Should Know

### Requirements

A database requirement is something the database needs to have or do in order to meet the business needs of the organization for which it is being built. For instance, in the Tutoring database, if Terry needs to make reports on student gender and ethnicity, then the database must have attributes that store those values. It is a requirement of the database. Another requirement might be that, for legal and privacy reasons, the personal data of students must be secured so that only those with valid reasons and permission can view or edit them.

**REQUIREMENT**

Something the database must do in order to meet the business needs of an organization.

There are different kinds of database requirements:

- **Data requirements**. This refers to the attributes the database must contain in order to store all the information an organization needs for its activities. To record a point-of-sale transaction, for example, the database would need to have attributes for the sale number, the date, the customer, the items and quantities purchased, and the prices of those items among others.
- **Report requirements**. Most databases need to generate several different kinds of reports, summary information often gathered from several different entities. The entities must contain the data needed to make these reports, as mentioned earlier, but also be related in a way that makes it possible to bring the various pieces of data together. This is a function of relational design which we shall look at in detail in the next chapter.
- **Access and Security Requirements**. Often some, or all, of the data in a database are confidential. Databases typically contain core business information that could be of great value of to a competitor, or it may contain things such as credit card numbers or social security numbers that could pose financial and legal risks if revealed to the wrong people. An essential requirement of most databases is to develop a security schema that determines who has access to what data. Anyone without the proper authentication credentials should be excluded.

Chapter 2 looked at most of the techniques for gathering requirements: interviews, questionnaires, review of documents, and job shadowing. From those, it is necessary to distill the requirements into a usable list. One of the techniques, used in this chapter, is to look at the requirements in terms of each user who will interact with the database. What does the database need to do and contain for that user to successfully complete his or her tasks? The chapter starts with the higher-level approaches, looking at the general requirements first and then getting down to the detail of what attributes and entities the database needs to contain. This approach can help organize what is admittedly a complex task.

Finally, it is essential to review the requirements you find with those who will be using the database. Having a full understanding of the requirements is crucial if you are to develop a successful database. Leaving out requirements, even small ones, may render the entire database useless to the organization.

Thinking about this, Sharon remembers that Professor Collins had told her to make sure that she looked at the requirements in terms of each of the stakeholders for the database. That gives her a place to start. First, she will look at the tutors. What does the database have to do for each tutor? She writes out a list:

- Allow tutors to enter their monthly schedules.
- Allow tutors to view the schedule to see for which sessions students have signed up.
- Allow tutors to cancel a session.
- Allow tutors to fill out and submit a session report.

She ponders for a moment trying to decide if there is anything else the database has to do for tutors. It has to allow their hours to be tracked for payment. But that requirement seems to belong more to the tutoring administrator.

Sharon next decides to list all the requirements she can for students. For them, the database must do the following:

- Allow students to register for tutoring (includes entering demographic data and current courses).
- Allow students to view session schedule.
- Allow students to sign up for session.
- Allow students to cancel a session.

Sharon isn't sure of the last one. Are students allowed to cancel their own sessions? She will have to check with Terry when they review the requirements together.

Thinking of Terry, Sharon decides to list the requirements for the tutoring administrator next. For Terry, the database must do the following:

- Allow her to view session schedules.
- Allow her to add and remove tutors.
- Allow her to add and remove courses.
- Allow her to view students' requests.
- Allow her to view and summarize session reports.

Sharon thinks about this for a moment. There are other reports Terry needs to view, besides just reports on the sessions. And it might be possible that she needs to be able to generate new reports. Sharon adds a few more items to Terry's list of requirements:

- View and generate reports.
- Summarize tutor hours for payroll.

There will be a couple more actors who will be involved in the database. In addition to the tutoring administrator, there will need to be a database administrator. He or she will need to maintain the database by backing it up regularly, and will need to maintain its security, especially for student information. IT staff members will need to make the database available over the network and secure access to it. Sharon decides not to list these for the moment.

Another set of requirements involves access and security. Sharon knows that she will have to fully develop these in the database itself, but for now she just makes a few notes. First, she looks at the access requirements for Terry:

- The database administrator should have select access to all the data. That means he or she can view all the data in the tables.
- The database administrator needs to be able to add, edit, and remove records for tutors and courses.
- The database administrator should be able to create queries as needed.
- The database administrator should not be able to create or remove tables or other database objects.

The last one she will have to check with Terry, but her basic instinct is that no one except the database administrator should be able to add or remove database objects.

**Caution**
*It is essential that you include security considerations in your planning from the beginning. Too often developers wait until after the database has been designed and developed to think about the security issues of a database. Adding security as an afterthought can result in an insecure database, vulnerable to data theft or to accidental violations that can result in a loss of data integrity.*

## THINGS TO THINK ABOUT

*For the moment, disregard any malicious intent by a user. What do you think would happen to the data in a database if every user could access and change every other user's data?*

Next, she thinks about the tutor:

- A tutor needs to be able to enter and edit his or her own schedules but no one else's.
- A tutor needs to be able to enter a session report.
- A tutor needs to be able to cancel one of his or her own sessions, but no one else's.
- A tutor should not be able to see student information.

Lastly, she looks at students:

- A student must be able to view all available sessions.
- A student must be able to enter his or her own demographic information.
- A student must be able to enter the courses in which he or she is currently enrolled.
- A student should be able to cancel one of his or her own sessions, but no one else's.

## Things You Should Know

### Access and Security

Security involves determining who has access to database objects and data and what kind of access they should have. The following table lists some of the types of access a user can have. Each type of access also represents a set of SQL commands. SQL will be covered in more detail in Chapter 7 and Security in Chapter 8.

*USER ACCESS*

It refers to what objects and data in a database a user has permission to use.

**Table 3-1**    Types of Database Permissions

| Type of Access | Description |
|---|---|
| Create | The permission to make new database objects such as tables or views |
| Alter | The permission to modify database objects |
| Drop | The permission to remove database objects |
| Select | The permission to see data in a table or view |
| Update | The permission to modify data in a table |
| Insert | The permission to add data rows to a table |
| Delete | The permission to remove data rows from a table |
| Execute | The permission to run database executables such as stored procedures |

Sharon makes a list of all the requirements she has identified.

The database must do the following:

- Allow tutors to enter their monthly schedules.
- Allow tutors to view the schedule to see which sessions have students signed up.
- Allow tutors to cancel a session.
- Allow tutors to fill out and submit a session report.
- Track and summarize tutor hours.
- Track and summarize student demographic data.
- Track and summarize tutoring sessions by subject area.
- Allow the administrator to view session schedules.
- Allow the administrator to add and remove tutors.

- Allow the administrator to add and remove courses.
- Allow the administrator to view student requests.
- Allow the administrator to view and summarize session reports.
- Allow students to register for tutoring (includes demographic data and current courses).
- Allow students to view session schedule.
- Allow students to sign up for session.
- Allow students to cancel a session.
- Secure student demographic information.

Sharon looked over her requirements. Do they provide the data needed to resolve all the issues she had identified? It should be easier for Terry to get demographic information. Most students will enter it, and those who don't will need to at least enter their student ID. That will make it easier to look them up on the school's system. The Session entity data should make it easy to track tutor's hours and the session usage. It should also make it much easier for students to locate appropriate sessions by time, class, and tutor. She isn't sure it will help with the sessions running over time, but the database should solve most of the issues.

## BUSINESS RULES

Sharon is starting to feel a little better. Listing the requirements is a big step toward being able to design the database. Next, she needs to list the business rules. Business rules, she knows, are rules about how the data are captured and used and what limits or constraints are placed on the data. Some of these rules can be enforced in the database, and some will need to be built into the client application that is built on the database. Once again, she looks through her notes.

### Things You Should Know

#### Business Rules

*BUSINESS RULE*

A rule that covers the way data are acquired, stored, or processed.

*TRIGGER*

A database code, usually written in SQL, which executes when "triggered" by an event such as an insert or a delete.

Business rules describe the rules that govern the way data are acquired, stored, and used by the business. They are important for a database developer, who must make sure the database he or she develops can support all the business rules and operations. Some of the business rules can be enforced directly in the database. For instance, consider a database to track students' grades and grade-point averages. If the school is on a 4-point system, most databases will support putting a "constraint" on the grade column that limits the value to a number between 0.0 and 4.0. A database developer can also limit the length of a column. If all states are to be represented by the two-letter abbreviation, then the length of the column can be set to two. There are several other ways to enforce rules within the database as well. But some kinds of rules require extra-programming to enforce. If a library has a limit of 20 items out at a time, for instance, there is no way to enforce this rule in the data table. It is possible though to create a "trigger," which will query the database every time someone checks out an item to see how many items are currently out. It can then flag or block a checkout if it exceeds the number of items. (We will talk more about triggers and procedures in chapter 8.) Still other business rules can only be enforced in the client application through which users will interact with the database.

First, Sharon knows the database is going to create a couple of new rules: Students must register for tutoring, and they must enter their current courses. As part of that registration, students will be encouraged to enter their demographic information. As Sharon understands it, they can't be forced to enter it, but she will check back with Terry. Students must be registered in the courses they want to be tutored for. Those are some of the business rules that apply specifically to students.

Next, Sharon tries to identify the business rules that apply to tutors. Here Sharon finds she still has some major questions. Do tutors enter their own contact information? She assumes that Terry will want to control that information. Are all tutors also students? She remembers from the interview that one of the tutors was an MBA student from a different college, so not all tutors are students of the same college. She knows that tutors enter their schedules every two weeks and that they are limited to 15 hours total a week. Tutors are paid for scheduled sessions even if no student shows up. She also knows from the form she was shown while job shadowing that if a tutor has too many empty sessions, the maximum hours could be reduced. In fact, that was spelled out on the Responsibilities form. She shuffles through her papers until she finds it: "If you have fewer than half of your sessions filled in a 4-week period, you will be asked to reduce the number of sessions you offer."

Now, thinks Sharon, "What do I know about the tutoring sessions themselves?" She starts to list what she has learned:

- Students sign up for tutoring sessions.
- Tutoring sessions are 30 minutes long.
- Tutors fill out a session report for every session they are scheduled for even if no student is scheduled or the student doesn't show.
- Tutors must show up for scheduled sessions even if no one is signed up.

Some of the most puzzling aspects of the session for Sharon were the rules around canceling. From the interview, she knew that tutors could cancel a session if there was no one scheduled. If someone were scheduled, they were required to try to contact the student scheduled. But what happened if the tutor couldn't contact the student? She also knew students could cancel a session, but were there any limits to that? And, were there any penalties for frequent cancelations for either the student or the tutor? She would have to ask Terry that.

While thinking of Terry, Sharon tries to identify some of the business rules related to the administrator's reports:

- Tutors' hours are calculated from the session schedule and session reports.
- Term reports are based on unduplicated student counts.

Sharon also realizes she doesn't know the rules for handling requests.

Sharon makes a list of all the rules she has so far:

- Students must register for tutoring and enter their current courses.
- Students are encouraged but not required to enter demographic data including ethnicity.
- The administrator will enter tutor information.
- Not all tutors are students of this college (so they won't all have a student ID).
- Tutors are limited to a maximum of 15 hours a week.
- Tutors are paid for scheduled sessions even if no student is scheduled or if the scheduled student fails to show.
- If over ½ of a tutor's sessions have no students signed up over a 4-week period, tutors may have their maximum weekly hours reduced.
- Students sign up for tutoring sessions.
- Tutoring sessions are 30 minutes long.
- Tutors fill out a session report every session they are scheduled for even if no student is scheduled or the student doesn't show.
- Tutors must show up for scheduled sessions even if no one is signed up.
- Tutors can cancel a session if no student is signed up. If a student is signed up for the session, the tutor must try to contact the student.
- A student can cancel a session.
- Tutors' hours are calculated from the session schedule and session reports.
- Term reports are based on unduplicated student counts.

## REVIEW OF REQUIREMENTS AND BUSINESS RULES WITH TERRY

Sharon calls Terry and sets up an appointment for the afternoon. When she arrives, Terry invites her in and offers her a chair. Sharon pulls out the printed use cases she made earlier. She tells Terry, "I made these diagrams to help review the database requirements. Sometimes pictures are much clearer than just words." Sharon explains the elements of the use case and then goes over the diagrams one at a time. She also shows Terry her list of requirements. "Do they cover everything the database needs to do or did I forget something?" Terry studies them for a moment and then says, "That looks complete to me. I wonder, though, if students should be allowed to cancel sessions."

Sharon responds, "Actually that brings me to a couple of questions I have about the business rules. The whole process of canceling a session is a bit confusing to me. As I understand it, a tutor can cancel a session if no student is scheduled. If a student is scheduled, they must try to notify the student. What happens if they can't notify the student?"

Terry muses, "It depends on the reason for canceling. If it is possible to make the session, the tutor should meet the student. Often, though, it's not. In that case, we leave a note on the schedule and at the computer desk."

"How about the students? How do they cancel?"

"Typically, they just don't show up. Sometimes they call me or the tutor."

"Is there any penalty for missing a session?"

"We have a general rule that if a student misses more than 3 sessions, they are no longer eligible for tutoring, though it is not always enforced."

"Thank you." Sharon pulls out the list of business rules. "I identified these other business rules. If you could look at them and tell me what I missed or what I got wrong."

Terry nods, "Those look good to me."

Sharon asks, "The rule about reducing a tutor's hours—is that always enforced."

Terry smiles, "No, but we really can't afford to have our tutors sitting around getting paid for doing nothing. If it is a pattern, I do have to reduce the hours sometimes. It is not necessarily the tutor's fault. It may just be that the students that term don't need a tutor, or maybe they don't know tutoring is available."

Sharon picks up the diagrams and the rules. "Thank you, Terry. I think I am ready to start putting things together. The next thing I will show you will be the design for the database."

*Caution*
*It is critical that you review the requirements and business rules with the clients for the database. You need to ensure that you haven't forgotten any requirements or misunderstood any of the business rules. It is also important that you document each of the requirements and business rules so that everyone involved is clear on what they have agreed to. Use cases and other diagrams are an important part of documentation, but you should also write them out.*

## A LITTLE BIT OF GRAMMAR

Now that Sharon has got a clear sense of what the issues, requirements, and rules are for the database, she feels ready to start brainstorming the major content of the database. The task is daunting though. Where does she start? She remembers a technique her professor Bill Collins taught them. She can start by just listing all the nouns she has encountered.

She remembers her first list of topics

- Tutor
- Student
- Session
- Request

Next she looks at the Tutor Session Report form.

| Tutor Session Report Form | |
|---|---|
| Tutor Name | |
| Session Date | |
| Session Time | |
| Student ID | |
| Student Name (NA if no student signed up) | |
| Materials covered (NS if no show) | |

**FIGURE 3-2** Tutor Session Report Form

There are several fields on the form. She writes them down:

student ID, session date, session time, tutor name, student name, and materials covered.

She looks at the scheduling form:

| Tutoring for the Week of 4/12 to 4/16/2009 | | | | | |
|---|---|---|---|---|---|
| | Monday | Tuesday | Wednesday | Thursday | Friday |
| 9:00 AM | TT:<br>CL:<br>ST:<br>----------------<br>TT:<br>CL:<br>ST:<br>----------------<br>TT:<br>CL:<br>ST: | TT:<br>CL:<br>ST:<br>----------------<br>TT:<br>CL:<br>ST:<br>----------------<br>TT:<br>CL:<br>ST: | TT:<br>CL:<br>ST:<br>----------------<br>TT:<br>CL:<br>ST:<br>----------------<br>TT:<br>CL:<br>ST: | TT:Aimes<br>CL:(Math 290)<br>ST:Laura Jones<br>----------------<br>TT:Carson<br>CL: (ITC 110)<br>ST:<br>----------------<br>Johnson<br>(ITC 224)<br>Shanna Taylor | TT:<br>CL:<br>ST:<br>----------------<br>TT:<br>CL:<br>ST:<br>----------------<br>TT:<br>CL:<br>ST: |

**FIGURE 3-3**   Scheduling Form

From it, she can gather "tutor," "class," and "student." There are also time indicators for "month," "week," "year," "time," and "weekday."

Then she scans the reports Terry gave her. A lot of this material is summarized so it is a little harder to get information. The payroll report, for instance, is all summarized and calculated data.

| Tutor Pay | | | | | |
|---|---|---|---|---|---|
| For weeks beginning 4/6/2009 and 4/16/2009 | | | | | |
| **Tutor** | **Week1** | **Week2** | **Total Hours** | **Wage** | **Gross Pay** |
| Aimes, Tabatha | 0.5 | 2 | 2.5 | $ 10.50 | $ 26.25 |
| Carson, Karen | 8 | 10 | 18 | $ 10.50 | $ 189.00 |
| Johnson, Luke | 3 | 4.5 | 7.5 | $ 10.50 | $ 78.75 |
| Lewis, Mary | 1 | 3.5 | 4.5 | $ 10.50 | $ 47.25 |
| Sanderson, Nathan | 3 | 3 | 6 | $ 10.50 | $ 63.00 |
| Stevens, Robert | 4 | 5.5 | 9.5 | $ 10.50 | $ 99.75 |
| **Totals** | **19.5** | **28.5** | **48** | | **$ 504.00** |

**FIGURE 3-4**   Tutor Payroll

The main thing the database needs to provide for is the tutor name or ID and the hours worked grouped by week, month, and year. Sharon remembers that as a rule, you should not store calculated fields in a database. You can always recreate the calculation in a query, and it will be more accurate because it is based on live data. The hours per week and the total hours can be calculated from the number of sessions a tutor has on the schedule.

The form that Terry bases her reports on also contains a great deal of summarized information.

For a moment, she ponders the word "unduplicated." But, "unduplicated" is an adjective rather than a noun. It is describing something in the database, not a new element in itself. But "gender," "ethnicity," "workforce retraining," and "subject area" can count as nouns. Time also crops up again in terms of "Fall Term 2010." That implies "quarter" and "year."

Sharon listens carefully to the notes she recorded during her interview with the tutors and students. Many of the same nouns show up. Sharon notes the noun

*Caution*
*It is easy to get the data attributes confused with the attributes themselves. An attribute is a general descriptor of an entity. For instance, "Last Name" would be an attribute of a Customer entity, but "John Smith" is a type of data that would be stored in that attribute. Attributes are the column heads that describe the data. One way to think of it is that on a computerized form, the attributes are in the labels and the data are what are entered into the textboxes.*

| Report Statistics | | | | |
|---|---|---|---|---|
| Fall Term 2010 | | | | |
| | **Students** | | | |
| **Total usage** | 2345 | **Workforce Retraining** | | 247 |
| **Unduplicated usage** | 1735 | | | |
| *Difference* | *610* | | | |
| Unduplicated Demographics | | | | |
| Gender | | | | |
| **Male** | 937 | | | |
| **Female** | 798 | | | |
| *Total* | *1735* | | | |
| Ethnicity | | | | |
| **White** | 868 | | | |
| **AfAm** | 312 | | | |
| **Asian** | 312 | | | |
| **PacIs** | 121 | | | |
| **NAmer** | 35 | | | |
| **Other** | 87 | | | |
| *Total* | *1735* | | | |
| By Subject Area | | | | |
| **ACC** | 139 | | | |
| **BUS** | 121 | | | |
| **ENG** | 347 | | | |
| **HIS** | 139 | | | |
| **ITC** | 139 | | | |
| **MAT** | 607 | | | |
| **SCI** | 243 | | | |
| *Total* | *1735* | | | |

**FIGURE 3-5**  Report Statistics

"schedule." It also appears in her notes about the observation of Mary's tutoring session.

Sharon looks at her list of nouns so far.

tutor, session, student ID, student name, session date, session time, tutor name, weekday, materials covered, class name, gender, ethnicity, subject area, schedule, term, year, month, workforce retraining, subject area, request

It is not a very long list, but it is a place to start from. The next step she knows is to list them into related groups. Again, she can use the original big themes she identified as a starting place. She writes down the word "tutor." Which elements go with tutor?

Tutor
Tutor Name

She thinks about Class name, but classes don't just belong to the tutor. Students take classes, and a tutoring session is focused on a class, so class must be a separate group. So now she has

Tutor                              Class
Tutor Name                         Class Name

There are also student, session, and request groups, of course. She adds the groups:

| Tutor | Class | Student | Session | Request |
|---|---|---|---|---|
| Tutor Name | Class Name | Student ID | Session Date | |
| | | Student Name | Session Time | |
| | | Gender | Term | |
| | | Ethnicity | Year | |
| | | | Month | |
| | | | Materials Covered | |

That leaves "Schedule" and "Subject area." From the report, she knows that the subject area is broader than just the class. It actually maps pretty well to the class department, such as ENG or MAT. She places it with the Class group. "She wonders if 'schedule' is just a synonym for 'Session'." She decides to hold it aside for the moment. Another issue she sees is in Session. Quarter, Year, and Month are really redundant. All that information can be gathered from the Date itself. She makes the modifications and then scans her list so far:

| Tutor | Class | Student | Session | Request |
|---|---|---|---|---|
| Tutor Name | Class Name | Student ID | Session Date | |
| | Subject Area | Student Name | Session Time | |
| | | Gender | Materials Covered | |
| | | Ethnicity | | |

She knows she can modify this list to some extent. Student Name and Tutor Name can be divided into first and last name. The Class Name can be divided into department, class number, and section. She also knows she needs to add term and year. Sharon isn't sure what additional demographic information Terry needs. She will have to talk to her again and get a precise list. She also isn't sure how much information the database will need to store about each tutor. Again, she will have to ask. She knows that a Session will also contain at least a tutor, a student, a class, and materials covered, so she adds them. Finally, she can be sure that a request will contain a student name or ID, a class name, and the date of the request. Now her list looks like this:

| Tutor | Class | Student | Session | Request |
|---|---|---|---|---|
| Tutor First Name | Class Name | Student ID | Session Date | Class Name |
| Tutor Last Name | Department | Student Last Name | Session Time | Request Date |
| | Class Number | Student First Name | Term | Student ID |
| | Term | Gender | Year | |
| | Year | Ethnicity | Month | |
| | Section | | Materials Covered | |

## ENTITIES AND ATTRIBUTES

Sharon looks at her lists of nouns. She knows that the big items, the group headings such as Tutor, Class, Student, Session, and Request, will probably be entities in her database design. The items listed under them will be attributes, or things that describe or belong to the entity. She also knows the list is not complete. It is only a beginning, but it does give her a good place to start when she gets down to the details of designing the database.

> ### Things You Should Know

### Entities and Attributes

As was mentioned in Chapter 1, entities are things that a database is concerned with, such as students, inventory, orders, or courses, and so on. Attributes are aspects of entities. They are things that describe an entity or belong to it. Entities are a part of the logical design of a database. The logical design is independent of any database management system. It doesn't take into account any of the implementation issues such as file locations or sizes or database tuning and efficiency. Logic design is concerned only with defining the entities, their attributes, and their relations to other entities.

One of the great features of logical design is that it is the same no matter what software or operating system you are using. Most entities will become tables in the final database, but there is not always a one-to-one correspondence. Entities, attributes, and relations will be covered in much greater depth in the next few chapters.

## CANDIDATE KEYS

Although she knows it is early in the process, Sharon decides to start identifying some potential keys. She knows that keys are used to uniquely identify each record in a database and to relate records to each other that are stored in different tables. So she begins trying to find some candidate keys.

> ### Things You Should Know

### Candidate Keys

Ideally, every entity should have a key attribute—one attribute that uniquely identifies an instance of that entity. Candidate keys are attributes that could possibly be used as identifying attributes. There is much discussion as to what makes a good candidate. It must be unique. That means it can never occur twice in the same entity. Last names, for instance, don't make good candidate keys. It is far too probable that more than one person will share the same last name. Telephone numbers might make a good candidate key, if all that needs to be unique is the household. Many Web sites use email addresses.

If there is no good candidate key singly, attributes can be combined to form a "composite key." For example, in an Appointment entity in a database tracking dental appointments, the date is not unique because several people could have appointments on the same day. The date and time together are not necessarily unique, because more than one appointment could be scheduled at the same time. The date, time, and patient name or ID should be unique, however. In combination, they are a candidate to be the entity's key.

Keys that are based on attributes that belong naturally to the entity are sometimes called "natural keys." Many advocate the use of natural keys because they protect data from accidental duplication. No two households, for instance, should have the same telephone number. If you accidentally enter a household a second time, the database management system will throw an error because the phone number of the second row will conflict with the uniqueness requirement of a primary key. Others argue, however, that all keys should be arbitrary. They argue that it is very difficult to always find a natural key and that often designers have to resort to awkward composite (multi-attribute) keys that add to a database's redundancy. Instead, they advocate just assigning a number to each instance of an entity. These are sometimes called "surrogate keys." Surrogate keys guarantee that the key will always be unique. However, it provides less protection against accidentally repeating an instance. A new instance (row) could be identical in every aspect except the key attribute. There will be much more discussion of these topics in later chapters.

*COMPOSITE KEY*

A key that consists of more than one attribute.

*NATURAL KEY*

A key made from one or more of an entity's "natural" attributes.

*SURROGATE KEY*

An artificially created key, often just auto-incremented numbers.

Sharon starts with Tutor. What would uniquely identify a tutor? The tutor's name is one idea, especially if you combined the first and last names. There are not many tutors, and the chance of any two tutors having exactly the same name is slight, but it does exist. Although it is not listed, students have student IDs, which could be used to uniquely identify each student. Most tutors are also students and would have a student

ID, but not all tutors are students. Perhaps there is some sort of employee ID. She will have to ask Terry. Each course has a unique name so that could be a potential key for that entity.

For the session, the session date or the session time, perhaps in combination, could be a key, but that wouldn't really be unique because different tutors could have sessions on the same day at the same time. If the tutor ID was added to the key, that could be unique.

After all the analysis, Sharon feels ready to get to work on the logical design of the database.

## DOCUMENTATION

Requirements and business rules are an essential part of the documentation of any database. A developer needs to refer to them many times during the development process. She needs to constantly check to see if the database is meeting all the requirements. Is anything being left out? Are there elements that weren't in the initial requirements? And, if there are, should they be added to the requirement list, or should they be removed? When the database is completed, the requirements and business rules guide how the database is tested. The developer should look at each requirement and rule and make sure the database satisfies it. Terry, for instance, requires the database to be able to produce reports with unduplicated counts of students. The database must be tested to make sure this is possible. If it isn't, then it must be adjusted until it is.

Additionally, anytime someone needs to change the database, make an addition, or replace it all together, that person will need to review the original requirements to see if the changes add to them or alter them in some way. If no one documented the original requirements and rules, the person will have to recreate them by talking to the users of the database. He or she will, in short, have to do the whole process of gathering requirements over again. If the database has been in use for a long time, this can be difficult. Often, many of the people involved in the original development of the database have retired or left for other jobs. It is possible that no one will remember exactly the reasons for creating the original database.

The requirements and business rules for a database should be clearly marked and stored with the other database documentation.

The initial attempts listing nouns and dividing them into attributes do not necessarily need to go into the formal database documentation, but it is a good idea to keep them and other project notes in a folder or notebook of some kind. It is always useful to be able to review your notes and revisit why you made the decisions you did. You may find that you need to modify the original ideas based on later evidence.

## Things We Have Done

*In this chapter we have*

- revisited the problem domain by reviewing the issues with the current system
- reviewed the business rules for the tutoring database
- reviewed the materials collected in the previous chapters and extracted nouns that may become entities and attributes

- organized the nouns into preliminary entities and attributes
- looked for attributes that could serve as candidate keys, that is, attributes that could potentially work as primary keys for the entities

## Vocabulary

*Match the definitions to the vocabulary words:*

| | | |
|---|---|---|
| **1.** User access | — a. | A program that requests a service |
| **2.** Server | — b. | A key that consists of more than one attribute |
| **3.** Surrogate key | — c. | A program in SQL that is triggered by a database event |
| **4.** Actor | — d. | A program that offers a service to requesting programs |

5. Requirement        — e. A key based on one or more "natural" attributes of an entity
6. Natural key        — f. A rule about how data are acquired, stored, or processed
7. Client             — g. The general problem area with which a database is concerned
8. Trigger            — h. An artificial key, often just an incremented number
9. Composite key      — i. Something a database must do to meet a business need
10. Business rule     — j. A person or program that makes some use of the database
11. Problem domain    — k. The permissions a user has to use or view database objects and data

## Things to Look Up

1. Look up "Requirement Analysis" on the Web. What kinds of topic headings do you find?
2. Look up two or more definitions for "Business Rules."
3. Look up an article on the Web that discusses natural versus surrogate keys in databases. Which does the author prefer?
4. What are some additional plusses or minuses of each?

## Practices

Use the following scenario for each of the practice exercises:

You have been asked to build a database for a pet foster and adoption shelter. The agency is a nonprofit that takes in stray or abandoned pets and places them with foster caregivers until the pet is adopted. Foster caregivers are volunteers, though they must first be screened. The database needs to track all animals in its care, their species, breed, name, and condition. It also needs to track all approved foster caregivers and the animals currently in their care. Foster caregivers are also supposed to turn in monthly reports on the animals in their care. The database also needs to track the adoptions of the animals.

Currently, volunteers come into the shelter and fill out a paper form. After a background check, they are added to a file. Some volunteers complain that they are never contacted again. The shelter staff admits, they tend to go with foster caregivers they know, and some people get forgotten in the file. The shelter has also occasionally lost track of an animal in foster care when the caregiver failed to turn in the monthly reports. Another recurring problem is that when someone comes into the shelter looking to adopt, it is not always easy or even possible to let them know about all the animals available for adoption.

Ideally, the shelter would like people to be able to register as a volunteer online. They would like to be able to call up a list of all available foster volunteers. They would also like to be able to pull up all the animals of the kind a potential adopter is interested in and know exactly where those animals are and who is caring for them.

1. Make a list of some of the major issues with the current system used in the shelter.
2. Identity who the major actors are and list them.
3. Would animals be an actor in this database? Explain why or why not.
4. Make a list of requirements for each of the actors showing how he or she would interact with the database.
5. Make a list of business rules for the shelter.
6. What might be some of the shelter database security issues?
7. Make a list of all the nouns in the description of the shelter.
8. Take the list from 7, and determine what you think would be the major entities.
9. List the attributes for each of the entities you listed in 8.
10. Identify some candidate keys.

## Scenarios

### WILD WOOD APARTMENTS

The Wild Wood Management team is ready to see some results. You have a meeting with them at the end of the week. It is time to analyze and organize all the information. Look back at the material from the last chapters.

1. Make a list of issues with the current system.
2. Make a list of the database requirements for each stakeholder involved in the database.
3. Make a list of business rules.
4. List some major security rules for the database.
5. Take a look at each of the forms, and make a list of all the nouns in them. Do the same for the interview, the questionnaire, and the Job Shadow Report. Then set up some preliminary entities and attributes.

6. Identify some candidate keys.
7. **Documentation**: Store the list of the requirements and business rules in your database notebook.

### VINCE'S VINYLS

You are eager to show Vince some progress on the database. You sit down to analyze all the materials you have gathered to see if you can make some sense of them. Make sure you review the material in the previous two chapters.

1. Make a list of issues with the current system.
2. Make a list that shows the database requirements for each stakeholder involved in the database.
3. Make a list of business rules.
4. List some major security rules for the database.

5. Take a look at each of the forms, and make a list of all the nouns in them. Do the same for the interview, the questionnaire, and the Job Shadow Report. Then set up some preliminary entities and attributes.
6. Identify some candidate keys.
7. **Documentation**: Store the list of the requirements and business rules in your database notebook.

## GRANDFIELD COLLEGE

It is imperative that the college get the software tracking database online as soon as possible. You have assured the management team that you will be able to show some progress very soon. It is time to set down and review all the forms and materials.

1. Make a list of issues with the current system.
2. Make a list of the database requirements for each stakeholder involved in the database.
3. Make a list of business rules.
4. List some major security rules for the database.
5. Take a look at each of the forms, and make a list of all the nouns in them. Do the same for the interview, the questionnaire, and the Job Shadow Report. Then set up some preliminary entities and attributes.
6. Identify some candidate keys.
7. **Documentation**: Store the list of the requirements and business rules in your database notebook.

## WESTLAKE RESEARCH HOSPITAL

The drug study is set to begin in just a few months' time. It is important to make some progress toward the database. It is time to gather all the materials you have collected and try to make some sense of them.

1. Make a list of issues with the current system.
2. Make a list of the database requirements for each stakeholder involved in the database.

3. Make a list of business rules.
4. List some major security rules for the database.
5. Take a look at each of the forms, and make a list of all the nouns in them. Do the same for the interview, the questionnaire, and the Job Shadow Report. Then set up some preliminary entities and attributes.
6. Identify some candidate keys.
7. **Documentation**: Store the list of the requirements and business rules in your database notebook.

## SUGGESTIONS FOR SCENARIOS

Review all the documents and interviews from the last chapter. It will probably be necessary to talk with your instructor or other students to answer some of the questions about you scenario that have not yet been answered. A certain amount of invention is expected here.

Look at the requirements in terms of each user or actor. It is much easier to do it this way rather than trying to just make a general list of requirements. The actor gives you a clearer focus on what the database needs to do in a particular instance. The same holds true of the database security. It is much easier to understand in terms of each actor's access needs.

When making the initial list of nouns, don't try to distinguish between entities and attributes. Just list them in the order you encounter them. Save the analysis until you are done.

When you do the analysis, remember entities are major themes or elements. They will tend to stand out. If you find a lot of words clustered around a single topic, that topic is likely the entity and the words clustered around it are probably attributes.

It is good to remember that this is a very preliminary stage of analysis. There aren't any absolutely right or wrong answers at this stage.

## CHAPTER 4

# Database Design

## ENTITY RELATION DIAGRAMS

Having organized her materials and determined the business rules, in this chapter, Sharon begins the logical design of the Tutoring database. Using Microsoft Visio, she defines the database entities, their attributes, and the relationships among them.

## CHAPTER OUTCOMES

**By the end of this chapter you will be able to:**

- Use the database modeling template in Microsoft Visio
- Create entities and add attributes
- Determine the appropriate relationship between entities
- Resolve many-to-many relationships with a linking table

## DESIGNING THE DATABASE

Sharon is ready to prepare the logical design of the database. The logical design, she knows, is separate from any consideration of which DBMS the database is going to be developed on. It doesn't take into account how the files will be stored or accessed. It ignores any features or limitations of the target DBMS. It is focused purely on the logical structure of the entities and their relationships with each other.

---

### THINGS TO THINK ABOUT

*The logical design of a database is the same no matter what the RDBMS is going to be.*

*Physical design is specifically tailored to the features and limits of a particular RDBMS.*

*What is the advantage of separating the logical from the physical design?*

---

**LOGICAL DESIGN**

The entity relation design without regard to what RDBMS or system it will be on.

**PHYSICAL DESIGN**

The design adapted to the RDBMS and system constraints and features.

For this process, she is going to use the data-modeling template in Microsoft Visio and create a new entity relation diagram or ERD. (For a complete description of opening the entity diagram in Visio, see Appendix C.)

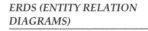

## Things You Should Know

### Entity Relation Diagrams

As the name suggests, an entity relation diagram (ERD) is a diagram of entities, their attributes, and the relations among the entities. Most ERDs represent the entities as rectangles divided into three horizontal parts—the entity name, the primary key, and then the other attributes—and two or more vertical parts, the first containing information about keys and indexes, and the second containing the attribute name.

| EntityName | |
|---|---|
| PK | **PrimaryKey** |
| | **Attribute1** |
| | Attribute2 |

*ERDS (ENTITY RELATION DIAGRAMS)*

One common method of depicting entities and relations in a diagram.

**FIGURE 4-1** Entity

Attributes in bold are required attributes.

Relationships between entities can be represented in different ways. In Microsoft Visio, the default way is as a line with an arrow on one end. The arrow always points to the *one* side of a relation, usually the side with a primary key. We discuss all these concepts more in the following sections. Here is an example using the arrow-headed line for the relationship:

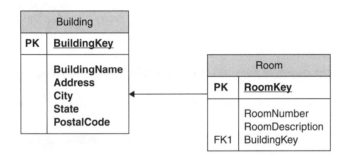

| Building | |
|---|---|
| PK | **BuildingKey** |
| | **BuildingName** |
| | **Address** |
| | **City** |
| | **State** |
| | **PostalCode** |

| Room | |
|---|---|
| PK | **RoomKey** |
| | RoomNumber |
| | RoomDescription |
| FK1 | BuildingKey |

**FIGURE 4-2** Arrow Symbol for Relationship

The relationship can also be represented in "crow's feet" notation. You can change the relationship representation in Visio by going to the Database tab on the ribbon and selecting "Display Options."

**Database Document Options**

General | Table | Relationship

Show
- ☑ Relationships
- ☑ Crow's feet
- ☐ Cardinality
- ☐ Referential actions

Name display
- ☐ Show verb phrase
  - ☑ Forward text
  - ☑ Inverse text
- ☐ Show physical name
- ☑ Don't display name

[?] | Defaults ▼ | OK | Cancel

**FIGURE 4-3** Crow's Feet Option

The crow's feet notation actually conveys more information about a relationship than the arrow notation. Look at the following example that uses the same two entities but uses the crow's feet notation.

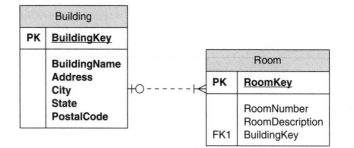

**FIGURE 4-4** Crow's Feet Notation

The end with three lines is the "crow's foot." It is the *many* side of the relation. The straight line and 0 on the building or *one* side mean that a building can have zero to many rooms. The straight line before the crow's foot indicates that every room must be associated with one building.

Although it may seem a bit confusing at first, this book will use the crow's foot notation. You will often encounter this notation in your database work, and it is good to get familiar with it as soon as possible. We won't, however, in this book, worry about all the subtle nuances of the notation.

Sharon opens a new data model template in Visio and drags an entity symbol onto the grid.

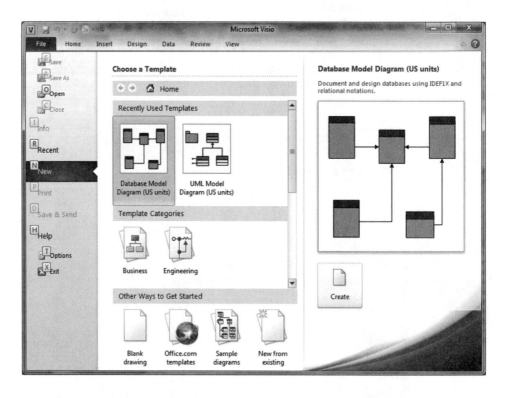

**FIGURE 4-5** New Database Model Diagram

She increases the zoom to 100% so she can see the entities better. She clicks on the new entity to select it and sets its name in the definition property: Tutor.

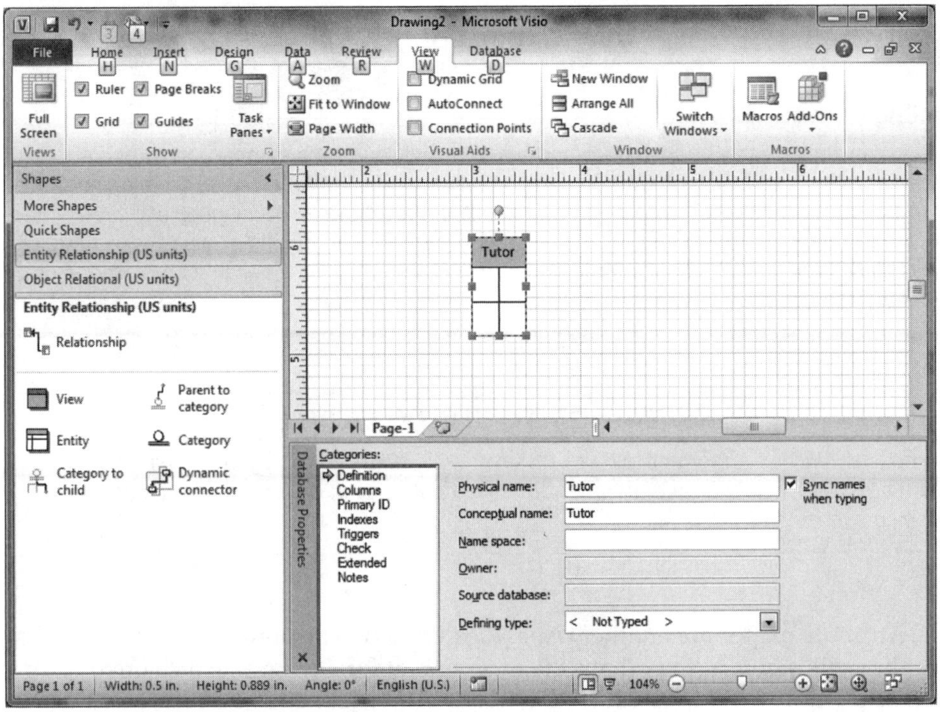

**FIGURE 4-6** Visio Entity

Next she selects the columns property and keys in the first attribute name *TutorKey*. She clicks on the check box to make it the primary key. Right now Sharon isn't worried about the data types of the columns. They are important, and in the design phase, it is a good idea to have some sense of what data type a particular attribute will require, but choosing specific data types belongs more to the physical side of database development. For now, Sharon is focusing on identifying all the entities, attributes, and relationships. We will discuss data types thoroughly in Chapter 6.

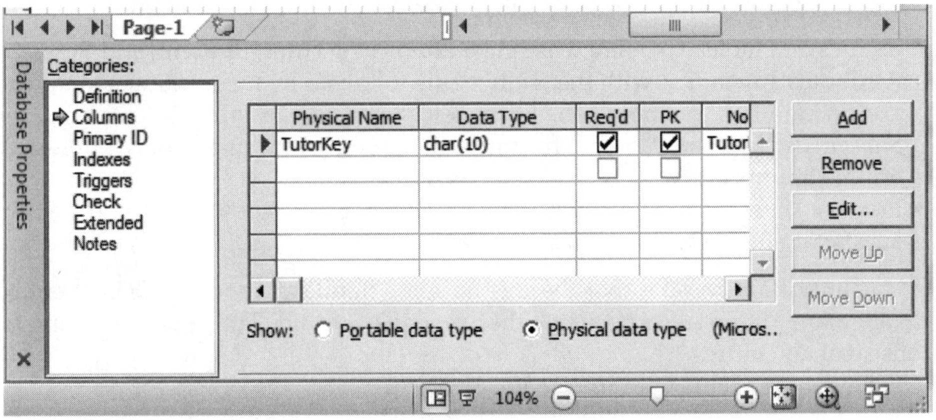

**FIGURE 4-7** Setting Primary Key

Now she types in the other attributes. She decides to use a naming convention that puts the entity name at the front of every attribute name. For instance, every tutor will have a first name and a last name in the database, so she names the attributes *TutorFirstName* and *TutorLastName*. It can get a bit awkward and make for long names, but it makes it clear which entity an attribute belongs to. Foreign keys, she decides, will be named the same as their corresponding primary keys.

**Things You Should Know**

### Naming Conventions

Naming conventions vary book to book, individual to individual, and company to company. The most important thing is to be consistent. Some people like to put "tbl" before all table names, but that doesn't make sense for the logical design. Entities are not yet tables. Some people always name entities with a plural noun on the theory that each entity will contain multiple instances or rows. Others always name them with a singular noun on the theory that they are an abstract representation of an element of the database.

### THINGS TO THINK ABOUT

*Why do you think it is important to be consistent in naming? What would be the disadvantage of not being consistent?*

*What role do you think naming conventions could play in documenting a database?*

Attribute names are another issue. Ideally no two attributes in a database should have the same name, with perhaps the exception of foreign keys, which often retain the name of the primary key to which they relate. The problem is that many entities have the same or similar attributes. A Customer entity, for instance, will have a LastName, FirstName, Address, and City. But an Employee entity also has these attributes. One way to differentiate them is to put the entity name in front of the attribute name or some abbreviation of the table name. Often these are separated with underscores, such as Customer_LastName or Cust_LastName.

Key attributes are also a naming issue. Often the key attribute is called an ID, like CustomerID or EmployeeID. Often the foreign key retains the name of the primary key it relates to. But the foreign key doesn't have to have the same name as its associated primary key. (It does have to have the same or at least a compatible data type.) If a foreign key is not named the same as the primary key, it should be named something that makes it clear that it is in fact a foreign key, and it should be clear what primary key it relates back to.

This book uses the following naming conventions:

- Entities and tables are named as single nouns like **Tutor**, **Student**, and **Session**.
- Attributes are named with the entity name followed by the attribute name. There are no underscores between. Each new word is capitalized: *TutorLastName*, *StudentLastName*, and so on. This can make for long attribute names, but it makes for maximum clarity.
- Primary keys end with the word "Key": *TutorKey*, *StudentKey*, and so on. Foreign keys retain the name of the primary key.

*Caution*
*A lack of naming conventions can lead to confusion and can make it much harder to maintain or extend a database.*

It is important to note that there is nothing standard about these conventions. There are many different conventions that are equally valid. The important thing is to be consistent and clear.

Following is a table with some equivalencies.

| Table 4-1 | Term Equivalencies | |
|---|---|---|
| **Logical Design** | **Physical Design** | **Theoretical** |
| Entity | Table | Relation |
| Attribute | Column, field | Attribute |
| | Row, record | Tuple |

Entities and attributes are used to describe the elements in logical design. Most often the entities become the tables, and the attributes become columns or fields when implementing the database in a particular DBMS. A row or record is one complete set of data—one customer, for instance, or one inventory item. "Relation" is a theoretical term for a table, and "tuple" is a theoretical term for a row of data. You can encounter these terms in more advanced books on database.

Though these categories are not as absolute as the table might make them seem, we will try to be consistent in our use of terms.

When Sharon finishes, her **Tutor** entity looks like this:

| Tutor | |
|---|---|
| **PK** | **TutorKey** |
| | TutorLastName |
| | TutorFirstName |
| | TutorPhone |
| | TutorEmail |
| | TutorHireDate |
| | TutorCourse |

**FIGURE 4-8**  Tutor Entity Version 1

Sharon looks at the entity for a moment. Something about it bothers her. Then it hits her. What if a tutor tutors for more than one course? She could modify the entity to look like this:

| Tutor | |
|---|---|
| **PK** | **TutorKey** |
| | TutorLastName |
| | TutorFirstName |
| | TutorPhone |
| | TutorEmail |
| | TutorHireDate |
| | TutorCourse1 |
| | TutorCourse2 |
| | TutorCourse3 |

**FIGURE 4-9**  Tutor Entity Revision 1

But as she looks at it, she knows it is wrong. What if a tutor does only tutor for one class? That means two of the attributes would always be null. What if a tutor tutored for four classes? There would be no place to put the fourth one. And, she realizes, if someone wanted to find out what tutors tutored a specific class, he or she would have to always query three separate columns to be sure. Also, if her memory serves her, the entity violates the first normal form. (Normal forms and normalization will be covered in detail in Chapter 5.)

Sharon revises the Tutor entity one more time. She realizes that course doesn't belong to **Tutor**. It is an entity in itself, with its own attributes and its own key. She creates another entity called **Course**.

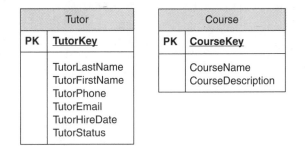

**FIGURE 4-10**  Tutor and Course Entities

Sharon looks at the two entities, trying to determine what kind of relationship exists between the two. It puzzles her for a moment and then she realizes it is a many-to-many relationship. One tutor can tutor for many courses, and each course can have many tutors. She smiles as she remembers her instructor in class going over just this situation again and again. "Whenever you have a many-to-many relationship, you must always make a linking table."

## Things You Should Know

### Relationships

There are three kinds of relationships that can exist between entities:

- one to one
- one to many
- many to many

### *One to One*

In databases, a one-to-one relationship is rare, but it can be useful. A one-to-one relationship specifies that for each row in the primary entity, there can be one and no more than one related record in the secondary entity. In a one-to-one relationship, the primary key of the first entity is often the primary key of the second entity.

In crow's feet notation, one-to-one relationships can be represented in two ways:

·H - - - - - - - - - - - - O+

**FIGURE 4-11** Zero or one

-H - - - - - - - - - - - - +⊢

**FIGURE 4-12** Exactly One

One use for this kind of relationship is to express a class/subclass relationship. Say a database is keeping a list of different resources. The resources can be in any of several different media, and the attributes to describe each media are significantly different. If you put all the attributes in one Resource entity, each entry will have several nulls for the attributes it doesn't need. To solve this, you can break the Resource entity into several one-to–one relationships.

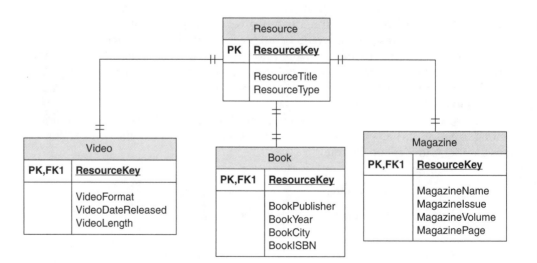

**FIGURE 4-13** One-to-One Relationships

The entities mentioned earlier don't include all the relevant attributes, just enough to show the relationship. Notice that each entity has the same primary key. That means each resource will appear once in the resource table and exactly once in one of the resource type tables. To get a clearer sense of this relationship, look at the following tables based on this design.

| ResourceKey | ResourceTitle | ResourceType |
|---|---|---|
| 235091 | Database Programming with ADO | Book |
| 244088 | PhotoShop Basics | Video |
| 200211 | Data Binding with LINQ | Magazine |
| 202883 | Relational Algebra | Book |

**FIGURE 4-14** Resource Table

| ResourceKey | BookPublisher | BookYear | BookCity | BookISBN |
|---|---|---|---|---|
| 235091 | Westland Press | 2005 | San Francisco | 123-77-6576-X |
| 202883 | PL University Press | 1998 | Seattle | 234-11-2345-0 |

**FIGURE 4-15** Book Table

| ResourceKey | MagazineName | MagazineIssue | MagazineVolume | MagazinePage |
|---|---|---|---|---|
| 200211 | Visual Studio Magazine | March 2008 | 3 | 76 |

**FIGURE 4-16** Magazine Table

One-to-one relationships are sometimes also used as part of a security structure. A single entity may be broken into two entities. One will contain publicly viewable content and the second private content. For example, an employee's information might be broken into two entities. The first one contains nonsensitive content such as the employee's name, department, business phone number, and position title. The second table contains sensitive material such as the employee's social security number, home address, home phone, and salary information. There is a one-to-one relationship between the tables. Each employee has exactly one related record in the private table.

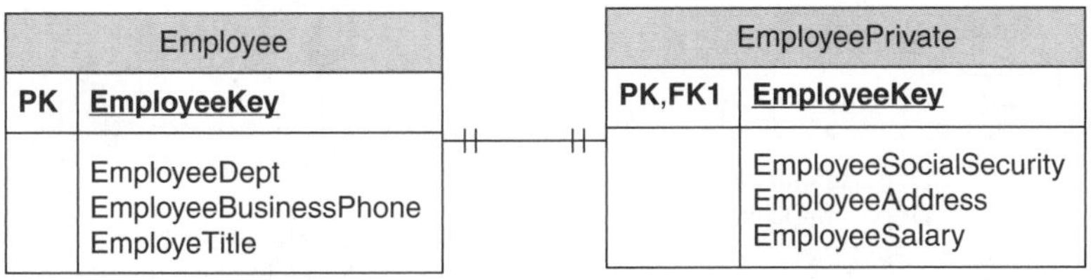

**FIGURE 4-17** One to One for Security

It should be noted, this is not necessarily the best way to deal with security issues. There are many ways to allow the public aspects of the Employee entity to be accessed while protecting the private information. Creating a view or using a stored procedure (see Chapter 7) to control which columns a user can access is generally a better strategy.

### One to Many

Most of the entities in any relational database will have a one-to-many relationship. A one-to-many relationship means that for each record in the primary entity there can be many associated records in the secondary or child entity. There are two crow's feet symbols for one-to-many relationships:

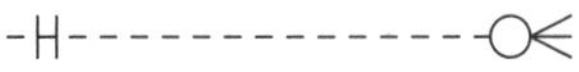

**FIGURE 4-18** Zero or More

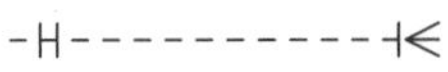

**FIGURE 4-19** At Least One or More

For an example of a one-to-many relationship, consider the relationship between a department in a business and its employees. Each department can contain zero or more employees. Each employee belongs to one department.

**FIGURE 4-20**   One to Many

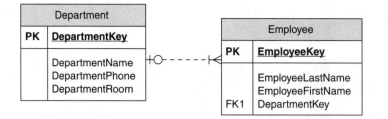

You need to enter the department information only once in the Department table. You use the primary key to link the table to a child table by repeating it in that table as a foreign key. The foreign key can repeat as often as needed in the child table.

**FIGURE 4-21**   Department Table

| DepartmentKey | DepartmentName | DepartmentPhone | DepartmentRoom |
|---|---|---|---|
| ACC | Accounting | (206)555-1234 | SB201 |
| IT | Information Technology | (206)555-2468 | NB100 |

**FIGURE 4-22**   Employee Table

| EmployeeKey | EmployeeLastName | EmployeeFirstName | DepartmentKey |
|---|---|---|---|
| FB2001D | Collins | Richard | IT |
| BN2004N | Faulkner | Leonore | IT |
| NC2004M | Brown | Carol | ACC |
| LL20060 | Anderson | Thomas | IT |

🖐 *Caution*
*It is important that you do not create a "cross relationship." There is a temptation to think that because a department contains employees, the Department entity should contain a foreign key for employee.*

*Doing this will create an impossible situation. In effect, a department will only be able to contain a single employee. The second employee will create a conflict with the DepartmentKey, which cannot repeat. This is a fairly common error among novice designers. It often isn't discovered until the attempt to enter data into the tables fails.*

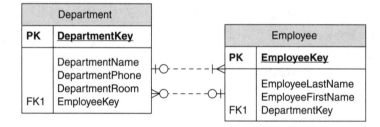

**FIGURE 4-23**   Cross-Relationship Error

### Many to Many

Many–to-many relationships are common, and they are legitimate relationships in logical terms, but no database can implement them. A many-to-many relationship means that each record in the primary entity can have many related records in a second entity and each record in the second entity can have many related records in the primary entity.

The symbol for a many-to-many relationship has a crow's foot on both sides of the relationship, as shown in the following figure:

**FIGURE 4-24**   Many to Many

Visio doesn't contain a symbol for this relationship.

For an example, consider the relationship between Subscribers and an entity designed to store a list of various magazines. Each customer can subscribe to many magazines, and each magazine can be subscribed to by many customers. That creates a many-to-many relationship.

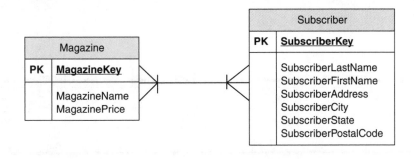

FIGURE 4-25   Many-to-Many Relationship

In any RDBMS, a many-to-many relationship must be resolved into two one-to-many relationships. This is done by creating a linking entity. In this case, the Magazine and the Subscriber entities are linked by a Subscription entity. A subscriber subscribes to one or more magazines. A magazine can be subscribed to by zero-to-many subscribers. Often, as in this case, creating the linking entity reveals a forgotten or undiscovered entity, Subscription is more than a linking entity. It is a legitimate entity with attributes of its own.

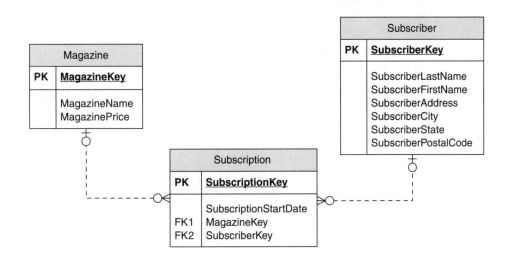

FIGURE 4-26   Linking Table

The following tables show how these entities would be translated into a database. These are, of course, much simplified. A real database would contain many more columns of essential information such as the subscription length, the magazine type (e.g., weekly and quarterly), the magazine publisher information, and so on. Also for the subscribers, it would be necessary to distinguish between the billing address and the shipping address, since they are not necessarily the same.

| MagazineKey | MagazineName | MagazinePrice |
|---|---|---|
| TM2K1 | Time | 35.50 |
| NW2K1 | Newsweek | 36.40 |

FIGURE 4-27   Magazine Table

| SubscriberKey | Subscriber LastName | Subscriber FirstName | Subscriber Address | Subscriber City | Subscriber State | Subscriber PostalCode |
|---|---|---|---|---|---|---|
| 4231 | Johnson | Leslie | 101 Best Ave. | Seattle | WA | 98007 |
| 4333 | Anderson | Mark | 1200 Western Blvd | Tacoma | WA | 98011 |
| 5344 | Manning | Tabitha | 100 Westlake | Seattle | WA | 98008 |

**FIGURE 4-28**   Subscriber Table

| SubscriptionKey | MagazineKey | SubscriberKey | SubscriptionStartDate |
|---|---|---|---|
| 1004 | TM2K1 | 4333 | 1/15/2009 |
| 1005 | NW2K1 | 4333 | 1/15/2009 |
| 1006 | NW2K1 | 4231 | 2/1/2009 |
| 1007 | TM2K1 | 5344 | 2/15/2009 |

**FIGURE 4-29**   Subscription Table

Sometimes, however, the linking entity only serves to resolve the many-to-many relationship. Consider the relationship between authors and books. Each book can have several authors, and each author can author several books. This relationship can be resolved with a linking table as in the following figure:

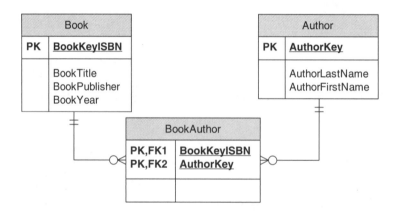

**FIGURE 4-30**   Linking Table Two

*LINKING ENTITY*
_____

An entity which resolves a many-to-many relationship into two one-to-many relationships.

*COMPOSITE KEY*
_____

A key that consists of more than one column.

*SURROGATE KEY*
_____

A random or arbitrary key often generated by just incrementing numbers.

It is not uncommon for a linking entity to have a composite key made up of the foreign keys from the two tables whose relationship it resolves. Another note: You may have noticed in the earlier diagrams that most relationships are represented by dashed lines. The preceding relationships and the one-to-one relationships are represented as solid lines. Visio distinguishes between *identifying* and *nonidentifying* relationships. An *identifying* relationship is one where the foreign key in the child table is also a part of the primary key of that child table. For instance, AuthorKey is both a foreign key and part of the composite primary key in the entity BookAuthor. A *nonidentifying* relationship is one in which the foreign key is *not* a part of the primary key of the child table.

Following are some examples of how these entities would be translated into tables in a database. Notice how the *Head First Object Oriented Analysis and Design* book has three authors.

| BookKeyISBN | BookTitle | BookPublisher | BookPublisherYear |
|---|---|---|---|
| 0-07-222513-0 | *Java 2 Beginners Guide* | Oracle Press | 2002 |
| 0674019999-1 | *After the Ice* | Harvard | 2003 |
| 0-596-00867-8 | *Head First Object Oriented Analysis and Design* | O'Reilly | 2007 |

**FIGURE 4-31**   Book Table

| AuthorKey | AuthorLastName | AuthorFirstName |
|---|---|---|
| HSCHLT | Schildt | Herbert |
| SMITHN | Mithen | Steven |
| BMCLAU | McLaughlin | Brett |
| GPOLLIC | Pollice | Gary |
| DWEST | West | David |

**FIGURE 4-32** Author Table

| BookKeyISBN | AuthorKey |
|---|---|
| 0-07-222513-0 | HSCHLT |
| 0674019999-1 | SMITHN |
| 0-596-00867-8 | BMCLAU |
| 0-596-00867-8 | GPOLLIC |
| 0-596-00867-8 | DWEST |

**FIGURE 4-33** Linking Table BookAuthor

 *Caution*
*Always resolve a many-to-many relationship by creating a linking table. An unresolved many-to-many relationship will cause your database to fail.*

Sharon adds a linking entity to resolve the many-to-many relationship.

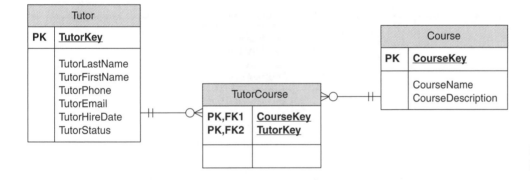

**FIGURE 4-34** TutorCourse Linking Table

Now **Tutor** has a one-to-many relationship with **TutorCourse**, and **Course** has a one-to-many relationship with **TutorCourse**, also. That is, one tutor can tutor for many courses, and one course can have many tutors. The composite key, which consists of the two foreign keys *TutorKey* and *CourseKey,* ensures that the same tutor won't be linked with the same course twice.

As she looks at her work, Sharon realizes that **Student** would have the same relationship with **Course** that **Tutor** does. One student can enroll in many courses, and one course can contain many students. It is another many-to-many relationship. Sharon adds a **Student** entity to her diagram. She reviews the attributes carefully to make sure she has all the demographic information included. Then she adds the linking tables and makes the relationship. Here is her whole diagram so far:

In the **Student** entity, Sharon decides to specify ethnicity as a foreign key. Her idea is that she will create a lookup table for the different ethnicities.

One big thing remains to be done. Sharon still needs to define the tutoring sessions themselves. Many databases have a central entity where everything is tied together. For this database, it is the **Session** entity. She reviews her notes. A session must have a date and time. It needs a course and a tutor. The student is optional because not every session that is available will be taken. She comes up with this entity diagram:

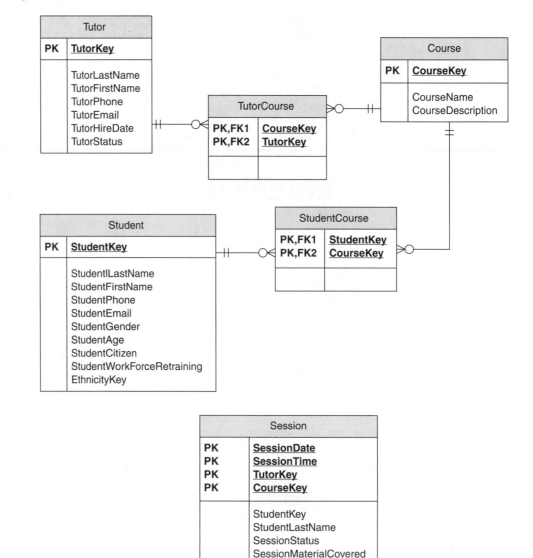

**FIGURE 4-35** Tutor ERD 1

**FIGURE 4-36** Session Entity

She is a bit uncomfortable with a four-attribute composite key, but it takes all four to uniquely identify a session, and she thinks Session won't have any child relations. She is also unsure of the attribute session status. *SessionStatus,* as she is thinking about it, would contain a value like "completed" if a student showed up and received tutoring, or "canceled" if the student did not—or maybe "tutor canceled" and "student canceled," respectively. She would also need a value if the session remained unused.

Another issue with Session, she realizes, is that there is a limit to the number of sessions a student can sign up for, and, for that matter, a limit to how many sessions a tutor can teach in a given time. She remembers that Bill, her professor, called these issues of cardinality. They can be important considerations for design and enforcing business rules, but generally they cannot be enforced in a database through the relationships themselves.

---

## THINGS TO THINK ABOUT

**Composite versus surrogate keys**

*Composite keys provide better protection for data integrity because they prevent accidental entry of identical information, but they can get awkward and can result in more redundant information.*

*Surrogate keys, like an identity or autonumber, remove those data redundancies but do nothing to protect data integrity.*

*Most database specialists choose one or the other, but all advise not to mix them.*

*Which do you think is the better option?*

| **Things You Should Know** | *CARDINALITY* |
|---|---|

*CARDINALITY*

The number of permitted records in a related entity.

*MAXIMUM CARDINALITY*

The highest number permitted.

*MINIMUM CARDINALITY*

The smallest number permitted.

*TRIGGERS*

Executable scripts of SQL code that are triggered by an event such as an insert, update, or delete. They can be used to enforce business rules that cannot be enforced by database design alone.

## Cardinality

Relationships can also have a property called cardinality. Cardinality refers to the number of allowed related rows between entities. The usual one-to-many relationship assumes that for each one record in the primary key entity, there can be any number of related rows in the foreign key entity. This is often expressed with an infinity sign. But a one-to-many relationship can have limits on the number of related rows. For example, say an Account entity can have no more than five email addresses in a related Email entity. That would mean that the relationship has a *maximum cardinality* of five. Let's also say that each account must have at least one email account. That would make the *minimum cardinality* of the relationship one.

RDBMSs really don't have ways to enforce cardinality rules directly. Usually, these kinds of rules are enforced by means of triggers and other extra-database code.

Next, Sharon adds a lookup entity for Ethnicity.

**Things You Should Know**

### Types of Entities

As you have seen in the preceding discussion, entities can play various roles in a database. It can be useful when designing a database to identify what roles different entities play.

| Ethnicity | |
|---|---|
| **PK** | **EthnicityKey** |
| | EthnicityDescription |

**FIGURE 4-37**   Lookup Entity

#### Domain Entities

Domain entities are the entities that relate directly to the business of the database. In a database to track customer orders, for instance, domain entities would probably include ones like Customer, Order, Inventory, and so on. In Sharon's Tutor database, the domain entities so far include Tutor, Student, Session, and Course.

#### Linking Entities

Linking entities are used to resolve many-to-many relationships into two one-to-many relationships. In Sharon's database, the TutorCourse and StudentCourse entities serve this purpose. Without these linking entities, RDBMSs would be unable to resolve the relationships between the entities involved, and the database would fail.

#### Lookup Entities

Lookup entities are essentially utility entities. They store lists of data that other tables need to look up, such as state names or abbreviations, country names, months of the year, postal codes, or any number of other things. Lookup entities help ensure consistency in data entry. If you want to use the two-letter abbreviation for a state rather than the full state name, a lookup table can help enforce it. Lookup tables also help protect against typing and other data entry errors.

#### Weak Entities

A weak entity is an entity that is dependent on another entity for its meaning. Consider, for instance, a situation where you needed to track an employee and his or her dependents. You can't just list a certain number of dependents in the Employee entity because you cannot know ahead of time how many dependents any one employee may have. It is also not a good idea just to list them separated by commas in a character attribute. It is better to create a separate entity called Dependents.

The Dependent entity is weak, because it depends on the Employee for meaning.

Another common weak entity relationship is the master/detail relationship. Typically an order, purchase, or sale is broken into two tables: the master CustomerOrder table and the child OrderDetail table.

FIGURE 4-38 Weak Entity

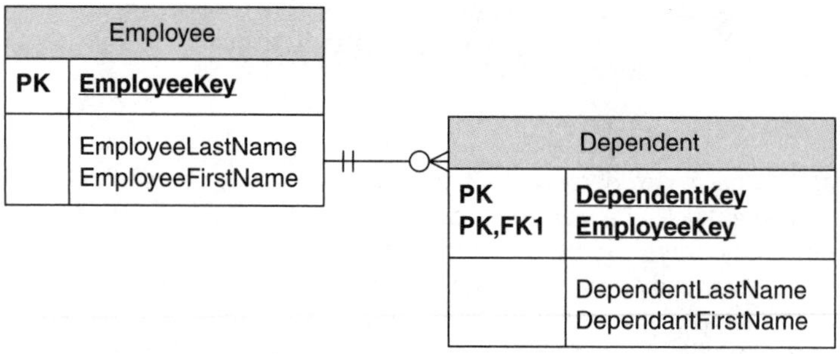


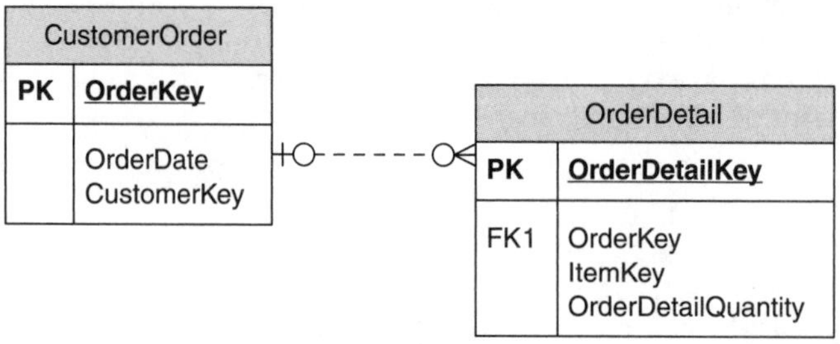


FIGURE 4-39 Master/Detail relation

A good way to understand this is to look at a receipt.

WestLake Grocery Emporium
(206-555-2020)

| | |
|---|---|
| TerminalID | 002 |
| Merchant# | 02340606060 |
| Visa | |
| ############1234 | |
| SALE | |
| Date | 2/1/2010 |
| Bread | 2.15 |
| Milk | 1.66 |
| Eggs | 1.25 |
| Hamburger | 4.62 |
| Subtotal | 9.68 |
| Tax | 0.00 |
| Total due | 9.68 |

The top of the receipt contains all the information necessary to identify the general transaction. It contains the order number, the date, the customer card number, possibly the employee code, and so on. The middle of the receipt contains the line items of the order, the specific items purchased, and the quantity purchased. The bottom of the receipt contains summary information. (In a database, this is achieved through queries.) The OrderDetail entity is dependent on the CustomerOrder for its meaning and is therefore a weak entity. It is also sometimes referred to as a master/detail relationship.

Here is a table of relationship types:

**Table 4-2** Entity Roles

| Entity Roles | Description |
|---|---|
| Domain | Entity describing a core business element of the database |
| Linking | Entity used to resolve a many-to-many relationship into two one-to-many relationships |
| Lookup | Entity used to store lookup values and help ensure data integrity and consistency |
| Weak (master/detail) | An entity that depends on another entity for its meaning |

Finally Sharon reviews all her entities.

As she reviews, she looks at each attribute and determines if it should be required or not. If the data in the attribute are critical to the integrity of the data in the database, it should be required. But if the data are not immediately known—such as which student might sign up for a session—or if it is not critical or if it is optional, it should not be required. You don't want to burden the process by forcing the users to enter data they may not have. For instance, you wouldn't want to force a tutor or student to invent an email address if he or she doesn't have one. But, equally, you don't want the user to leave out necessary data.

After her review, she has this logical design for the Tutoring database.

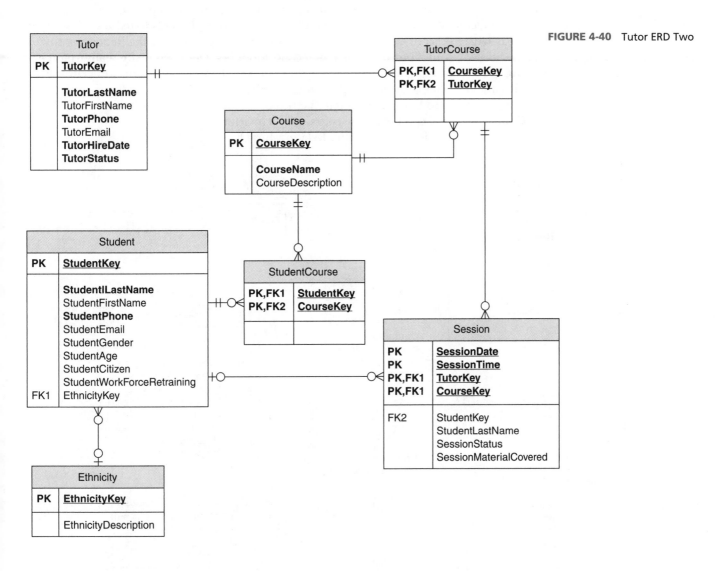

FIGURE 4-40   Tutor ERD Two

The required fields are in bold. For the Student table, Sharon knew that by law she couldn't require that a student enter the demographic information.

Now Sharon looks over the diagram one more time. She decides it might be a good exercise to define what role each entity is playing in her design. First, she identifies the domain entities:

- Tutor
- Student
- Course
- Session

Next, she lists her linking entities:

- StudentCourse
- TutorCourse

She has only one lookup entity, which is Ethnicity. So far she has no weak entities.

---

### THINGS TO THINK ABOUT

*What is the benefit of reviewing the entities according to the role they play in design?*

---

Looking over her list, Sharon realizes there is one domain entity that she still hasn't included. That is the Request entity, which allows students to request tutoring in areas where it is not already provided. Her first instinct is to link the Request entity to the Student entity, but then she has second thoughts. Does she really want to force a student to register to request tutoring for a course where there isn't tutoring currently? The student making the request is quite probably not being tutored at the moment. Still she would like to link the table into the rest of the database. As she understands it, the Course table will contain all the courses for a quarter.

Here, then, is her final Entity Relationship Diagram.

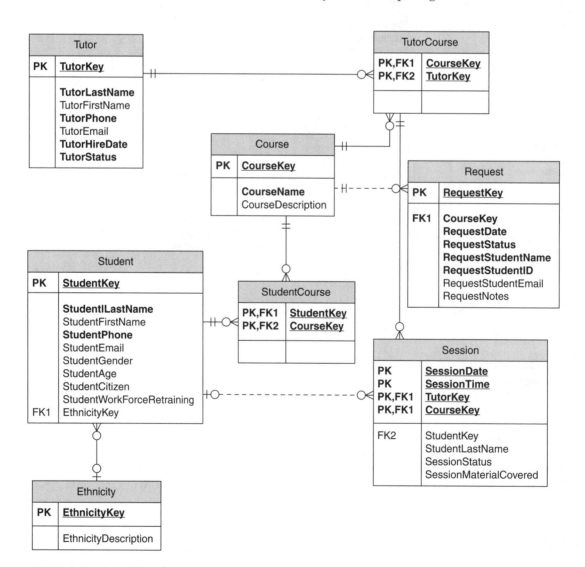

**FIGURE 4-41** Final ERD Before Review

Before taking this diagram to Terry, Sharon decides to have her instructor Bill Collins review it. She emails him, requesting an appointment, and attaches the diagram so he can go over it before they meet. Within minutes, he sends an email back, agreeing to meet the next morning. He said he would look over the design and make sure that it was normalized.

## DOCUMENTATION

Diagrams often communicate more clearly than words. It is important to keep ERDs in your database notebook. It is also a good idea to keep a history of diagrams. As your design progresses, you will make changes to the diagrams, adding and removing entities and attributes. Rather than just discarding the older diagrams, it can be valuable to keep dated versions of the ERD along with notes defining what changes were made and why. Coming back later, this can help you or a later developer understand the thought process that culminated in the final database design.

## Things We Have Done

*In this chapter we have*
- worked through the logical design of the database
- created entities
- added attributes to entities
- analyzed and created relationships among our entities
- identified the roles the entities play in our design

## Vocabulary

*Match the definitions to the vocabulary words:*

1. Cardinality
2. Composite keys
3. Crow's feet notation
4. Domain entities
5. Entity relation diagrams
6. Linking entity
7. Logical design
8. Lookup entity
9. Maximum cardinality
10. Minimum cardinality
11. Naming conventions
12. Physical design
13. Surrogate keys

14. Triggers
15. Weak entities

— a. The entity relation design without regard to what RDBMS or system it will be on
— b. The design adapted to the RDBMS and system constraints and features
— c. One common method of depicting entities and relations in a diagram
— d. A set of rules or suggestions that promote consistency in the naming of database objects
— e. Notation for relationships that uses lines and circles to depict cardinality
— f. An entity which resolves a many-to-many relationship into two one-to-many relationships
— g. Refers to the number of permitted records in a related entity
— h. An entity that depends on another entity for its meaning
— i. The highest number permitted
— j. The smallest number permitted
— k. A random or arbitrary key often generated by just incrementing numbers
— l. An entity that captures a chief element of the business problem
— m. Executable scripts of SQL code that are triggered by an event such as an insert, update, or delete.
— n. A key that consists of more than one column
— o. Are used to store a set of values that can be looked up, such as state abbreviations or zip codes

## Things to Look Up

1. Look up other database-naming conventions. Is there one that makes the most sense to you? Explain why?
2. Look up Entity Relation Diagrams. What other ways of diagramming entities and relations did you find?

3. Look for online tutorials on relational database design. Make a list of the five best. Share with the class to make a resource list of tutorials.

## Practices

1. Create an entity to describe the products in a sandwich shop. These can include sandwiches, of course, but also pastries and drinks.
2. Which attributes of the products entity should be required?

3. Which attributes would make a good primary key?
4. Here are two entities. (Only the primary keys are included.) What kind of relationship exists between these entities? Explain.

FIGURE 4-42

| Recipe | |
|---|---|
| PK | **RecipeKey** |
| | |

| Ingredient | |
|---|---|
| PK | **IngredientKey** |
| | |

5. Create a diagram that shows how you would resolve the relationship in Practice 4.
6. An instructor has decided that he needs a relational database to store grades in. He has defined the following three entities: **Student**, **Course**, and **Assignment**. What kind of relationship exists between these entities?
7. Create an entity relation diagram for the instructor's database. Don't worry about the attributes, but give each entity a primary key attribute. Remember to watch out for many-to-many relationships.
8. A dentist office has three dentists, two hygienists, five dental assistants, and two administrative assistants to maintain the office paper work. They are creating a database to track appointments and also to track who works with each patient. So far the database developer has defined the following entities: Employee (which includes all categories of employee including the dentists), Customer, and Appointment. Which entities have many-to-many relationships?
9. Create an ERD that shows the relationships among the entities in the dentist office mentioned in Practice 9. Remember several employees (a dentist, an assistant, a hygienist, etc.) can be involved in a single appointment for a customer.
10. Look at the diagram for Practice 8. Identify which entities are domain entities, which are linking entities, which are lookup, and which, if any, are weak entities.

## Scenarios

### WILD WOOD APARTMENTS

The managers at Wild Wood Apartments are anxious to see some progress on their database. They have answered your questions and now want to see some results. They really want the new database to be in place before the beginning of the new fiscal year in July. It is time to design the database.

1. Review all the requirements and business rules.
2. Define your entities and attributes and the relations that exist between them.
3. Create a logical model using crow's feet notation in Visio or hand draw it on graph paper, if you prefer.
4. Add all the entities and their attributes. You don't need to worry about data types for now.
5. Identify the key fields for each entity and the foreign keys.
6. Analyze the diagram. Identify which role (i.e., domain, linking, lookup, or weak) each entity plays in your database.
7. Have another student or a group review it for the following:

   a. Are all the major components of the Wildwood Apartments business model represented by domain entities?
   b. Does each entity contain the appropriate attributes to fully describe it and meet the business rules you have gathered so far?
   c. Does every entity have an appropriate primary key defined?
   d. Are all many-to-many relationships resolved into one-to-many relationships by linking tables?
   e. Are the relationships valid (no cross relationships)? Is the appropriate entity defined as the one side of a one-to-many relationship? Do the tables have appropriate foreign keys? Also check for other such issues.
   f. Are lookup tables used for attributes that have a set list of values?

8. **Documentation:** Be sure to store your ERDS in your database notebook.

### VINCE'S VINYL

Vince is convinced he is losing money on several of his transactions. He is anxious to get the new database in place to help him get control over his business. He has been polite but keeps checking on your progress. It is time to show some results.

Create a logical design of Vince's database. Use the following steps:

1. Review all the requirements and business rules that you have gathered from your interviews and after reviewing Vince's records.
2. Define your entities and attributes and the relations that exist between them.
3. Create a logical model using crow's feet notation in Visio or hand draw it on graph paper, if you prefer.
4. Add all the entities and their attributes. You don't need to worry about data types for now.
5. Identify the key fields for each entity and the foreign keys.
6. Analyze the diagram. Identify which role (i.e., domain, linking, lookup, or weak) each entity plays in your database.

7. Have another student or a group review it for the following:

    a. Are all the major components of the Vince's business model represented by domain entities?

    b. Does each entity contain the appropriate attributes to fully describe it and meet the business rules you have gathered so far?

    c. Does every entity have an appropriate primary key defined?

    d. Are all many-to-many relationships resolved into one-to-many relationships by linking tables?

    e. Are the relationships valid (no cross-relationships)? Is the appropriate entity defined as the one side of a one-to-many relationship? Do the tables have appropriate foreign keys? Also check for other such issues?

    f. Are lookup tables used for attributes that have a set list of values?

8. **Documentation:** Be sure to store your ERDs in your database notebook.

## GRANDFIELD COLLEGE

A team from the Software Alliance could show up any day. The IT services manager is eager to get the tracking database in place. It is time to show some progress. Create the logical design of the database following these steps:

1. Review all the requirements and business rules.
2. Define your entities and attributes and the relations that exist between them.
3. Create a logical model using crow's feet notation in Visio or hand draw it on graph paper, if you prefer.
4. Add all the entities and their attributes. You don't need to worry about data types for now.
5. Identify the key fields for each entity and the foreign keys.
6. Analyze the diagram. Identify which role (i.e., domain, linking, lookup, or weak) each entity plays in your database.
7. Have another student or a group review it for the following:

    a. Are all the major components of the software tracking system represented by domain entities?

    b. Does each entity contain the appropriate attributes to fully describe it and meet the business rules you have gathered so far?

    c. Does every entity have an appropriate primary key defined?

    d. Are all many-to-many relationships resolved into one-to-many relationships by linking tables?

    e. Are the relationships valid (no cross-relationships)? Is the appropriate entity defined as the one side of a one-to-many relationship? Do the tables have appropriate foreign keys? Also check for other such issues?

    f. Are lookup tabtles used for attributes that have a set list of values?

8. **Documentation:** Be sure to store your ERDs in your database notebook.

## WESTLAKE RESEARCH HOSPITAL

It is imperative that the database be ready before the actual clinical trials begin. The staff at Westlake is anxious to see some results. It is time you show them the logical design of their database. Follow these steps:

1. Review all the requirements and business rules.
2. Define your entities and attributes and the relations that exist between them.
3. Create a logical model using crow's feet notation in Visio or hand draw it on graph paper, if you prefer.
4. Add all the entities and their attributes. You don't need to worry about data types for now.
5. Identify the key fields for each entity and the foreign keys.
6. Analyze the diagram. Identify which role (i.e., domain, linking, lookup, or weak) each entity plays in your database.
7. Have another student or a group review it for the following:

    a. Are all the major components of the clinical trial represented by domain entities?

    b. Does each entity contain the appropriate attributes to fully describe it and meet the business rules you have gathered so far?

    c. Does every entity have an appropriate primary key defined?

    d. Are all many-to-many relationships resolved into one-to-many relationships by linking tables?

    e. Are the relationships valid (no cross-relationships)? Is the appropriate entity defined as the one side of a one-to-many relationship? Do the tables have appropriate foreign keys? Also check for other such issues.

    f. Lookup tables are used for attributes that have a set list of values.

8. **Documentation:** Be sure to store your ERDs in your database notebook.

## SUGGESTION FOR THE SCENARIOS

These scenario exercises are probably the most difficult in the book. The first suggestion is to not panic. Creating ERDs is an iterative process. No one expects you to have a perfect diagram on the first attempt. The trick is to add entities one at a time. Don't try to imagine the whole diagram all at once. Look at each entity separately. Does it have the appropriate attributes? Is the primary key defined? After the main entities are on the diagram, look at the relationships between two entities at a time. What kind of relationship do they have? Do you need a linking table? Also check for other such issues. Remember, also, that some entities have no direct relationship between them. Don't fall into the trap of trying to relate every entity to every other entity.

Discussion helps. Others can see issues and approaches that you might have missed. It is always good to have another pair of eyes looking over your work.

## CHAPTER 5

# Normalization and Design Review

Sharon takes her entity relation diagram to her database professor, Bill Collins. Together they review it for completeness and conformity to the first three normal forms. Then Sharon takes the design to Terry for a final discussion and review before beginning the physical design of the database.

## CHAPTER OUTCOMES
**By the end of this chapter you will be able to:**

- Evaluate an entity against the first three normal forms
- Remove all repeating lists or arrays (First Normal Form)
- Remove functional dependencies (Second Normal Form)
- Remove all transitive dependencies (Third Normal Form)
- Understand the importance of design review

## THE DESIGN REVIEW

Sharon knocks on Professor Collins's door early in the morning. He greets her and offers a chair. He has the diagram printed out with a few handwritten notes and arrows. He shows her the diagram and begins to explain his notes. "This is a pretty good diagram. You have all the basic elements in place."

"I owe it all to what I learned in your class."

"Thanks." He looks at the diagram, "I think we should begin by looking at the entities and making sure they are all properly normalized. Then we should check to make sure all the relationships are correct, and finally, we can discuss whether the diagram completely captures everything needed to meet the business requirements."

"Sound's good. Let's start."

"OK, let's start with normalization. First, we will see if it conforms to the first normal form."

### Things You Should Know

### Normalization

Normalization is the process of removing anomalies and redundancies from database design. There are three specific kinds of anomalies that can occur in database design:

- Insertion anomalies
- Update anomalies
- Deletion anomalies

**NORMALIZATION**

The process of removing anomalies and redundancies from database design.

### Insertion Anomalies

An insertion anomaly occurs when you can't enter certain information because you are missing some other information. Consider, for example, a case, where a company has a business rule that every employee must be assigned to a project. They have set up the Employee entity in their database to look like this:

| Employee | |
|---|---|
| **PK** | **EmployeeKey** |
| | EmployeeLastName |
| | EmployeeFirstName |
| | ProjectName |
| | ProjectDescription |

**INSERTION ANOMALY**

This is when you can't enter data because some other data is missing.

**FIGURE 5-1** Employee Entity

The data in the table would look like this:

| EmployeeKey | EmployeeLastName | EmployeeFirstName | ProjectName | ProjectDescription |
|---|---|---|---|---|
| 4123 | Brown | Richard | DB245 | New Employee database |
| 4124 | Sanderson | Lisa | DB134 | Tune the point of Sales database |
| 4215 | Lewis | Wallace | DB245 | New Employee database |

**FIGURE 5-2** Employee Table

The project is required. A new employee, who hasn't been assigned a project, cannot be entered into the table. One strategy is to create a dummy project for new employees. But this is a bad idea. It puts meaningless data in your database and is a risk to data integrity.

### Update Anomalies

Update anomalies occur when the same data is stored in more than one place. If the data needs to be changed or "updated," the user has to find every instance of that data and change it to make sure the data is consistent. It is all too easy to miss an instance or to make a mistake on one of the records so that it reads differently from the others. In the example given earlier, for instance, employees Brown and Lewis are working on the same project. Suppose the project name was changed by management. When the database is updated, the project name is changed for all employees in the project except for Lewis. Now if someone queries the database, it would look like Lewis and Brown are working on different projects.

**UPDATE ANOMALY**

An instance where the same information must be updated in several different places.

---

## THINGS TO THINK ABOUT

*How do you think it would affect the users of a database to have these anomalies appear after the database had been put into production?*

---

This may seem unlikely with the three records shown earlier, but imagine a data table with hundreds or thousands of records. Whenever there is redundancy—the same data repeated in several places—update anomalies are likely to occur.

### Deletion Anomalies

The preceding table also illustrates how deletion anomalies occur. A deletion anomaly happens when deleting one piece of data accidentally deletes all information about a different piece of data. For instance, the Employee table mentioned earlier. If Lisa Sanderson were to quit and be deleted from the table, we would also lose all information about the project DB134. Even if she were the only employee assigned to the project, information about the project should be available after she leaves.

*DELETION ANOMALY*

Where deleting one piece of data inadvertently causes other data to be lost.

### Normal Forms

Over the years, database experts have developed a series of "normal forms." Each form was designed to eliminate one or more of these anomalies. The normal forms are as follows:

- First Normal Form
- Second Normal Form
- Third Normal Form

- Boyce Codd Normal Form
- Fourth Normal Form
- Fifth Normal Form
- Domain Key Normal Form

*NORMAL FORMS*

Each normal form is a set of rules designed to reduce or eliminate various anomalies.

The first three normal forms are the most critical for developing a working database. The other normal forms add refinements that are valuable but not as critical.

The concepts of normalization and the process of "normalizing" can be quite difficult to master initially. To help, we will look at two different examples.

### A Note on Terminology

In the following examples, the term "entity" is used to describe the logical structure as seen in design. The term "table" is used for physical manifestation of the entity which contains actual rows of data.

## Example 1

The first example looks at a simple database to track albums, artists, and songs. Here is the first incarnation of the table.

This table could potentially fall prey to all three anomalies. If the *ArtistCountry* was required, it would be impossible to insert a new album if you did not know the country of the artist. If you deleted an album, you could accidently remove all data about a given artist. Updating tracks could be difficult and result in errors because of the way they are listed in the cell.

| Album | Tracks | Artist | ArtistCountry |
|---|---|---|---|
| Abby Road | Here comes the sun, Octopus Garden, Something, etc. | Beatles | UK |
| Blond on Blond | Rainy Day Woman, Sad eyed lady of the lowlands, Stuck in Memphis with the mobile blues again | Bob Dylan | US |

**FIGURE 5-3** Album Table Not Normalized

## Example 2

Converting a spreadsheet into a relational database is a common task for database developers. The task is not as straightforward as it might seem. Although you can often import data from a spreadsheet directly into a database management system, spreadsheets are almost never well designed for relational databases. The following figure is a spreadsheet that stores contact information for a university. Some sample rows are included.

The contact list works fairly well as a spreadsheet, but it presents several difficulties for a database developer. For one thing, there is a great deal of redundancy. Among others, the Building and BuildingAddress entities repeat numerous times. While this may seem innocuous enough, it does present the possibility of update anomalies. Consider what would need to be done if the IT Department moved to the Broadway Edison building. The building code, building name, and address would have to be changed for every employee that works in the IT Department. If any row remains unchanged, the information for that employee would be incorrect. When a value is repeated many times, such mistakes can happen quite easily.

| LastName/Dept. | FirstName | Phone | BuildingCode | Building | BuildingAddress |
|---|---|---|---|---|---|
| Able | Susan | 206.555.2356 | BE | Broadway Edison | 1700 Broadway |
| Admissions | | 206.555.1000 | BE | Broadway Edison | 1700 Broadway |
| Anderson | Elliot | 206.555.1029 | SA | South Annex | 1650 Broadway |
| Anderson | Jolene | 206.555.9001 | SA | South Annex | 1650 Broadway |
| Bradley | Lisa | 206.555.2323 | BE | Broadway Edison | 1700 Broadway |
| Brown | Martin | 206.555.1200 | SA | South Annex | 1650 Broadway |
| Information Technology | | 206.555.1200 | SA | South Annex | 1650 Broadway |

**FIGURE 5-4** Contact Spreadsheet (a)

| Office | Dept. | Type | Status | Title | Email |
|--------|-------|------|--------|-------|-------|
| 314 | HUM | Instruction | FT | Professor | sable@university.edu |
| 124 | ADM | | | | |
| 212 | IT | Instruction | PT | Professor | eanderson@univeristy.edu |
| 113 | IT | Instruction | PT | Professor | janderson@university.edu |
| 114 | MAT | Staff | FT | Program Assistant, Lab Assistant | lbradely@university.edu |
| 201 | IT | Exempt | | Dean IT | mbrown@university.edu |
| 200 | | | | | |

**FIGURE 5-5** Contact Spreadsheet (b)

The spreadsheet is also open to deletion anomalies. Consider what would happen if Martin Brown were to quit and be removed from the list. The position of Dean would also be lost. While it is extremely unlikely that all the Deans would quit at once, it still points out a problem. Removing one thing, a person, requires that you also remove another thing, a department.

Insertion anomalies could also occur. If Office and Phone were required, it would be impossible to insert a new employee until he or she had been assigned an office and a phone.

### First Normal Form

The First Normal Form [FN1] involves getting rid of repeating groups or arrays. Each attribute should contain only a single value of a single type. This means a couple of things. For one, all the values under an attribute should be about the same thing. An attribute called "Email," for instance, should contain emails only, no phone or pager numbers. A second meaning is that each value stored under an attribute should be a single value, not an array or list of values. It would be wrong, for example, to store two or three emails for the same person separated by commas.

An entity is in First Normal Form if

- Every attribute represents only one value.
- There are no repeating groups or arrays.
- Each row is unique.

*FIRST NORMAL FORM*

It removes all repeating groups or arrays.

## Example 1

This Album table does not meet the criteria for First Normal Form. The main problem is in the *Track* column. The column *Track* contains a list of songs rather than a single value. This would make it very difficult to locate information about any single song.

One solution that often occurs to novice database developers is to enumerate a list of columns such as Track1, Track2, Track3, and so on, to some arbitrary number of tracks. This also violates the First Normal Form by creating a repeating group. Say, for argument's sake, you made 13 track columns. What happens to an album with fourteen tracks? What if an album has only one or two tracks? Also consider what you would need to do to find any individual track. You would need to query 13 separate columns.

The following table is in First Normal Form:

| AlbumTitle | Track | Artist | ArtistCountry |
|------------|-------|--------|---------------|
| Abby Road | Here comes the sun | Beatles | UK |
| Abby Road | Octopus's Garden | Beatles | UK |
| Abby Road | Something | Beatles | UK |
| Blond on Blond | Rainy Day Woman | Bob Dylan | US |
| Blond on Blond | Sad Eyed Lady of the lowlands | Bob Dylan | US |
| Blond on Blond | Stuck in Mobile with the Memphis blues again | Bob Dylan | US |

**FIGURE 5-6** Album Table in 1NF

It is obvious from looking at the preceding table that First Normal Form is not sufficient. Every column contains a single value, and there are no arrays or repeating groups, but there is a great deal of redundancy.

## Example 2

In our spreadsheet example, the first attribute LastName/Dept. stores two different types of values, last names and department names. The attribute Title also has an issue. Lisa Brown has two titles, "Program Assistant" and "Lab Assistant." In First Normal Form, each row of an attribute must contain only a single value.

It may not be obvious at first why these things are a problem. Think about it from the point of view of someone querying the database. If they want to find a department's phone number, they have to search through all the faculty and staff names to find it. They could apply various filters, such as searching for values that have no status or position, but that is not guaranteed to return just what they want. A database user expects to be able to just ask for the department names and find them. The Title column is even more problematic for the database searcher. Suppose you want to find all the employees who have the title "Lab Assistant." When the attribute contains a list of values, you can't simply search for that title. You would have to use some kind of pattern search or string function to extract the title from the list. There is also no way to ensure consistency or data integrity when you have a list of values for an attribute.

To get the data to conform to First Normal Form, the first thing to do is to separate LastName and Dept. into two attributes. Since there is already a Dept. attribute, call the new attribute DeptName. Here is the first half of the spreadsheet with the correction:

| LastName | FirstName | DeptName | Phone | BuildingCode | Building |
|----------|-----------|----------|-------|--------------|----------|
| Able | Susan | | 206.555.2356 | BE | Broadway Edison |
| Admissions | | Admissions | 206.555.1000 | BE | Broadway Edison |
| Anderson | Elliot | | 206.555.1029 | SA | South Annex |
| Anderson | Jolene | | 206.555.9001 | SA | South Annex |
| Bradley | Lisa | | 206.555.2323 | BE | Broadway Edison |
| Brown | Martin | | 206.555.1200 | SA | South Annex |
| | | Information Technology | 206.555.1200 | SA | South Annex |

**FIGURE 5-7** Department and Name Separated

The next problem is more difficult. Title can have multiple values for a single employee. One temptation is to add columns such as Title1, Title2, and Title3, but this solution generates more problems than it solves. For the vast majority of employees who have only one title, Title2 and Title3 would be always empty. Also, what if some enterprising employee were working in four positions and had four titles. There would be no room for the fourth. For someone querying the database, this solution opens up even worse problems. If you were searching for all the employees who held a particular job title, you would have to query three different attributes.

The only way to solve this problem is to break the entity into two or more separate entities. Job title will be a separate entity. We will also need a linking entity, since there is a many-to-many relationship between employees and job titles.

One last issue remains. As you learned in the last chapter on database design, each entity should have a primary key, an attribute that uniquely identifies each row stored in the entity. In the Tutor database and most examples, the book has used natural keys, that is, keys that arise from some combination of the natural attributes of an entity. But in this example, just to show an alternative approach, we will use surrogate keys. Each row will be assigned an arbitrary number in sequence. Most relational database management systems have a utility to provide such keys. In SQL Server, it is "Identity"; in Access, it is called an "autonumber."

The overall Contact entity will have the key "ContactKey." The new Title entity will have "TitleKey" for a primary key and the linking entity will have a composite key consisting of "ContactKey" and "TitleKey."

When we are done, the data will look like this:

Following is an ERD of our efforts so far:

| ContactKey | LastName | FirstName | DeptName | Phone | BuildingCode |
|---|---|---|---|---|---|
| 1 | Able | Susan | | 206.555.2356 | BE |
| 2 | Admissions | | Admissions | 206.555.1000 | BE |
| 3 | Anderson | Elliot | | 206.555.1029 | SA |
| 4 | Anderson | Jolene | | 206.555.9001 | SA |
| 5 | Bradley | Lisa | | 206.555.2323 | BE |
| 6 | Brown | Martin | | 206.555.1200 | SA |
| 7 | | | Information Technology | 206.555.1200 | SA |

**FIGURE 5-8**   Contact Table 1NF

| Building | BuildingAddress | Office | Dept. | Type | Status | Email |
|---|---|---|---|---|---|---|
| Broadway Edison | 1700 Broadway | 314 | HUM | Instruction | FT | sable@university.edu |
| Broadway Edison | 1700 Broadway | 124 | ADM | | | |
| South Annex | 1650 Broadway | 212 | IT | Instruction | PT | eanderson@univeristy.edu |
| South Annex | 1650 Broadway | 113 | IT | Instruction | PT | janderson@university.edu |
| Broadway Edison | 1700 Broadway | 114 | MAT | Staff | FT | lbradely@university.edu |
| South Annex | 1650 Broadway | 201 | IT | Exempt | | mbrown@university.edu |
| South Annex | 1650 Broadway | 200 | | | | |

**FIGURE 5-9**   Contact Table (cont.)

| TitleKey | TitleName |
|---|---|
| 1 | Professor |
| 2 | Program Assistant |
| 3 | Dean |
| 4 | Lab Assistant |

**FIGURE 5-10**   Title Table

| ContactKey | TitleKey |
|---|---|
| 1 | 1 |
| 3 | 1 |
| 4 | 1 |
| 5 | 2 |
| 5 | 4 |
| 6 | 3 |

**FIGURE 5-11**   Contact Title Table

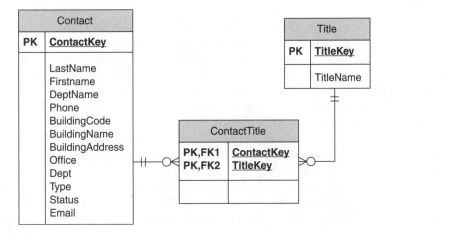

**FIGURE 5-12**   Contact ERD 1NF

Professor Collins lays out the Tutor diagram so that both he and Sharon can see it clearly.

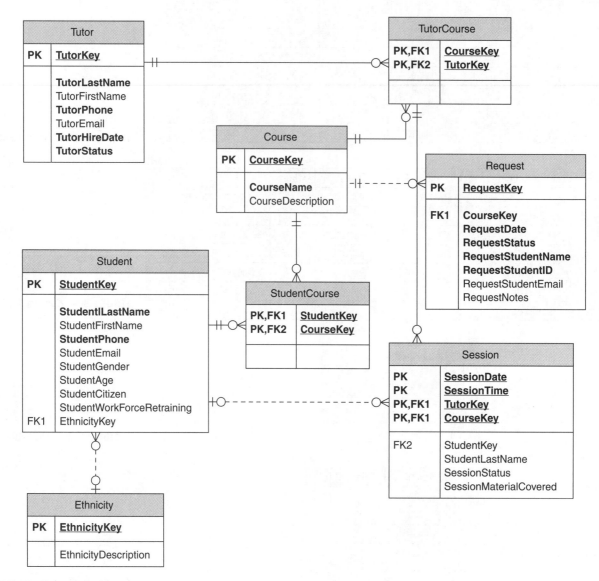

**FIGURE 5-13**  Tutor ERD

"As you recall," he begins, "to conform to First Normal Form, you need to eliminate all repeating groups or arrays and all multivalued dependencies." Together they go through each table. Professor Collins pauses at the Request table. "All the tables look good, but I do have a question about the attribute 'Request Notes.' Will there be instances with more than one entry for notes? If so, it would be better to make a new entity called RequestNotes, or something to that end. That way each request can have several notes if necessary, and you won't be wasting disk space by reserving note space for requests that don't have any notes. The primary key could be the date and time the note was entered, and it would be tied to the Request table by the RequestKey repeated as a foreign key."

Sharon nods. "I hadn't thought about that. I suppose there could be several notes as the status of the request changes. I will ask Terry about it to be sure. But the idea of separating it just to save disk space makes sense too. I'll change it."

"Ok, let's look to see how well your diagram conforms to Second Normal Form."

## Things You Should Know

Second Normal Form removes what are called "functional dependencies." One way to think of functional dependencies is as separate groups or themes within an entity. The members of the group are dependent on each other. If one member of the group repeats, so will the others in the group. An entity should only be about one thing. All the members should be dependent on the key, not on each other.

*SECOND NORMAL FORM*

It removes functional dependencies by creating new entities.

*FUNCTIONAL DEPENDENCIES*

Groups of related attributes that form subthemes within an entity.

## Example 1

In the Album table, there are really at least two large subjects. One is the Album itself. The other is the Track.

| AlbumTitle | Track | Artist | ArtistCountry |
|---|---|---|---|
| Abby Road | Here comes the sun | Beatles | UK |
| Abby Road | Octopus's Garden | Beatles | UK |
| Abby Road | Something | Beatles | UK |
| Blond on Blond | Rainy Day Woman | Bob Dylan | US |
| Blond on Blond | Sad Eyed Lady of the lowlands | Bob Dylan | US |
| Blond on Blond | Stuck in Mobile with the Memphis blues again | Bob Dylan | US |

**FIGURE 5-14**  Album Table 1FN

The Artist information depends on the Track. (Think about an album with tracks by multiple artists.) To conform to the Second Normal Form, the two functional dependencies—big themes—must be broken into separate entities.

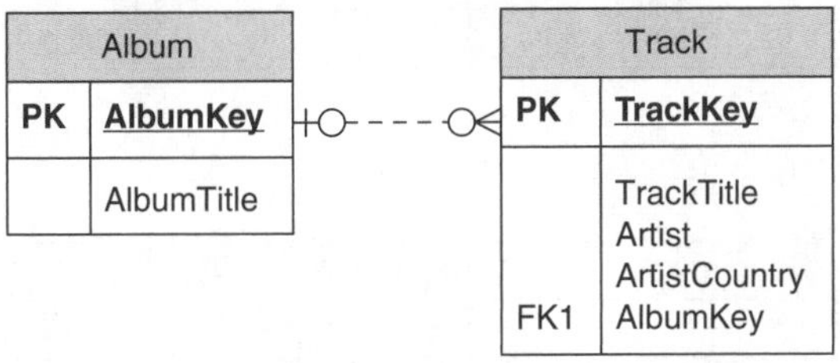

**FIGURE 5-15**  Album ERD 2NF

To relate the Album entity to the Track entity, it is necessary to create a primary key for the Album entity that can be used to create a key–foreign key relationship with the Track entity. It is also a good idea to give the Track entity a primary key. Here is what the tables look like now:

| AlbumKey | AlbumTitle |
|---|---|
| ABRD | Abby Road |
| BLBL | Blond On Blond |

**FIGURE 5-16**  Album table 2NF

| TrackKey | TrackTitle | AlbumKey | Artist | ArtistCountry |
|---|---|---|---|---|
| HCTS | Here Comes the Sun | ABRD | Beatles | UK |
| SMTH | Something | ABRD | Beatles | UK |
| OPGD | Octopus's Garden | ABRD | Beatles | UK |
| RDWM | Rainy Day Woman | BLBL | Bob Dylan | US |
| SELL | Sad Eyed Lady of the Lowlands | BLBL | Bob Dylan | US |
| SMMB | Stuck in Memphis with the Mobile Blues | BLBL | Bob Dylan | US |

**FIGURE 5-17**  Track table 2NF

## Example 2

In the Contact spreadsheet example, there are two distinct types of contacts: employees and departments. They have separate attributes within the entity. Employee has LastName and FirstName attributes, for instance, which are always blank for Department. Separate themes should be given their own entities.

Following is the sample data reflecting the new entities. Creating the Employee entity required some additional changes. The ContactTitle entity is changed to EmployeeTitle, and ContactKey is changed to EmployeeKey. The numbers have been changed to reflect the new relationship. Additional information not present in the original table has been added to fill in the Department entity.

| EmployeeKey | LastName | FirstName | Phone | BuildingCode | Building |
|---|---|---|---|---|---|
| 1 | Able | Susan | 206.555.2356 | BE | Broadway Edison |
| 2 | Anderson | Elliot | 206.555.1029 | SA | South Annex |
| 3 | Anderson | Jolene | 206.555.9001 | SA | South Annex |
| 4 | Bradley | Lisa | 206.555.2323 | BE | Broadway Edison |
| 5 | Brown | Martin | 206.555.1200 | SA | South Annex |

**FIGURE 5-18**   Employee Table

| BuildingAddress | Office | DeptKey | Type | Status | Email |
|---|---|---|---|---|---|
| 1700 Broadway | 314 | 1 | Instruction | FT | sable@university.edu |
| 1650 Broadway | 212 | 2 | Instruction | PT | eanderson@univeristy.edu |
| 1650 Broadway | 113 | 2 | Instruction | PT | janderson@university.edu |
| 1700 Broadway | 114 | 3 | Staff | FT | lbradely@university.edu |
| 1650 Broadway | 201 | 2 | Exempt | | mbrown@university.edu |

**FIGURE 5-19**   Employee Table (cont.)

| DeptKey | DeptAbrv | DeptName | DeptPhone | BuildingCode |
|---|---|---|---|---|
| 1 | Hum | Humanities | 206.555.1300 | BE |
| 2 | IT | Information Technology | 206.555.1200 | SA |
| 3 | MAT | Math | 206.555.1400 | BE |
| 4 | ADM | Admissions | 206.555.1000 | BE |

| Building | BuildingAddress | Office | | |
|---|---|---|---|---|
| Broadway Edison | 1700 Broadway | 301 | | |
| South Annex | 1650 Broadway | 200 | | |
| Broadway Edison | 1700 Broadway | 245 | | |
| Broadway Edison | 1700 Broadway | 124 | | |

**FIGURE 5-20**   Department Table

| TitleKey | TitleName |
|---|---|
| 1 | Professor |
| 2 | Program Assistant |
| 3 | Dean |
| 4 | Lab Assistant |

**FIGURE 5-21**   Title Table

| EmployeeKey | TitleKey |
|-------------|----------|
| 1 | 1 |
| 2 | 1 |
| 3 | 1 |
| 4 | 2 |
| 4 | 4 |
| 5 | 3 |

**FIGURE 5-22**  Employee Title Table

There is still one major functional dependency in the entities remaining. Both the Employee and the Department entities contain a group related to building. "Building Name" and "Building Address" both depend on "Building Code" and repeat whenever the attribute "Building Code" is present. Building is another separate theme and should have its own entity.

The NewBuilding entity looks like this:

| BuildingKey | BuildingCode | BuildingName | BuildingAddress |
|-------------|--------------|--------------|-----------------|
| 1 | BE | Broadway Edison | 1700 Broadway |
| 1 | SA | South Annex | 1650 Broadway |

**FIGURE 5-23**  Building Table

The "BuildingCode," "Building," and "BuildingAddress" attributes in Employee and Department are replaced by the "BuildingKey" attribute. So they now look like these:

| EmployeeKey | LastName | FirstName | Phone | BuildingCode |
|-------------|----------|-----------|-------|--------------|
| 1 | Able | Susan | 206.555.2356 | 1 |
| 2 | Anderson | Elliot | 206.555.1029 | 2 |
| 3 | Anderson | Jolene | 206.555.9001 | 2 |
| 4 | Bradley | Lisa | 206.555.2323 | 1 |
| 5 | Brown | Martin | 206.555.1200 | 2 |

**FIGURE 5-24**  Employee Table 2NF

| Office | DeptKey | Type | Status | Email |
|--------|---------|------|--------|-------|
| 314 | 1 | Instruction | FT | sable@university.edu |
| 212 | 2 | Instruction | PT | eanderson@univeristy.edu |
| 113 | 2 | Instruction | PT | janderson@university.edu |
| 114 | 3 | Staff | FT | lbradely@university.edu |
| 201 | 2 | Exempt | | mbrown@university.edu |

**FIGURE 5-25**  Employee Table (cont.)

| DeptKey | DeptAbrv | DeptName | DeptPhone | BuildingCode | Office |
|---------|----------|----------|-----------|--------------|--------|
| 1 | Hum | Humanities | 206.555.1300 | 1 | 301 |
| 2 | IT | Information Technology | 206.555.1200 | 2 | 200 |
| 3 | MAT | Math | 206.555.1400 | 1 | 245 |
| 4 | ADM | Admissions | 206.555.1000 | 1 | 124 |

**FIGURE 5-26**  Department Table 2NF

The ERD of the data in Second Normal Form looks like this:

**FIGURE 5-27** Employee
ERD 2NF

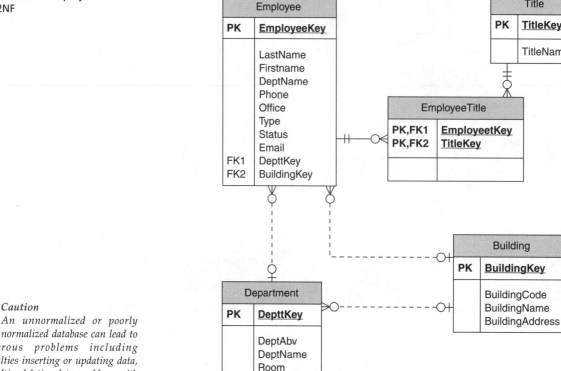

*Caution*
*An unnormalized or poorly normalized database can lead to numerous problems including difficulties inserting or updating data, difficulties deleting data, problems with data integrity, and the inability to retrieve the data you need.*

Professor Collins looked through each of the entities for functional dependencies. He stops again at the Request entity.

**FIGURE 5-28** Request Entity

"We already talked about the *RequestNotes*, but look at the entity again," he says. "Can you see two different things going on?"

Sharon looks at it for some time before she finally sees it. "Request is one theme, and student is another."

"Yes, there is a functional dependency there. *RequestStudentName* and *RequestStudentEmail* depend on *RequestStudentID*, rather than on the *RequestKey*."

"I see that, but I was thinking that a student shouldn't have to register as a tutoring student to make a request for additional tutoring. In particular, they shouldn't have to enter all the demographic information. In fact, if they do register just to make a request, it may make it more difficult for Terry to develop her demographic reports."

"I understand, but if you leave the entity the way it is, it could cause problems. The student information would be repeated with every request the student makes. That could lead to update and other anomalies."

Bill thinks about it for a while. "I can think of a couple of solutions. The best solution would be to have the students register in the Student table. As I understand it, any student who wants tutoring must register. Being registered, in and of itself, does not mean they are actually signing up for tutoring sessions. To do the demographics, Terry would have to compare the student information to the student keys in the Session table anyway. The other option is to create a Requester table that contains the student information for those requesting tutoring. I don't think this option is as strong because it creates a lot of potential redundancy."

"Which one do you think I should go with?"

"I think you should talk it over with Terry. Use the Student entity if possible."

"Thanks."

"OK, Let's see how it looks for Third Normal Form."

## Things You Should Know

### Third Normal Form

For an entity to be in Third Normal Form, it has to first be in Second Normal Form. Third Normal Form is about removing "transitive dependencies." A transitive dependency describes an attribute that depends on another attribute—not the primary key—for its meaning. The idea is that every attribute should directly describe the entity itself. If you have a Customer entity, every attribute should describe the customer. There shouldn't be any attributes that describe another attribute.

While transitive dependencies may seem trivial, they do add to redundancy and therefore open the possibilities for update and other anomalies.

*THIRD NORMAL FORM*

It refers to removing transient dependencies.

*TRANSIENT DEPENDENCIES*

Where one attribute depends on another attribute for its meaning and not on the key.

### Example 1

Take another look at the Track table.

| TrackKey | TrackTitle | AlbumKey | Artist | ArtistCountry |
|----------|-----------|----------|--------|---------------|
| HCTS | Here Comes the Sun | ABRD | Beatles | UK |
| SMTH | Something | ABRD | Beatles | UK |
| OPGD | Octopus's Garden | ABRD | Beatles | UK |
| RDWM | Rainy Day Woman | BLBL | Bob Dylan | US |
| SELL | Sad Eyed Lady of the Lowlands | BLBL | Bob Dylan | US |
| SMMB | Stuck in Memphis with the Mobile Blues | BLBL | Bob Dylan | US |

FIGURE 5-29    Track Table

There is a transitive dependency in the table. *ArtistCountry* doesn't describe the track; it describes the Artist. The solution, as usual, is to break out a separate table. Artist should be its own entity.

| AlbumKey | AlbumTitle |
|----------|-----------|
| ABRD | Abby Road |
| BLBL | Blond On Blond |

FIGURE 5-30    Album Table

| ArtistKey | ArtistName | ArtistCountry |
|-----------|-----------|---------------|
| BTLS | Beatles | UK |
| BDLN | Bob Dylan | US |

FIGURE 5-31    Artist Table

| TrackKey | TrackTitle | AlbumKey | ArtistKey |
|----------|------------|----------|-----------|
| HCTS | Here Comes the Sun | ABRD | BTLS |
| SMTH | Something | ABRD | BTLS |
| OPGD | Octopus's Garden | ABRD | BTLS |
| RDWM | Rainy Day Woman | BLBL | BDLN |
| SELL | Sad Eyed Lady of the Lowlands | BLBL | BDLN |
| SMMB | Stuck in Memphis with the Mobile Blues | BLBL | BDLN |

**FIGURE 5-32**   Track-Table 3NF

Here is an entity relation diagram for the three tables:

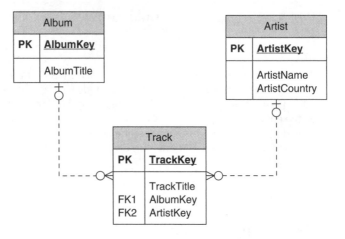

**FIGURE 5-33**   Album ERD 3NF

## Example 2

A careful review of the entities developed from the address spreadsheet can show two related transitive dependencies. In the Employee entity, the office number depends on the BuildingKey. That is, a particular office number only has meaning in the context of a particular building. The same issue exists in the Department entity. The room number for the Department depends on the Building.

One solution is to create a new entity called BuildingRoom that resolves the building and room relationship. Use of surrogate keys will give the new entity BuildingRoomKey a primary key.

Now the tables look like this:

| EmployeeKey | LastName | FirstName | Phone | BuildingRoomKey |
|-------------|----------|-----------|-------|-----------------|
| 1 | Able | Susan | 206.555.2356 | 5 |
| 2 | Anderson | Elliot | 206.555.1029 | 9 |
| 3 | Anderson | Jolene | 206.555.9001 | 6 |
| 4 | Bradley | Lisa | 206.555.2323 | 1 |
| 5 | Brown | Martin | 206.555.1200 | 8 |

**FIGURE 5-34**   Employee Table

| DeptKey | Type | Status | Email |
|---------|------|--------|-------|
| 1 | Instruction | FT | sable@university.edu |
| 2 | Instruction | PT | eanderson@univeristy.edu |
| 2 | Instruction | PT | janderson@university.edu |
| 3 | Staff | FT | lbradely@university.edu |
| 2 | Exempt | | mbrown@university.edu |

**FIGURE 5-35**   Employee Table
(cont.)

| DeptKey | DeptAbrv | DeptName | DeptPhone | BuildingRoomKey |
|---------|----------|----------|-----------|-----------------|
| 1 | Hum | Humanities | 206.555.1300 | 4 |
| 2 | IT | Information Technology | 206.555.1200 | 7 |
| 3 | MAT | Math | 206.555.1400 | 3 |
| 4 | ADM | Admissions | 206.555.1000 | 2 |

FIGURE 5-36   Department Table

| TitleKey | TitleName |
|----------|-----------|
| 1 | Professor |
| 2 | Program Assistant |
| 3 | Dean |
| 4 | Lab Assistant |

FIGURE 5-37   Title Table

| EmployeeKey | TitleKey |
|-------------|----------|
| 1 | 1 |
| 2 | 1 |
| 3 | 1 |
| 4 | 2 |
| 4 | 4 |
| 5 | 3 |

FIGURE 5-38   Employee Title Table

| BuildingKey | BuildingCode | BuildingName | BuildingAddress |
|-------------|--------------|--------------|-----------------|
| 1 | BE | Broadway Edison | 1700 Broadway |
| 1 | SA | South Annex | 1650 Broadway |

FIGURE 5-39   Building Table

| BuildingRoomKey | BuildingKey | Room |
|-----------------|-------------|------|
| 1 | 1 | 114 |
| 2 | 1 | 124 |
| 3 | 1 | 245 |
| 4 | 1 | 301 |
| 5 | 1 | 314 |
| 6 | 2 | 113 |
| 7 | 2 | 200 |
| 8 | 2 | 201 |
| 9 | 2 | 212 |

FIGURE 5-40   Building Room Table

The new entity diagram looks like this:

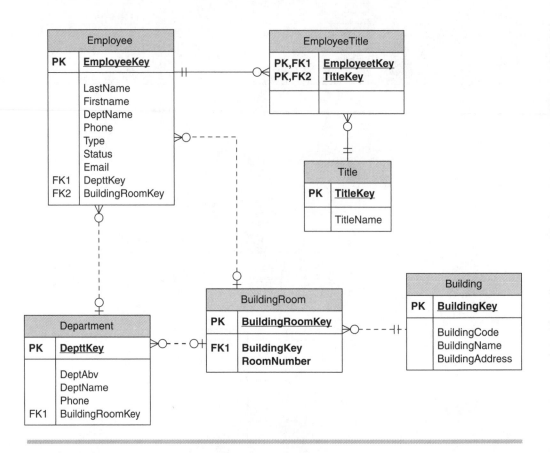

**FIGURE 5-41**   Employee ERD 3NF

Once again Professor Collins reviewed the entities, this time checking to make sure they conform to Third Normal Form. "I see only one issue," he says and points to the Session entity:

| Session | |
|---|---|
| PK,FK1 | **TutorKey** |
| PK,FK1 | **CourseKey** |
| PK | **SessionDate** |
| PK | **SessionStartTime** |
| FK2 | StudentKey |
| | StudentLastName |
| | SessionStatus |

**FIGURE 5-42**   Session Entity

*Caution*
*It is easy to add an attribute to an entity because you feel intuitively that you would want to see it there when looking at the data. But adding the column creates unnecessary redundancy and opens the possibility of anomalies. One way to think about it is that normalization is about designing tables so that they work best on the computer. They are not designed to be necessarily readable by human users. Queries and views are used to bring the data back in a form that is easy to understand and use. Queries will be covered in Chapter 7.*

"StudentLastName modifies the StudentKey and not the SessionKey. I know it seems natural to want the student last name in the Session, but it is unnecessary and redundant. The session is related to the Student table by means of the 'StudentKey,' and you can always retrieve any student information you need by means of a query."

Sharon says, "I knew that. I don't know what possessed me to put it in there."

Bill Collins smiles. "Like I said, it is a natural reaction. You want the student name to be a part of the tutoring session. But I notice you didn't put in the tutor's name. That shows you understood the principle, you just slipped up. That's what reviews are for." He turns to another of his notes.

"Looking the diagram over a third time, I noticed another potential problem. Here you made a linking table between Student and Courses with a composite key consisting of StudentKey and CourseKey. That makes perfect sense, but it does have a problem. That means a student can only take a particular course once, ever, or, at least, he or she can get tutored for that course only once. If a student takes a course a second time, it would violate the primary key constraint. I don't think that is a policy of the tutoring center. I think you can get tutoring for any course you are enrolled in, even if it is your second or third try."

---

### THINGS TO THINK ABOUT

*You should always have someone else review your entity relation diagrams before you use them to start developing the database itself.*

*Who do you think should review the diagram? What should he or she look for? What are the dangers of going ahead without reviewing the diagram?*

---

Sharon studies the diagram for a minute. "How would I fix that?"

"I think all it would take is to add another column to the composite key, ideally one that specifies quarter and year. I would suggest something like this."

| StudentCourse | |
|---|---|
| PK,FK1 | **StudentKey** |
| PK,FK2 | **CourseKey** |
| PK | **StudentCourseQuarter** |
| | |

**FIGURE 5-43**  StudentCourse Entity

Sharon nods in agreement, "Anything else?"

"No, I think with those changes it should be fine. Remember to review the diagram with Terry to make sure it covers everything she needs. Don't expect her to understand the diagram. She probably won't understand normalization and relational modeling, but she will be the best source to determine if you have captured everything that needs to be captured. The main thing you need to do is look at all the attributes and make sure that everything she needs is included."

"I will do that, and thank you for your help."

"You are most welcome."

---

### THINGS TO THINK ABOUT

*Do you think it is easier to modify a database in design mode or after the database has been actually built? Why do you think that way?*

---

After Sharon leaves Bill Collins's office, she goes to the cafeteria and gets a cup of coffee. She opens her laptop and adjusts her entity relation diagram to incorporate all of Bill's suggestions. This is the version she will take to Terry.

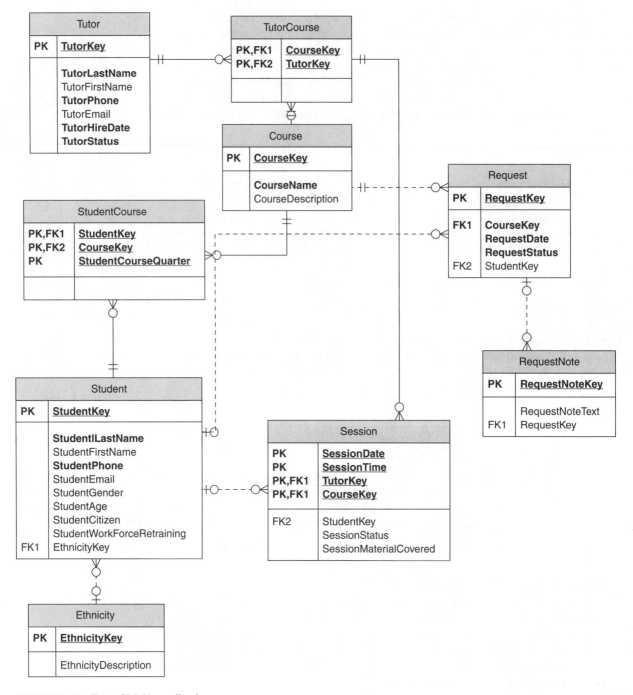

**FIGURE 5-44**  Tutor ERD Normalized

## FINAL CONTENT REVIEW

Terry agrees to see her the next day. After she has sat down, she presents Terry with a printout of the diagram. "I have reviewed the design with Professor Collins," she says, "what I need to do with you is figure out if I have captured all the information you need to capture."

"All right, that sounds good. Where do we start?"

"I think the best way might be to look at each major entity and go through the attributes. Let's start with the Tutor entity up here. I have the tutors' first and last names, their phone numbers and email addresses, and the dates they were hired on."

Terry asks "What do you mean by *'TutorStatus'*?"

"I was thinking that would record whether a tutor is active or not. You don't necessarily want to delete the information regarding tutors and what they tutored when they leave. In fact, I am pretty sure you want to keep that information so you can compare current data to past data. So I thought this field would make it simple to determine which tutors were currently tutoring versus which ones were no longer tutoring. It is possible that you could get the same information by querying the Session tables. If a tutor doesn't have any current or future dates listed, will he or she be inactive?"

"That wouldn't always be true. A tutor could be active but not have scheduled anything for the next two weeks. I think the status field is better. What is the *TutorKey*?"

Sharon smiles, "I am not entirely sure. A student has a student ID and that can be the *StudentKey*. Most tutors are students but not all of them. Do you create an identifying number?"

"Yes. We give all tutors an employment ID. If they are students, it is the same as their student ID; if not, we give them one that looks just like a student ID."

"Good. That makes that easy."

They review each of the remaining entities. Terry has questions for each, but after the full review, she is satisfied that it captures all the information that she will need.

Sharon thanks her. "Now I am ready to actually build the database. We will need to get together again to decide what we want to build it in."

Terry looks down at her calendar. "How soon do you want to meet?"

"How about Monday? I think I know what we should use, but I would like to do a little research."

"OK, how does 9:00 AM work?"

"That should be fine."

## DOCUMENTATION

It is useful to keep multiple versions of the entity diagram, noting changes made to conform to normal forms. Again, these can be useful to later developers who need to make changes to your original design. One change that is often made on high-volume transaction databases is to apply a process called "denormalization." In denormalization, some entities that were separated in the normalization process are rejoined. This is done for processing and query speed. It is not a process that should be done lightly. Every act of denormalization reopens the possibility of the various anomalies. But sometimes the sheer size and volume of transactions on a database make it necessary to denormalize if the users are not to experience delays.

A database should always be fully normalized first and denormalized only as necessary for performance. Both the fully normalized design and the changes made for denormalization should be fully documented.

*DENORMALIZATION*

Joining tables that were separated in the normalization process to improve performance.

## Things We Have Done

*In this chapter we have*

- looked at three types of database anomalies: insert, update, and delete
- introduced normal forms

- reviewed database designs for First Normal Form
- reviewed database designs for Second Normal Form
- reviewed database designs for Third Normal Form
- reviewed database designs for completeness

## Vocabulary

*Match the definitions to the vocabulary words:*

**1.** Normal forms      —   a. Where deleting some data inadvertently also removes other data

**2.** Update anomalies      —   b. Removes transient dependencies

**3.** Deletion anomalies      —   c. Where the same data must be updated in several places creating the possibility of mismatched or inaccurate data

4. First Normal Form     — d. Attributes that are related to each other rather than the key. They form subthemes within the entity

5. Denormalization     — e. Rules for removing anomalies and redundancies

6. Insertion anomalies     — f. An attribute that depends on another attribute, not the key, for its meaning

7. Second Normal Form     — g. Removes functional dependencies

8. Transient dependencies     — h. The inability to insert data because some other unknown data is required

9. Functional dependencies     — i. Removes repeating groups and arrays

10. Third Normal Form     — j. The process of rejoining tables that were separated during the normalization process to improve performance

## Things to Look Up

1. Look up database anomalies. See if you can find a good example explaining each kind of anomaly.
2. Look up the definition of functional dependency. Can you find a good example?
3. Look up the definition of transitive dependency. Can you find a good example?
4. Look up one of the normal forms we did not cover. See if you can explain it to someone in the class.
5. Look up "denormalization," and why anyone would want to do it.

## Practices

Martin wants to make a database to track his extensive DVD & Blue Ray collection. He has been tracking them in a spreadsheet with these columns:

1. Title
2. Studio
3. Media (Blue Ray or DVD)
4. Year (year released)
5. Genre (action, sci-fi, comedy, animated, western, documentary, etc.)
6. Actors (all the listed actors separated by commas)
7. Special Features (all the listed special features separated by commas)
8. Rating (R, PG-13, PG, G, N for unrated)
9. Price (the price he paid for it)

You may want to create the spreadsheet and enter some sample data, if it helps clarify the process.

1. What are some of the potential problems with this layout if carried directly into a database? Specifically address each of the three anomaly types: insert, update, and delete.
2. Which of the columns in the spreadsheet are multivalued?

3. Create an entity diagram that shows how you would translate the preceding spreadsheet into a database that conforms to First Normal Form.
4. Describe the process you went through to arrive at the diagram for Practice 3.
5. List any "functional" dependencies, any major themes, you find.
6. Create a second entity diagram that shows how you would translate the spreadsheet into a database that conforms to Second Normal Form.
7. Describe the process you used for Practice 6. If you did not make any changes, provide your reasons for why you think your previous diagram also conforms to Second Normal Form.
8. List any "transitive" dependencies you find. Describe why you believe they depend on a column that is not the key of the table.
9. Create a third entity diagram that shows how you would bring the database into conformity with Third Normal Form.
10. Describe your process for Practice 9, even if you made no changes from the previous diagram.

## Scenarios

### WILD WOOD APARTMENTS

It is almost time to actually begin building the Apartment database, but you must make sure that the design is solid and that it captures all the data required by Wild Wood Apartments. The first step is a design review; then you must review the diagram for completeness.

### To Do

1. Review the diagram you made from the previous chapter for all three levels of normalization.
2. Change the diagram to reflect the fully normalized design.
3. Document in writing why you made the changes you did, or why you did not need to make changes.
4. Review the normalized diagram for completeness. Do the entities capture all the data needed to meet the business rules and needs of Wild Wood Apartments?
5. **Documentation**: Save the normalized diagram with notes about changes made during the normalization process to your database notebook.

## VINCE'S VINYL

You have told Vince that you can begin building the database very soon now, maybe even next week. But before you do that, you need to make sure the design is solid and complete.

### To Do

1. Review the diagram you made from the previous chapter for all the three levels of normalization.
2. Change the diagram to reflect the fully normalized design.
3. Document in writing why you made the changes you did, or why you did not need to make changes.
4. Review the normalized diagram for completeness. Do the entities capture all the data needed to meet the business rules and needs of Vince's Vinyl?
5. **Documentation**: Save the normalized diagram with notes about changes made during the normalization process to your database notebook.

## GRANDFIELD COLLEGE

You have promised to begin building the database within the next couple of days. But before you do that, you have to review the design for normalization and completeness.

### To Do

1. Review the diagram you made from the previous chapter for all three levels of normalization.
2. Change the diagram to reflect the fully normalized design.

3. Document in writing why you made the changes you did, or why you did not need to make changes.
4. Review the normalized diagram for completeness. Do the entities capture all the data needed to meet the business rules and needs of Grandfield College IT Department?
5. **Documentation**: Save the normalized diagram with notes about changes made during the normalization process to your database notebook.

## WESTLAKE RESEARCH HOSPITAL

The start of the double-blind test is approaching rapidly. There is a great deal of pressure on you to begin building the actual database. Before you can do that, though, you must perform a final review to make sure the database is normalized and complete.

### To Do

1. Review the diagram you made from the previous chapter for all three levels of normalization.
2. Change the diagram to reflect the fully normalized design.
3. Document in writing why you made the changes you did, or why you did not need to make changes.
4. Review the normalized diagram for completeness. Do the entities capture all the data needed to meet the business rules and needs of Westlake?
5. **Documentation**: Save the normalized diagram with notes about changes made during the normalization process to your database notebook.

## Suggestions for Scenarios

Normalization is difficult. The trick is to take each normal form one at a time. Look at each entity one at a time, to see if each conforms to the First Normal Form. Make sure there are no repeating groups or mutivalued attributes. If there are, then break them out into new entities. Then repeat the process for the Second Normal Form. Look at each entity, and make sure that each is about only one thing. Again, if you find an entity that is about more than one thing, break it into new entities. Finally, repeat the process for Third Normal Form, looking for transitive dependencies, attributes that depend on an attribute that is not the key, for their value.

As with the design process itself, the normalization process benefits from discussion and multiple inputs. It is crucial to have others review the results.

## CHAPTER 6

# Physical Design

Now that she has the logical design completed, Sharon works on the physical design of the database. The first thing to decide is what database management system to use. After considering several, Sharon decides on SQL Server Express. She creates a new database with a data file and a log file. She creates the tables in the new database, selecting the appropriate data type and setting any constraints for each column. She also sets up the relationships among the tables. Finally, when she has set up all the database objects, she enters 5 or 10 rows of sample data so she can test the database.

## CHAPTER OUTCOMES

**By the end of this chapter you will be able to:**

- Compare database management systems and determine which best suits current needs
- Implement a physical design of the database based on the logical ERDs
- Choose appropriate data types for columns
- Enter sample data into tables

## CHOOSING THE MANAGEMENT SYSTEM

Sharon finally feels comfortable with her design. Now it is time to begin actually creating the database. The first question she must resolve is which database management system to use. One of the first criteria is that it shouldn't cost the school anything. That still leaves open several options. Oracle Express or DB2 Express is tempting because she would love to explore both. But the fact that she doesn't know either also means a longer learning curve. Additionally, she knows that the IT staff is unfamiliar with them. The same holds true, though to a lesser extent, for MySQL and PostGres SQL. Both are free and actually more powerful than any of the express editions, but she is less familiar with them. The IT staff has some familiarity with MySQL, but still Sharon doesn't think she can afford the learning curve at this time. That leaves Access and SQL Server Express.

 **Things You Should Know**

### Choosing a DBMS

Choosing the appropriate DBMS requires a great deal of analysis. There are several important factors to consider.

- Compatibility with your network and operating systems
- Hardware and software requirements for the DBMS
- Features of the DBMS in relation to your database requirements
- Familiarity and expertise in the DBMS for database developers and IT personnel
- Price and licensing requirements
- Product reliability and support

### Compatibility and Hardware Requirements

It might seem obvious that if an RDBMS is not compatible with your system, you would exclude it from the list of possible candidates. For example, if your system is running exclusively Unix or Linux operating systems, SQL Server would be out of the question because it will run only on Microsoft Windows operating systems. Equally, if the DBMS requires more hard disk space and RAM than your system currently supports, you probably will look for a less demanding alternative. However, it is possible that an RDMS has features that make it compelling enough to add hardware or integrate another operating system into the network.

### Features of the DBMS

What features a DBMS supports is crucial to the decision. For a simple database, such as the Tutor Management database, almost any DBMS will do. All they need for features is to support a database with enough room for the records and support a relatively small number of multiple simultaneous users. Even these requirements may be more than some free RDBMSs support. Both SQL Server and Oracle Express, for instance, have file-size limits. They may be sufficient for a small or moderately sized database, but larger databases will rapidly run up against the limits. Additionally, the free databases often have limits on how they can utilize the hardware. It is not uncommon to have limits on the amount of RAM that can be accessed or the number of processors. They will not be adequate for systems that require higher levels of performance.

Open-source databases such as MySQL or PostGres are often good choices, especially for Web-based applications. As with other RDBMSs, you need to match the features to your needs.

Larger companies often have need for "enterprise"-level features. Often their databases need 24-hour, 7-days-a-week availability. If their database goes down, they lose money. One of the enterprise features is "failover." This feature ensures that if a server goes down, it will fail over to a copy of that server. The customer never knows a server failed. Enterprise features also include tools for load balancing. If one server gets too much traffic, some of the traffic is shifted to another server. Other features might include log shipping, mirroring, and so on. Generally, only the more expensive commercial servers such as SQL Server, Oracle, and DB2 support these enterprise-level features.

One additional set of features has grown increasingly important. These are the business intelligence features that can be used for data warehousing and advanced data analysis. Again, typically, these are only available with commercial RDBMSs.

### Familiarity and Expertise

Familiarity and expertise are also important factors to consider. It is much easier to develop a database with tools with which you are familiar. It is also easier for IT to support such a database. New systems, such as an unfamiliar RDBMS, typically require training and learning time. However, if the features and need are compelling enough, it may be worth the expense and time to train developers and support staff.

### Price and Licensing

It is crucial to understand the pricing and licensing agreements that come with a DBMS. In a school, for instance, it is common for SQL Server or Oracle to be licensed for use in instructional classrooms. But using the RDBMS to support the actual school infrastructure, such as the Tutoring program, requires an entirely different license agreement. You must make sure that the product you wish to use is licensed for the use you intend for it.

Prices can vary from free to many thousands of dollars. Free isn't always best, but you must balance the features of the DBMS against the budget and capabilities of the institution.

### Product Reliability and Support

The reliability of a DBMS product is crucial if it is to meet your needs. Reliability includes things like processing data without errors, hours of availability, and maintenance requirements. You should carefully research the reliability record for any DBMS you are thinking of adopting. Support can also be important. If you have questions about the product, or problems with it, what kind of help and response can you expect? Most DBMSs have online support and online community discussions. Some have live support. When you choose a DBMS, you should factor in the amount and kind of support you think you will need.

Microsoft Access isn't free, but the school has a site license for it, for both student and staff use. Access does offer some significant benefits. For one, it is familiar. Most staff members had Access on their desktops and had at least opened it a couple of times. Also, Access contains its own form and report builders, making it easier to create a user-friendly database application. But Access has its drawbacks as well. It has limits to how many simultaneous connections it can support. These limits can make it a questionable choice if you wish to create an Internet front end. Also, Sharon had always found Access difficult to secure properly.

SQL Server, on the other hand, has no limits on the number of simultaneous connections. It could work well as the back end of a Web-based application. Also, Sharon knows, the school uses SQL Server for a lot of its internal record keeping. Using SQL Express would make it easier to integrate with these systems at a later date. SQL Express was also scalable. It was easy to upgrade from Express to a standard edition of SQL Server. She also knows how to secure SQL Server, and she prefers its SQL Query window to Access'. The chief drawback was the lack of form builders. To create an application, she would have to use an external programming environment such as ASP.Net.

Thinking about it, she decides she prefers SQL Server Express, but the final decision is Terry's. At 9:00 when Sharon meets with her, she presents her arguments. After some assurances that Sharon can build an application for her and the tutors to use, Terry gives the go ahead to use SQL Express.

## CREATING THE DATABASE

*PHYSICAL DESIGN*

Database design adapted to the features and limitations of a particular RDBMS.

Later, Sharon opens her laptop and starts the SQL Server Management Studio. She connects to the instance of SQL Server Express. Then in the Object Explorer window, she right clicks on "Databases" and chooses "New Database."

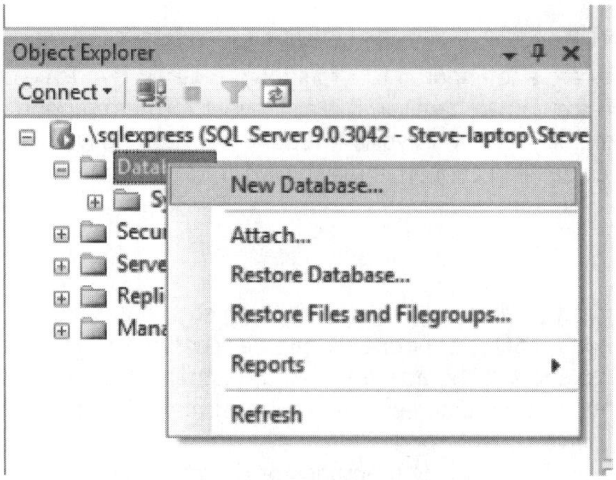

**FIGURE 6-1**  New Database

*DATABASE TRANSACTION*

Any action that a database takes, creating objects, adding rows, changing data in rows, removing rows, and so on.

The New Database dialog window opens. This dialog lets Sharon name the database and its files. An SQL Server database always has at least two files: a data file that contains all the data including the data on table structures and relationships and a log file that contains a running record of database transactions. She could add additional files, and she could change the locations of the files, but for now she will go with the default settings. She names the database "Tutor" and clicks the OK button.

It takes just a couple of seconds to create the new database.

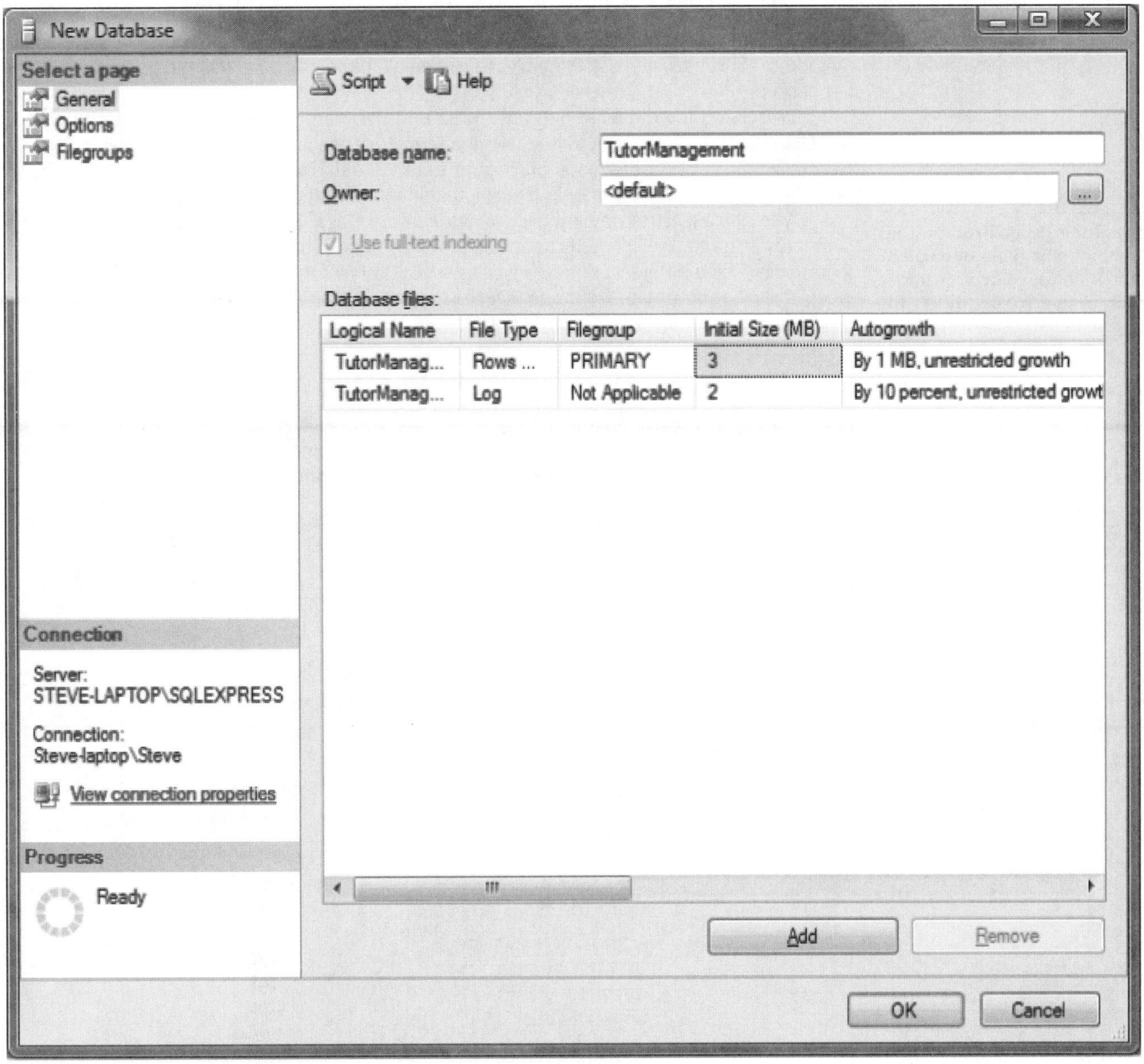

FIGURE 6-2   New Database Dialog

## Things You Should Know

### Physical Design

The logical design of a database is the same no matter what database management system you intend to use. The entities, attributes, and relationships are looked at purely in terms of the logical structure of the data. Physical design involves adapting the logical design to the features and limitations of a particular database product.

One of the first considerations in physical design is the location and structure of the database files themselves. Different database management systems manage files in different ways. Part of creating the physical design is understanding how your product stores and manages files. SQL Server databases have at least two files, a data file with the extension ".mdb" and a log file with the extension ".ldf." The first or *primary* data file contains not only the data in the database but also the metadata containing information about table structures, relations, and other database objects. You can arrange for an SQL Server database to save its data in multiple files, but one must always be designated the primary file. The log files track database transactions. If you have set the restore method to "Full," you can use these files to restore all the transactions that have occurred since your last backup.

By Default, the database files are stored in C:\Program Files\Microsoft SQL Server\MSSQL.1\ MSSQL\Data, though this may vary on your computer depending on how SQL Server was installed. Generally though, it is not a good practice to store the database files and the log files on the same disk. We'll look at this more fully in the chapter on administration and security.

A second aspect of physical design involves data types. There is a general American National Standards Institute (ANSI) specification for basic data types, but each RDBMS adapts and adds to these types. These differences in data types are responsible for many of the difficulties encountered when trying to move data from one RDBMS to another. Date and time data types especially vary from product to product. SQL Server 2008 supports the following data types:

*DATA TYPES*

The column specification that determines what kind of data can be stored in that column, character versus numeric or date, for example.

**Table 6-1** Numeric Data Types

| Data Type | Description | Range/Examples |
|-----------|-------------|----------------|
| Bigint | 8 bytes integer | −2^63 (−9,223,372,036,854,775,808) to 2^63−1 (9,223,372,036,854,775,807) |
| Int | 4 bytes | −2^31 (−2,147,483,648) to 2^31−1 (2,147,483,647) |
| Smallint | 2 bytes | −2^15 (−32,768) to 2^15−1 (32,767) |
| Tinyint | 1 byte | 0 to 255 |
| Bit | 1 bit | 0, 1, or null |
| Decimal | User can set precision up to 10^38 | decimal(10,2) |
| Money | 8 bytes | −922,337,203,685,477.5808 to 922,337,203,685,477.5807 |
| Smallmoney | 4 bytes | −214,748.3648 to 214,748.3647 |
| Numeric | User can set precision up to 10^38 | Same as decimal |
| Float | Approximate numeric type, the number of bytes depends on the number | −1.79E + 308 to −2.23E−308, 0 and 2.23E−308 to 1.79E + 308 |
| Real | Also approximate, 4 bytes | −3.40E + 38 to −1.18E − 38, 0 and 1.18E − 38 to 3.40E + 38 |

**Table 6-2** Date Time Types

| Data Type | Description | Examples/Range |
|-----------|-------------|----------------|
| Date | New in 2008, stores date values. | January 1, 1 A.D. through December 31, 9999 A.D |
| datetime2 | New. Stores date and time and allows user to set precision in fractions of seconds. | Same date range as given earlier. Time range = 00:00:00 through 23:59:59.9999999 |
| datetimeoffset | Date and time but with time-zone awareness. | Same |
| smalldatetime | Smaller date and time type. | January 1, 1753, through December 31, 9999 00:00:00 through 23:59:59.997 |
| Time | New. You can set the precision in fractions of a second. | 00:00:00.0000000 through 23:59:59.9999999 |

**Table 6-3** String and Character Types

| Data Type | Description | Examples |
|---|---|---|
| Char | Fixed-length ASCII text. | "Jefferson"—max 255 characters |
| Text | Text stores large blocks of text data. The text and ntext data types are deprecated; use varchar(MAX) or nvarchar(MAX). | 2,147,483,647 bytes |
| Varchar | Variable-length ASCII. | "Los Angeles," maximum 255 characters unless MAX (MAX allows 2^31 – 1 bytes) |
| Nchar | Unicode fixed length | Uses Unicode UCS_2 character set |
| Ntext | Unicode large block. Deprecated. | |
| nvarchar | Unicode variable-length text. | |

**Table 6-4** Some Data Types

| Data type | Description | Examples |
|---|---|---|
| Image | Variable-length binary data. The image data type is deprecated and will go away. | 2^31–1 bytes |
| Binary | Fixed-length binary. | 1 to 8000 bytes |
| varbinary | Variable-length binary. | 1 to 8000 bytes unless you specify MAX, 2 ^31–1 bytes |
| uniqueidentifer | Generates a unique identifier. | 6F9619FF-8B86-D011-B42D-00C04FC964FF |
| XML | Stores XML data as XML, can be validated against schema collections, and queried with xquery. | \<employee\> \<name\>Sue Larson \</name\>\</employee\> |

Sharon expands the database node in the Object Explorer and finds the new database Tutor. Then she clicks on the + sign to expand Tutor and see its folders. She clicks on the folder Tables and then right clicks and selects "New Table."

### THINGS TO THINK ABOUT

**Fixed-Length versus Variable-Character Data Types**

*The char and nchar data types are fixed length. That means if you set a width of 50 characters, they will always write 50 characters to the disk even if you use only 20. The varchar and nvarchar are variable length. That means if you set the maximum length to 50 but use only 20, the variable-length data type will write only 20.*

*When do you think fixed length would be a better choice? When do you think variable length would be better? Which uses more processing power? Which uses more disk space?*

The table designer opens. The table designer has three columns: one for the column name, one for the data type, and one with check boxes to allow or not allow nulls. Below the column designer is a window which lists all the properties of the selected column. For now, Sharon is going to ignore the properties and just focus on the columns and their data types.

Sharon decides to start with the table Tutor. She opens Visio and looks back at her entity relation diagram.

|            | Tutor     |
|------------|-----------|
| PK         | **TutorKey** |
|            |           |
|            | **TutorLastName** |
|            | TutorFirstName |
|            | **TutorPhone** |
|            | TutorEmail |
|            | **TutorHireDate** |
|            | **TutorStatus** |

**FIGURE 6-3**   Tutor Entity

The first attribute is TutorKey, which she enters under the column name. She thinks that the data contained in the column will be something like the student ID number. Even though it is a number, it will not be used as a number. That is, nobody would ever use it to add, subtract, multiply, or divide. Also, some student IDs have leading zeros. A numeric type would drop any leading zeros. She looks through the drop-down list of data types. There are four good candidates: *char*, *nchar*, *nvarchar*, and *varchar*. All four store character data. She knows that *char* and *nchar* are "fixed-length" data type. That means if you set the width of a *char* or *nchar* to 50, it will always write a 50-character block to the disk even if the actual content of the column is only 20 or 30 characters. The difference between *char* and *nchar* is the character set. *Char* uses the ASCII (American Standard Code for Information Interchange) character set, and *nchar* uses the larger and more complete Unicode character set. *Nvarchar* and *varchar* are variable-length data types. That means, the database only writes the actual length of the data to the disk up to the set limit. So if you assigned the *nvarchar* data type to a column and set the upper limit to 50 characters but entered only 30 characters, the database would only write a 30-character block to the disk.

Sharon decides to use the *nchar* data type. Student IDs, she knows, are of a fixed width. And setting the width to a particular value is one way of helping ensure the validity of the IDs. She also decides to go with the Unicode version. It takes no more space to store each character since the first 255 characters are identical to the ASCII codes, and it allows greater flexibility and compatibility.

**UNICODE**

An expanded character set that includes non-Latin character sets such as Russian or Japanese.

Finally, she goes the toolbar and clicks the key icon. This designates it as a primary key and also unchecks the allow nulls box, since a primary key cannot be null.

Now she enters the other columns from the Tutor entity into the table designer. She decides that only the tutor's first name and email should be optional and allow nulls. When she is done, the table definition looks like this:

| Column Name    | Data Type    | Allow Nulls |
|----------------|--------------|-------------|
| *TutorKey      | nchar(10)    |             |
| TutorLastName  | nvarchar(50) |             |
| TutorFirstName | nvarchar(50) | X           |
| TutorPhone     | nchar(10)    |             |
| TutorEmail     | nvarchar(50) | X           |
| TutorHireDate  | Date         |             |
| TutorStatus    | nchar(10)    |             |

**FIGURE 6-4**   Tutor Table (*) Key

She clicks the disk icon on the toolbar to save the table and names the table Tutor.

She clicks OK. Next, just to confirm to herself that it is there, she goes to the Object Explorer and expands the table folder. The Tutor table is there. She knows that if she expands the table itself, she can view the columns and their data types.

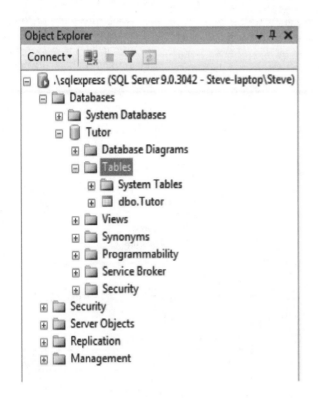

**FIGURE 6-5** Save Table Dialog

**FIGURE 6-6** Object Explorer Tables

---

**Things You Should Know**

### Nulls

Nulls represent an important concept in relational databases. A null is not a value as such. It signifies that a value is unknown. For a numeric type, a null is not the same as a zero. A zero is a value; null is a missing or unknown value. For a string or character type, the null is not the same as an empty string. Again, it is unknown. Nulls have many consequences for a database. When you are summing a column in a table, nulls are excluded from the sum by default. This doesn't really affect the end answer. But consider the effect when you are averaging a column. The mean average consists of the sum of the values in a column divided by the total number of rows. Here nulls do have an effect. If you count all the rows, even those with null, it will be as if each null was a zero. The average returned will be lower than the actual average would have been because of the nulls. The default action usually is to exclude them from the average. This makes more sense. The average returned reflects the actual values in the database, but the average is still only approximate because of the missing values.

When you create a table, you have a choice to allow nulls or not. If you allow nulls, you can leave that column blank when you are entering data. If you do not allow nulls, you must enter a value into the column to continue. Generally, you should not allow nulls for the columns that are crucial to your business rules. Assume, for example, that your business requires a customer name and a contact phone number for every transaction. Those fields should not allow nulls. But let's say your business also prefers to have the complete address of each customer for sending emails and updates later. The decision you have to make is whether to require the address by not allowing nulls

*NULL*

A null represents the absence of a value. A null value is unknown.

or to accept that some customers may not give their address and allow nulls for those columns. Consider that making too many fields required by not allowing nulls can make a database too rigid to use in everyday situations. If a customer refuses to give his or her address, and those columns are required, the person entering the record either has to turn the customer down or enter meaningless data into the columns.

## THINGS TO THINK ABOUT

### Nulls versus Out-of-Bounds Data

*In many older databases that did not have a provision for nulls, unknown data was represented by entering a value that was clearly out of bounds. A database tracking historical temperatures of a particular location, for instance, might put a value like 999.99 for an unknown temperature.*

*What are some of the drawbacks you can see to using out-of-bounds data for a column?*

*What advantages or disadvantages do you see in using nulls for unknown data?*

Now she turns to the task of taking each of the other entities in her diagram and translating them into SQL Server tables. First, she creates the course table.

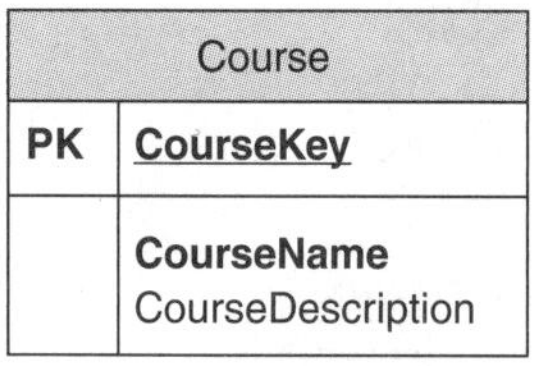

| Course | |
|---|---|
| **PK** | **CourseKey** |
| | **CourseName**<br>CourseDescription |

**FIGURE 6-7**   Course Entity

| Column Name | Data Type | Allow Nulls |
|---|---|---|
| *CourseKey | nchar(10) | |
| CourseName | nvarchar(50) | |
| CourseDescription | nvarchar(200) | X |

**FIGURE 6-8**   Course Table

## Things You Should Know

### Creating a Table in SQL

Creating tables in the graphical interface is not the only way to create a table. It is also possible to create the table using the SQL programming language. SQL will be covered in Chapter 7. To create the course table in SQL, you would open a New Query window. You would type in the following code:

```
CREATE TABLE Course
    (
        CourseKey NCHAR(10) PRIMARY KEY,
        CourseName NVARCHAR(50) NOT NULL,
        CourseDescription NVARCHAR(200) NULL
    )
```

Creating tables in code can be more efficient, but it does require that you have a full understanding of the structure of the database, its data types, and its relationships.

Next Sharon creates the Ethnicity lookup table.

For the student table, she is careful to make only the *StudentKey* and the *StudentLastName* columns required. She also must make sure that the *EthnicityKey* data type matches the data type of the *EthnicityKey* in the Ethnicity table. They must match for the foreign key constraint to work. Sharon is not going to add the foreign key constraint now; she will do that after the tables have been created.

| Ethnicity | |
|---|---|
| **PK** | **EthnicityKey** |
| | EthnicityDescription |

**FIGURE 6-9** Ethnicity Entity

| Column Name | Data Type | Allow Nulls |
|---|---|---|
| *EthnicityKey | nchar(10) | |
| EthnicityDescription | nvarchar(50) | X |

**FIGURE 6-10** Ethnicity Table

| Student | |
|---|---|
| **PK** | **StudentKey** |
| | **StudentILastName** |
| | StudentFirstName |
| | **StudentPhone** |
| | StudentEmail |
| | StudentGender |
| | StudentAge |
| | StudentCitizen |
| | StudentWorkForceRetraining |
| FK1 | EthnicityKey |

**FIGURE 6-11** Student Entity

| Column Name | Data Type | Allow Nulls |
|---|---|---|
| *StudentKey | nchar(10) | |
| StudentLastName | nvarchar(50) | |
| StudentFirstName | nvarchar(50) | X |
| StudentEmail | nvarchar(100) | X |
| StudentPhone | nvarchar(10) | X |
| StudentGender | nchar(1) | X |
| StudentAge | int | X |
| StudentCitizen | bit | X |
| StudentWorkerRetraining | bit | X |
| EthnicityKey | nchar(10) | x |

**FIGURE 6-12** Student Table

For the TutorCourse table, she needs to create a composite key.

| TutorCourse | |
|---|---|
| **PK,FK1** | **CourseKey** |
| **PK,FK2** | **TutorKey** |
| | |

**FIGURE 6-13** TutorCourse Entity

It takes her a moment to figure out how to make it work in the designer. She finds that if she selects both the columns and then clicks the key icon, both are marked as part of the key.

| Column Name | Data Type | Allow Nulls |
|---|---|---|
| *TutorKey | nchar(10) | |
| *StudentKey | nchar(50) | |

**FIGURE 6-14** TutorCourse Table

Now she works through the rest of the tables in her diagram.

| StudentCourse | |
|---|---|
| PK,FK1 | **StudentKey** |
| PK,FK2 | **CourseKey** |
| PK | **StudentCourseQuarter** |
| | |

**FIGURE 6-15** StudentCourse Entity

| Column Name | Data Type | Allow Nulls |
|---|---|---|
| *StudentKey | nchar(10) | |
| *CourseKey | nchar(10) | |
| *StudentCourseQuarter | nchar(10) | |

**FIGURE 6-16** StudentCourse Table

| Session | |
|---|---|
| PK | **SessionDate** |
| PK | **SessionTime** |
| PK,FK1 | **TutorKey** |
| PK,FK1 | **CourseKey** |
| | |
| FK2 | StudentKey |
| | SessionStatus |
| | SessionMaterialCovered |

**FIGURE 6-17** Session Entity

| Column Name | Data Type | Allow Nulls |
|---|---|---|
| *SessionDateKey | Date | |
| *SessionTimeKey | Time | |
| *TutorKey | nchar(10) | |
| *CourseKey | nchar(10) | |
| StudentKey | nchar(10) | X |
| SessionStatus | nchar(10) | X |
| SessionMaterialCovered | nvarchar(255) | X |

**FIGURE 6-18** Session Table

| Request | |
|---|---|
| PK | **RequestKey** |
| | |
| FK1 | **CourseKey** |
| | RequestDate |
| | RequestStatus |
| FK2 | StudentKey |

**FIGURE 6-19** Request Entity

| Column Name | Data Type | Allow Nulls |
|---|---|---|
| *RequestKey | nchar(10) | |
| CourseKey | nchar(10) | |
| RequestDate | Date | |
| RequestStatus | nchar(10) | |
| StudentKey | nchar(10) | |

**FIGURE 6-20** Request Table

For the RequestNotes table, Sharon realizes she needs something other than a *nvarchar* data type for the *RequestNoteText* column.

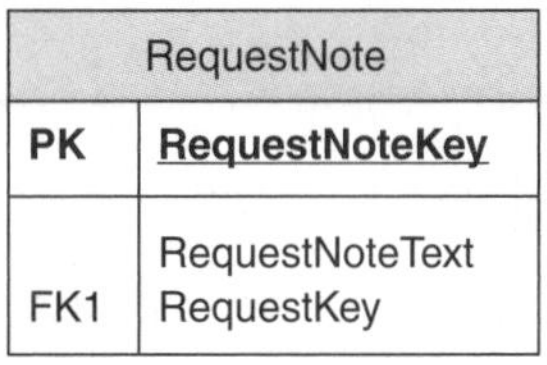

| RequestNote | |
|---|---|
| PK | **RequestNoteKey** |
| FK1 | RequestNoteText RequestKey |

**FIGURE 6-21** RequestNote Entity

The *varchar* and *nvarchar* data types have a maximum length of 255 characters. But there is another option called "MAX." Use of the MAX option allows the column to contain up to two gigabytes worth of data. The only drawback is that a column that uses the MAX data type can't be searched directly or indexed.

| Column Name | Data Type | Allow Nulls |
|---|---|---|
| *RequestNoteKey | DateTime | |
| RequestNoteText | nvarchar(Max) | |
| RequestKey | nchar(10) | |

**FIGURE 6-22** RequestNote Table

Sharon has created all the tables. Now she wants to define the relationships among the tables. There are several ways to do this, but one of the easiest is to create a database diagram and do it graphically. She right clicks on the Database Diagram folder under Tutor and chooses New Database Diagram. She gets the following warning:

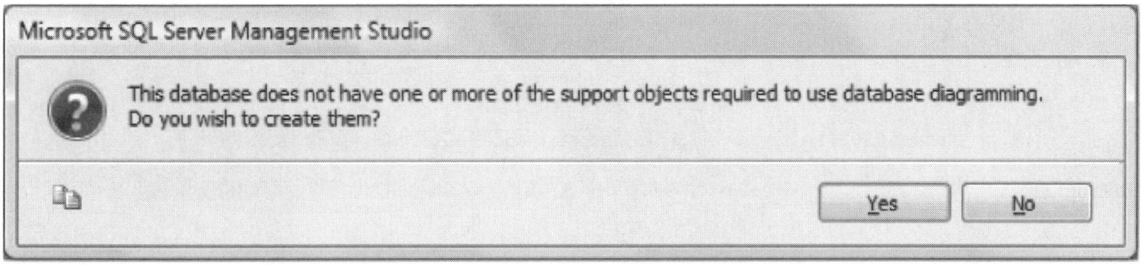

Microsoft SQL Server Management Studio

This database does not have one or more of the support objects required to use database diagramming. Do you wish to create them?

Yes    No

**FIGURE 6-23** Support Objects Query Dialog

This puzzles her for a second. She wonders what she did wrong, but then she reads the dialog box more carefully: "Do you wish to create them?" She clicks "Yes," and then right clicks on the Database Diagram folder again. This time she gets a new diagram and a list of all the tables in her database.

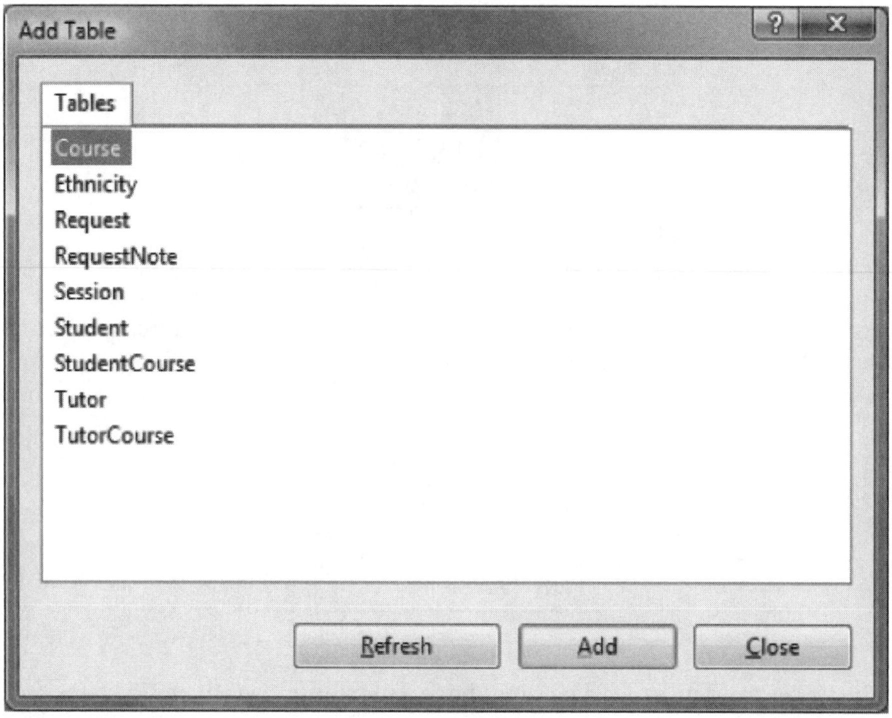

FIGURE 6-24   Add Table Dialog

She adds all the tables and moves them around until they fit on her screen.

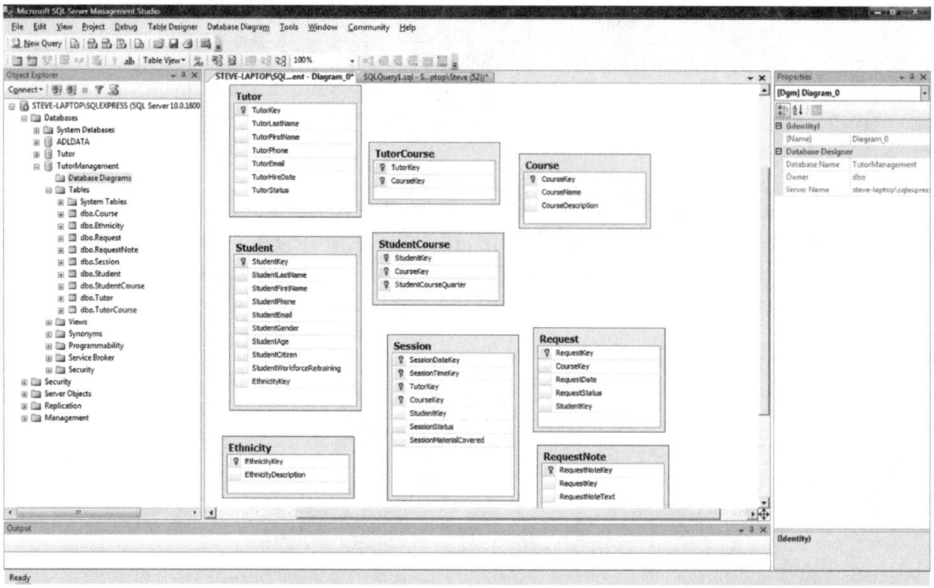

FIGURE 6-25   Database Diagram

She decides to start with the relationship between **Tutor** and **TutorCourse**. She selects *TutorKey*, puts the cursor in the gray to the left of the column, holds the mouse button down, and drags the mouse to the TutorCourse table. Then she releases the mouse. A Table and Columns relationship dialog box appears.

She confirms that the Primary Key table and Foreign Key table are correct and that the columns names are correct. She accepts the default name for the relationship and clicks OK. A second dialog box appears that allows a user to set additional properties for the foreign key relationship.

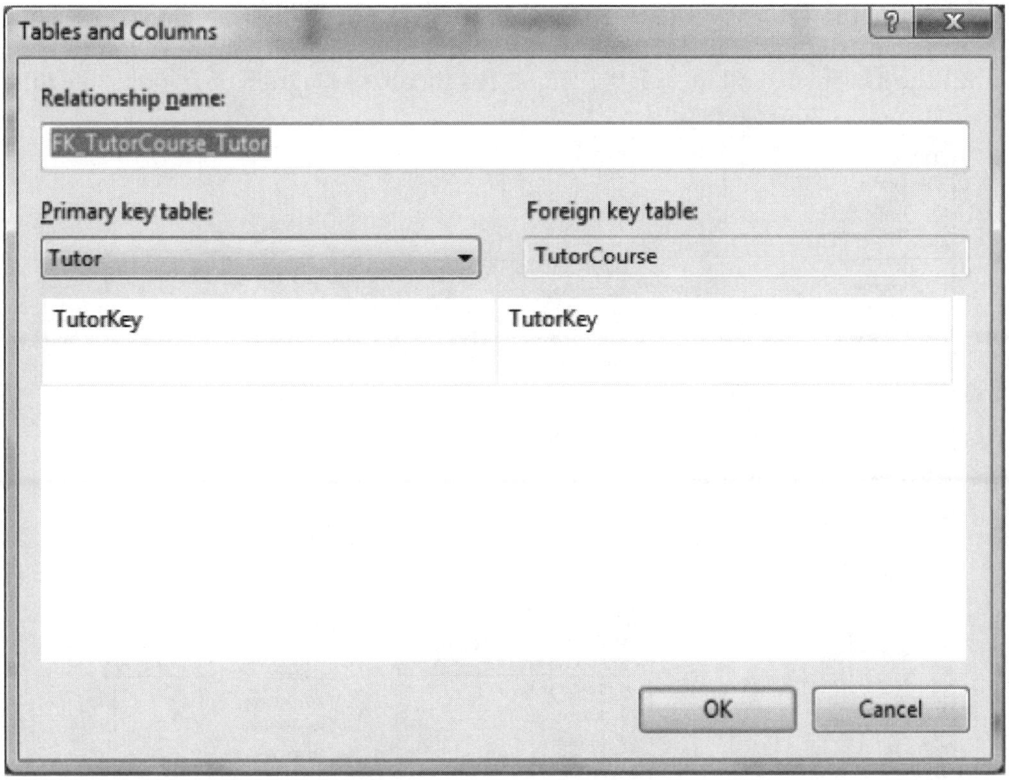

**FIGURE 6-26** Table and Columns Dialog

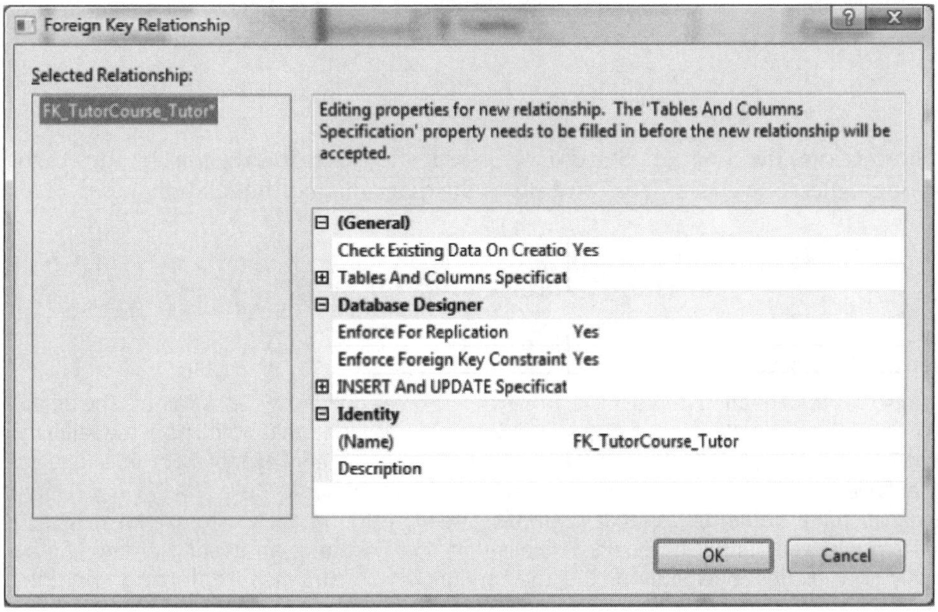

**FIGURE 6-27** Foreign Key Relationship

For now she just clicks OK, and the relationship is created. In the diagram, the relationship is represented as a line with a key on the end pointing to the table on the *one* side of the relationship, the table with the primary key. The connecter to the *many* side of the relationship is represented by an infinity sign. Now Sharon adds the relationship between **Course** and **TutorCourse**.

Again the Tables and Columns dialog appears. She makes sure it is correct and presses OK, and then OK again for the second dialog. Sharon continues in this way until she has created all the relationships. The database diagram now looks like this:

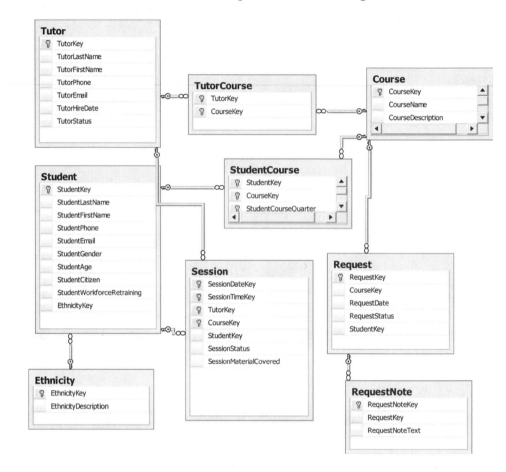

**FIGURE 6-28** Tutor Database Diagram

Sharon saves the diagram. SQL Server asks if she wants to save the changes to the underlying tables. She clicks "Yes" and saves the diagram and the relationships.

**Things You Need to Know**

### Referential Integrity

In the properties for a relation, there is the property "Enforce Foreign Key Constraint." The default value is "Yes." Enforcing the foreign key constraint means ensuring that no foreign key value can be entered that does not have a corresponding value in the primary key table. For instance, you cannot enter a customer key in a Sales table (where the customer key is a foreign key relating back to a Customer table) unless that customer already exists in the Customer table. Or, for another example, you cannot have order details that don't relate to an existing order. Another commonly used expression for enforcing the foreign key constraint is "enforcing referential integrity."

Enforcing referential integrity protects your database from orphan data. Consider the Order/Order Details table mentioned earlier. It is almost always necessary to break an order or sale into two tables. The first table, Order, contains what you might consider the header information: the date, the customerID, and the ID of the employee processing the order. The second or "detail" table consists of the line items, one row for each item ordered. The details are tied to the order by an order key. Enforcing referential integrity ensures that there won't be any details, any line items, that aren't associated with a valid order. Choosing not to enforce referential integrity opens the risk of having details that are not associated with any order. They are fragments of garbage data that can seriously affect any data analysis. A database is only as good as its data.

*REFERENTIAL INTEGRITY*

This exists when every foreign key relates to an existing primary key. There are no orphan records in child tables that have no reference in a parent table.

Changes to the data in a database are the result of one of three actions: insert, update, or delete. Inserts enter new data into the database. Updates change existing data. Deletes remove rows of data from the database. Enforcing referential integrity does impose some important restrictions on these actions.

| **Table 6-5** | Referential Integrity |
|---|---|
| **Action** | **Effect of Enforcing Referential Integrity** |
| INSERT | You must enter data into the parent (primary key) table before you can enter data into a child(foreign key) table. For example: You must enter the Customer information before entering the Sale information. |
| UPDATE | 1. You cannot change the primary key value for any record in the parent table without also changing the related foreign key. This creates a dilemma because both must be changed simultaneously. You can either suspend referential integrity while making the update or use cascading updates (see the following point).<br>2. You can only update or change a foreign key in a child table to one that has a matching value in a parent or primary key table. |
| DELETE | You cannot delete a row in a primary key table unless all related records are first deleted in the foreign key table. Example: You can't delete an order unless all the order details for that order are first deleted. |

---

## THINGS TO THINK ABOUT

**Using Referential Integrity**

*Can you think of any reasons why you might not want to set the referential integrity constraints?*

*What would you gain by not setting them? What would you risk?*

---

In the properties of a relationship, you have the option of setting what are called referential integrity actions. One of those actions is *cascade update* and another is *cascade delete*. Setting cascade update means that if you change the primary key of a row in the parent table, the database management system will automatically update all the related foreign keys in the child table. This can be useful, especially if you have a volatile value for your primary key—something like a telephone number or an email address. Setting cascade delete means that if you delete a row in a primary key table, all related rows in a child table will also be deleted. This protects the referential integrity and prevents orphan rows, but it is very dangerous. Imagine accidentally deleting a Customer entity and having all his or her transactions vanish as well. Cascade delete is something that should be used with great caution.

Sharon sets back and sighs. She has done it. She has taken the logical design she created in Visio and has translated it into the physical tables of SQL Server Express. Her next step is to add some sample data to the tables so she can test the database and make sure the database meets all the requirements and fulfills all the business rules.

Once again, she starts with the Tutor table. She right clicks on the table in the Object Explorer and selects Open Table. This opens the table for reading or entering data. She decides she needs about five tutor records for now. She enters some typical tutor data.

When she is done, she closes the Tutor table and right clicks on the Course table in the Object Explorer. She opens it for data entry. There is some method in which tables she chooses to do first. She knows that she needs to enter data into the tables on the primary key or *one* side of relationships before she can enter data into the foreign key side. Otherwise, she will get "data integrity" errors saying there must be a related record in the primary key table.

| TutorKey | TutorLastName | TutorFirstName | TutorPhone | TutorEmail | TutorHireDate | TutorStatus |
|----------|---------------|----------------|------------|------------|---------------|-------------|
| 980010000 | Roberts | Martha | 2065551467 | mroberts@yahoo.com | 1/6/2010 | Active |
| 980010001 | Brown | Susan | 2065553528 | Sb4@hotmail.com | 2/1/2009 | Active |
| 980010002 | Foster | Daniel | 2065553490 | Foster32@aol.com | 2/12/2009 | Active |
| 980010003 | Anderson | Nathan | 3065556320 | Null | 3/2/2009 | Inactive |
| 980010004 | Lewis | Ginger | 2065552985 | ginger@hotmail.com | 3/15/2009 | Active |

**FIGURE 6-29**  Tutor Table Data

## Things You Should Know

### Sample Data

Before you put any database into use, you should test it to make sure that it meets all the requirements and business rules. Part of this is entering sample data. The sample data should be as real as possible. Incorporating existing data is ideal. If you don't have existing data, you can make up sample data. But there are some things you should consider:

- Make sure your sample data are complete enough to test all the business rules.
- Make sure the data are varied enough to represent a variety of likely situations.
- Make sure the data contain some exceptions and possibly even errors so you can test how the database handles those.

Sharon adds a few samples course to the Course table.

| CourseKey | CourseName | CourseDescription |
|-----------|------------|-------------------|
| ITC110 | Beginning Programming | Programming using C# |
| ITC220 | Introduction to Database | Overview of database design and topics |
| ITC255 | Systems Analysis | Systems analysis and design |
| MAT107 | Applied Math | Applied math for computers |
| ENG211 | Technical Writing | Technical writing for information technology |
| WEB110 | Beginning Web Page Design | Basic xhtml |
| ITC226 | Database Administration | SQL Server administration |

**FIGURE 6-30**  Course Table Data

Next she enters the ethnicities into the Ethnicity table.

| EthnicityKey | EthnicityDescription |
|--------------|----------------------|
| Caucasian | White, European origin |
| Asian | Chinese, Japanese, Korean, Southeast Asian |
| AfrAmer | African American or of African origin |
| Hispanic | Mexican, Central or South American, Caribbean |
| Pacific | Pacific islander |
| Mideast | Arabic or Persian |
| Other | Other or not disclosed |

**FIGURE 6-31**  Ethnicity Table Data

The TutorCourse table consists of only foreign keys. Sharon reopens the Tutor and Course tables and makes sure that each of the keys she enters is correct.

| TutorKey | CourseKey |
|----------|-----------|
| 980010002 | ITC255 |
| 980010002 | ENG211 |
| 980010004 | MAT107 |
| 980010000 | WEB110 |
| 980010001 | ITC220 |
| 980010001 | WEB110 |
| 980010003 | ITC110 |

**FIGURE 6-32** TutorCourse Table Data

She enters twelve students.

| StudentKey | StudentLastName | StudentFirstName | StudentEmail | StudentPhone |
|------------|-----------------|------------------|--------------|--------------|
| 990001000 | Peterson | Laura | Null | 2065559318 |
| 990001002 | Carter | Shannon | Shannon@Carter.Org | 2065554301 |
| 990001003 | Martinez | Sandy | sandym@gmail.com | 2065551158 |
| 990001004 | Nguyen | Lu | lstar@yahoo.com | 2065552938 |
| 990001005 | Zukof | Mark | Null | Null |
| 990001006 | Taylor | Patty | P147@marketplace.com | 2065552076 |
| 990001007 | Thomas | Lawrence | Null | Null |
| 980001008 | Bradbury | Ron | rbradbury@mars.org | 2065557296 |
| 980001009 | Carlos | Juan | Carlos23@hotmail.com | 2065559134 |
| 009001010 | Min | Ly | lymin@hotmail.com | 2065552789 |

**FIGURE 6-33** Student Table Data

| StudentGender | StudentAge | StudentCitizen | StudentWorkerRetraining | EthnicityKey |
|---------------|------------|----------------|-------------------------|--------------|
| F | 23 | True | False | Caucasian |
| F | 32 | True | True | AfrAmer |
| F | 18 | True | False | Hispanic |
| M | 19 | False | False | Asian |
| Null | Null | Null | Null | Null |
| F | 42 | True | True | Caucasian |
| M | 24 | True | False | Caucasian |
| M | 53 | True | True | Caucasian |
| M | 25 | False | False | Hispanic |
| F | 20 | False | False | Asian |

**FIGURE 6-34** Student Table Data (cont.)

Each student can take multiple courses, so Sharon considers each student and ties him or her to two or three courses. She also separates the enrollments into two quarters, because she knows the database will need to store several quarters at a time, and it will be necessary to make sure you can pull out the data for only the quarter in question.

| StudentKey | CourseKey | StudentCourseQuarter |
|---|---|---|
| 990001000 | ITC220 | Fall09 |
| 990001000 | ITC110 | Fall09 |
| 990001000 | WEB110 | Fall09 |
| 990001002 | ITC220 | Fall09 |
| 990001002 | ITC110 | Fall09 |
| 990001004 | MAT107 | Fall09 |
| 990001004 | WEB110 | Fall09 |
| 990001007 | ITC110 | Fall09 |
| 980001009 | ITC110 | Fall09 |
| 980001009 | ITC220 | Fall09 |
| 980001009 | MAT107 | Fall09 |
| 990001002 | ENG211 | Winter10 |
| 990001002 | ITC255 | Winter10 |
| 990001003 | ENG211 | Winter10 |
| 990001003 | ITC255 | Winter10 |
| 990001005 | MAT107 | Winter10 |
| 009001010 | MAT107 | Winter10 |
| 009001010 | ITC255 | Winter10 |
| 009001010 | ENG211 | Winter10 |
| 990001000 | ITC255 | Winter10 |
| 990001000 | MAT107 | Winter10 |

**FIGURE 6-35** StudentCourse Table Data

The Session table is one of the most difficult to create sample data for. Sharon wants to enter some historical data for sessions that have already been held as well as for some open sessions. Sessions that haven't been completed have "Null" mentioned under the column *SessionStatus*. Sessions that haven't been signed up for yet also have "Null" mentioned under *StudentKey* and *SessionStatus*. The difficulty is making sure that the data match the data in the other tables. The tutors should only be listed for the courses they have signed up to tutor, and the students should only receive tutoring for those classes they are attending that quarter.

**FIGURE 6-36** Session Table Data

| SessionDateKey | SessionTimeKey | TutorKey | CourseKey | StudentKey | SessionStatus | SessionMaterialCovered |
|---|---|---|---|---|---|---|
| 10/20/2009 | 14:00 | 980010001 | WEB110 | 990001000 | C | CSS |
| 10/20/2009 | 13:00 | 980010003 | ITC110 | 990001000 | C | For next loop |
| 11/20/2009 | 10:30 | 980010001 | ITC220 | 990001002 | C | Relations |
| 11/5/2009 | 10:00 | 980010001 | ITC220 | Null | NS | Null |
| 11/10/2009 | 13:00 | 980010004 | MAT107 | 990001004 | C | Binary Numbers |
| 11/10/2009 | 14:00 | 980010001 | WEB110 | 990001000 | C | Web Forms |
| 1/15/2010 | 9:30 | 980010002 | ITC255 | 990001000 | C | Use Cases |
| 1/20/2010 | 11:00 | 980010002 | ENG211 | 990001003 | C | Document structure |
| 1/22/20120 | 14:00 | 980010004 | MAT107 | 990001005 | NS | Null |
| 2/5/2010 | 10:30 | 980010002 | ITC255 | 990001000 | C | Feasibility |
| 2/10/2010 | 13:30 | 980010004 | MAT107 | Null | Null | Null |
| 2/10/2010 | 14:00 | 980010004 | MAT107 | Null | Null | Null |
| 2/13/2010 | 10:00 | 980010002 | ITC255 | Null | Null | Null |
| 2/14/2010 | 11:00 | 980010002 | ENG211 | Null | Null | Null |

Finally, for the request table, she enters only a single request.

| RequestKey | RequestDate | CourseKey | RequestStatus | StudentKey |
|---|---|---|---|---|
| 1001 | 1/5/2010 | ITC226 | Active | 009001010 |

FIGURE 6-37 Request Table Data

The request notes include two notes in the RequestNotes table.

| RequestNoteKey | RequestID | RequestNoteText |
|---|---|---|
| 1/6/2010 2:00 PM | 1001 | Only offered once a year and not a lot of requests for this class |
| 1/10/2010 10:00 AM | 1001 | No students available, because a capstone class would have to get someone off campus |

FIGURE 6-38 RequestNote Table Data

Sharon has completed creating the database, building the tables, and adding some sample data. Now she is ready to start testing it with some SQL queries.

## DOCUMENTATION

In many ways, the database is self-documenting. The structure of each table, the columns, their data types, and all constraints are already stored in system tables and can be queried. But it is not uncommon, and can be quite useful, to create a separate data dictionary that lists all the database objects such as tables, along with their column names and data types. If the database is corrupted or lost somehow, a separate data dictionary can be used to help rebuild it. It can also serve as an excellent reference for application developers or future administrators of the database.

## Things We Have Done

*In this chapter we have*

- translated our logical design into a physical design
- created a database in SQL Server
- created tables
- assigned data types to columns
- determined which columns should allow nulls and which should not
- set primary keys
- created a database diagram
- created relationships among the tables
- entered sample data into those tables

## Vocabulary

*Match the definitions to the vocabulary words:*

1. Data types
2. Database transactions
3. Null
4. Physical design
5. Referential integrity
6. Unicode

— a. An extended language set that includes non-Latin characters
— b. A missing or unknown value for a column in a table
— c. Every action in a database
— d. Where every foreign key refers to an existing primary key in a related table
— e. Database design adapted to the features and limits of a particular RDBMS
— f. Column specifications that refer to what kind of data can be stored in a column

## Things to Look Up

1. What are some best practices for managing data files and logs?
2. Look up the data types for Oracle. How do they differ from SQL Server's?
3. Look up the ANSI data types. How do they differ from that of SQL Server and Oracle?

## Practices

Perfect Pizza is a pizza delivery shop. They only create pizzas for home delivery. They have recently designed a new database to track their sales. They use the customer's telephone number for a Key column in the Customer table. They are interested in households, not individuals. They need the street address and zip code for the delivery. They only deliver to three zip codes: 98001, 98002, and 98003. With the zip code, they can fill in city and state information later, though they prefer to do it when they enter a new customer. In the OrderDetail table, they store the price charged for two reasons: First, it may be different than product price due to a discount or special allowance, and second, it keeps a historic record of the price. That way, if they change the price in the product table, it doesn't affect the prices charged in past sales. Here is the entity relation diagram for the database. (We will use this database again in future practices.)

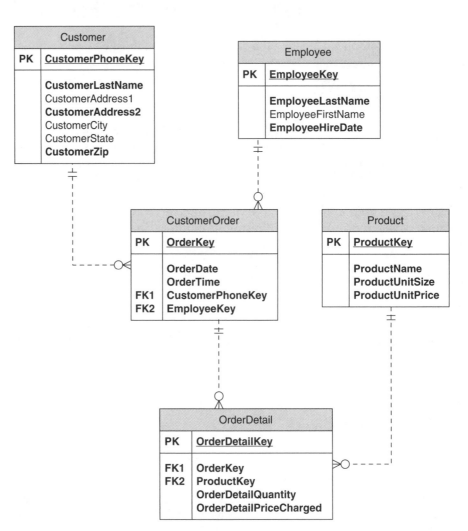

**FIGURE 6-39**   Pizza ERD 1

1. What do you think would be the appropriate data types for CustomerPhoneKey and CustomerZip? Explain.
2. What do you think would be the appropriate data types for ProductUnitSize and ProductUnitPrice? Explain.
3. Create the database in SQL Server.

4. Build the database tables depicted in the entity relation diagram (Figure 6-39) in SQL Server, choosing appropriate data types. (Use the following sample data as a guide.)
5. Create a database diagram, and use it to create the relationships among the tables.
6. Add these sample records to the appropriate tables.

**Customers**

| | | | | | | |
|---|---|---|---|---|---|---|
| 2065552123 | Lamont | NULL | 161 South Western Ave | NULL | NULL | 98001 |
| 2065553252 | Johnston | Apt. 304 | 1215 Terrace Avenue | Seattle | WA | 98001 |
| 2065552963 | Lewis | NULL | 520 East Lake Way | NULL | NULL | 98002 |
| 2065553213 | Anderson | Apt 10 | 222 Southern Street | NULL | NULL | 98001 |
| 2065552217 | Wong | NULL | 2832 Washington Ave | Seattle | WA | 98002 |
| 2065556623 | Jimenez | Apt 13 B | 1200 Norton Way | NULL | NULL | 98003 |

**Employee Table**

| | | | |
|---|---|---|---|
| cmanning | Manning | Carol | 3/12/2010 |
| btaylor | Taylor | Bob | 4/16/2009 |
| skristoph | Kristopherson | Stephen | 6/2/2010 |

**Product Table**

| | | | |
|---|---|---|---|
| soda | Soda bottle | 2 Liter bottle | 3.75 |
| brdstks | Breadsticks | 8 per pack | 2.50 |
| basicS | Basic Pizza small | 8 inch | 5.35 |
| basicM | Basic Pizza medium | 12 inch | 7.35 |
| basicL | Basic Pizza large | 18 inch | 13.50 |
| specialS | Specialty small | 8 inch | 6.35 |
| specialM | Specialty medium | 12 inch | 9.25 |
| specialL | Specialty large | 18 inch | 15.00 |
| top | Additional toppings | I cup | 1.00 |

**CustomerOrder Table**

| | | | | |
|---|---|---|---|---|
| 1000 | 10/8/2010 | 2:15 PM | 2065552963 | cmanning |
| 1001 | 10/8/2010 | 2:21 PM | 2065556623 | cmanning |
| 1002 | 10/8/2010 | 2:30 PM | 2065552963 | cmanning |
| 1003 | 10/8/2010 | 3:15 PM | 2065552123 | skristoph |
| 1004 | 10/10/2010 | 11:15 AM | 2065552217 | btaylor |
| 1005 | 10/10/2010 | 12:02 PM | 2065556623 | btaylor |

**Order Detail Table**

| | | | | |
|---|---|---|---|---|
| 1 | 1000 | Soda | 2 | 7.25 |
| 2 | 1000 | Brdstks | 1 | 2.50 |
| 3 | 1000 | specialM | 1 | 7.35 |
| 4 | 1001 | specialL | 1 | 15.00 |
| 5 | 1002 | Soda | 2 | 7.25 |
| 6 | 1002 | basicM | 3 | 20.00 |
| 7 | 1003 | basicM | 1 | 7.35 |
| 8 | 1003 | Top | 4 | 4.00 |
| 9 | 1004 | basicL | 1 | 13.50 |
| 10 | 1005 | basicM | 2 | 14.70 |

# Scenarios

## WILD WOOD APARTMENTS

You have completed the designs for the apartment management database. You reviewed it and all the business rules with the owners, and they are eager to proceed. Now you need to take your design and translate it into an actual database. Once

you have done that, you know that you will need to enter data to test the database, to make sure it does, in fact, store all the required data.

1. Review your diagram for the database, making sure that the design is complete and normalized.

2. Create the database in SQL Server.
3. Create the tables in the new database, selecting appropriate data types for the columns, setting a primary key for each table, and setting allow nulls as appropriate.
4. Create a database diagram, and create the relationships among tables.
5. Add some sample data to each table.
6. **Documentation:** Make a data dictionary that lists each table, all the columns for that table, and the data types for each column.

## VINCE'S VINYL

Vince is eager to get going. Just today, he had a customer come in and sell him a dozen old albums. One is quite rare and could be worth a lot of money. Vince doesn't want to lose track of it. He is ready to get organized and start entering his transactions in the database. You review your design with him and promise that you will begin building the database immediately. But, you remind him, it is important to test the database before actually starting to use it for the business.

1. Review your diagram for the database, making sure that the design is complete and normalized.
2. Create the database in SQL Server.
3. Create the tables in the new database, selecting appropriate data types for the columns, setting a primary key for each table, and setting allow nulls as appropriate.
4. Create a database diagram, and create the relationships among tables.
5. Add some sample data to each table.
6. **Documentation:** Make a data dictionary that lists each table, all the columns for that table, and the data types for each column.

## GRANDFIELD COLLEGE

The management is afraid of a software audit. The chief systems manager just came from a meeting where he heard that a school had just been fined $25,000 for illegally installed software. The current tracking system probably couldn't hold up to an audit. It is crucial that this new database be up and running soon. You assure the management that it will be done as soon as is possible, but you want to make sure that it really does what it is supposed to do. If you implement before it is ready, it might make matters worse rather than better.

1. Review your diagram for the database, making sure that the design is complete and normalized.
2. Create the database in SQL Server.

3. Create the tables in the new database, selecting appropriate data types for the columns, setting a primary key for each table, and setting allow nulls as appropriate.
4. Create a database diagram, and create the relationships among tables.
5. Add some sample data to each table.
6. **Documentation:** Make a data dictionary that lists each table, all the columns for that table, and the data types for each column.

## WESTLAKE RESEARCH HOSPITAL

The Drug study is falling into place. Several potential participants have already been interviewed. It is vital that the database be in place soon. You assure the management that you are ready to begin actually making the database objects but that it is essential you test and evaluate it before they start to commit data to it. You promise that you will deliver it as soon as possible.

1. Review your diagram for the database, making sure that the design is complete and normalized.
2. Create the database in SQL Server.
3. Create the tables in the new database, selecting appropriate data types for the columns, setting a primary key for each table, and setting allow nulls as appropriate.
4. Create a database diagram, and create the relationships among tables.
5. Add some sample data to each table.
6. **Documentation:** Make a data dictionary that lists each table, all the columns for that table, and the data types for each column.

## SUGGESTIONS FOR SCENARIOS

Make sure your primary keys and foreign keys have the same data type and same precision (length). Follow your diagram and make one table at a time. In the database diagram, always drag the relationship from the primary key to the foreign key. Before confirming the relationship, always make sure that the table and column names are correct in the dialog box.

If you need to adjust a table in the database diagram, you can right click on it and under View, select Normal. That will display the column names, data type, and whether it will accept nulls. You can edit the table in this view.

When entering data, you must enter data in the primary key tables before you can enter into the child or foreign key tables. The foreign key must match the primary key exactly.

## CHAPTER 7

# SQL

Now that Sharon has built the database and entered some data, she sets out to test the design and make sure she can satisfy the business requirements. To do this, she is going to use SQL and SQL Express's query analyzer.

**CHAPTER OUTCOMES**

**By the end of this chapter you will be able to:**

- Name the main events in the development of SQL
- Run SELECT queries with a variety of criteria
- Use the Aggregate functions COUNT, AVG, SUM, MIN, and MAX
- Use date, time, and other built-in functions
- Join two or more tables in a query
- INSERT, UPDATE, and DELETE records
- Use SQL to test business rules

## RUNNING QUERIES

It has been a long day. Sharon had two classes of her own today, and then she tutored three students in beginning database. But she feels some pressure to finish with the Tutoring database. Before she can give it to Terry, she needs to test it to make sure it can do all the things that are required of it. She has entered the sample data; now she is going to run some sample queries.

She takes out her laptop and sits at the kitchen table. She starts the SQL Server Management Studio and opens up the databases in the Object window. She selects the Tutor database and right clicks. Then she selects New Query window:

*SQL*

The programming language used to manipulate data and data objects in a relational database.

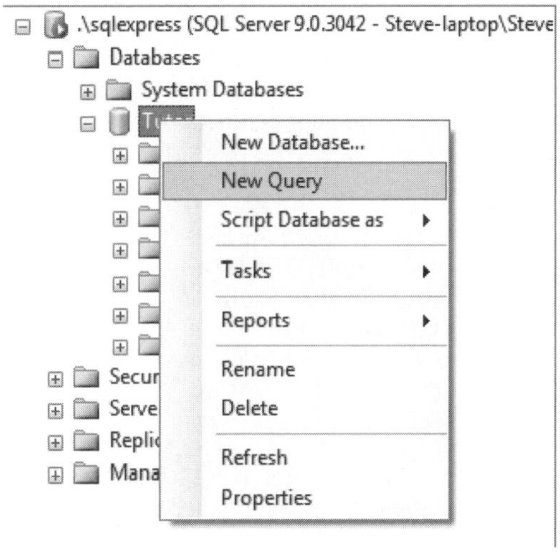

**FIGURE 7-1** New Query

123

To get started, in the Query window she types

```
SELECT * FROM Tut
```

SQL Server 2008 provides some intellisense to help her pick a table:

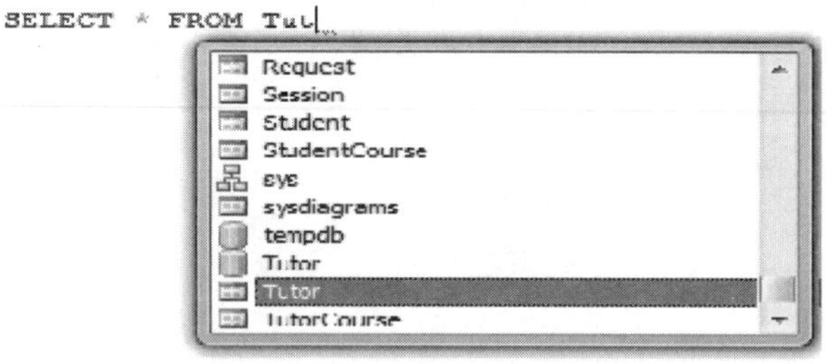

**FIGURE 7-2** Intellisense

She clicks Tutor in the list and then clicks the Execute button and gets these results:

| TutorKey | TutorLastName | TutorFirstName | TutorPhone | TutorEmail | TutorHire Date | TutorStatus |
|----------|---------------|----------------|------------|------------|----------------|-------------|
| 980010000 | Roberts | Martha | 2065551467 | mroberts@yahoo.com | 2010-01-06 | Active |
| 980010001 | Brown | Susan | 2065553528 | Sb4@hotmail.com | 2009-02-01 | Active |
| 980010002 | Foster | Daniel | 2065553490 | Foster32@aol.com | 2009-02-12 | Active |
| 980010003 | Anderson | Nathan | 3065556320 | NULL | 2009-03-02 | Inactive |
| 980010004 | Lewis | Ginger | 2065552985 | ginger@hotmail.com | 2009-03-15 | Active |

**FIGURE 7-3** Result Set

## Things You Should Know

SQL is the programming language used for manipulating database objects and data in relational databases. It is both an ANSI (American National Standards Institute) and an ISO (International Standards Organization) standard.

The first version of SQL was developed at IBM in the 1970s to work with their RBase relational database. The first ANSI standard for SQL was issued in 1986. The ISO committee ratified the standard in 1987. This first standard was not widely used. Database technologies had already moved past it. Most database manufacturers had already added features that were not included in the standard. A major revision was issued in 1992. This standard was much more robust and is still the de facto standard of many RDBMSs today. More changes were added to the standard in 1999 to define the use of triggers and procedures. Revisions in 2003 and 2006 defined how to incorporate XML and XQuery into SQL.

Most RDBMSs comply with the standard to a fairly high degree. What this means for the user is that the SQL they write for one product will translate fairly easily to another product. Much of the SQL you write for SQL Server, for instance, will work without change in Oracle or MySQL. Each RDBMS, however, is free to add proprietary features onto SQL as well as to implement the standard. Typically, these features are additional functions or administrative extensions.

### The Nature of SQL

SQL is a declarative language. This means it is different from the procedural languages you may have encountered in other programming languages such as C++ or Java or C# or Visual Basic. In those languages, you have to specify *how* something is to be done. You have to carefully list each step in the proper order to accomplish a task. In SQL, you say what you want done, not how to do it. In the preceding example, for instance, Sharon writes

```
SELECT * FROM Tutor
```

The **SELECT** tells the DBMS you want to retrieve data. The * is a wildcard that says "select all columns." The **FROM** keyword directs the RDBMS to a table in the current database. The statement as a whole declares "return all the columns and all the rows from the table Tutor." Again, it declares what you want to do, not how to do it. The RDBMS determines how to process the request. Different RDBMSs will process it differently because they have developed different query optimization engines in order to produce the results as efficiently and quickly as possible.

**DECLARATIVE LANGUAGE**

A language in which programmers declare what they want to do, not how they want to do it.

**PROCEDURAL LANGUAGE**

A language in which a programmer defines how to do a given procedure.

---

## THINGS TO THINK ABOUT

*What are the advantages of a declarative language as opposed to a procedural language?*

*What advantages might a procedural language have over a declarative language?*

---

SQL is not case sensitive, though the column names and values can be if the database options are set to be case sensitive. It is traditional, however, to type SQL keywords in all uppercase for readability. SQL also ignores most white spaces. That means you can organize an SQL statement on the page any way that makes it most readable to you. In many DBMSs, SQL statements are terminated by a semicolon. SQL Server does not require the semicolon, though using one can be a good habit to develop. In this book, the semicolons are not included.

Usually, SQL is divided into at least two broad areas of functionality: Data Manipulation Language (DML), which includes all the commands for selecting and manipulating database data, and Data Definition Language (DDL), which includes all the commands for creating, altering, and dropping database objects such as tables, procedures, constraints, and indexes. In this book, we are only going to focus on the DML.

*DDL*

Data Definition Language.

*DML*

Data Manipulation Language.

---

Sharon decides to run another query just to check the data. She types another SQL statement into the Query window. She selects the statement so that only it will run when she clicks Execute.

```
SELECT StudentLastName, StudentFirstName, StudentEmail
       FROM Student
```

**FIGURE 7-4**  Selected SQL Statement

She executes the statement and gets these results:

| StudentLastName | StudentFirstName | StudentEmail |
|---|---|---|
| Min | Ly | lymin@hotmail.com |
| Bradbury | Ron | rbradbury@mars.org |
| Carlos | Juan | Carlos23@hotmail.com |
| Peterson | Laura | NULL |
| Carter | Shannon | shannon@carter.org |
| Martinez | Sandy | sandym@gmail.com |
| Nguyen | Lu | lstar@yahoo.com |
| Zukof | Mark | NULL |
| Taylor | Patty | p147@marketplace.com |
| Thomas | Lawrence | NULL |

**FIGURE 7-5**  Result Table

## Things You Should Know

### The Basic SELECT Statement

The syntax for the simplest **SELECT** statement is

```
SELECT [Column1], [Column2], etc.
FROM [Table]
```

You can select any number of columns from the database table. The columns are separated by commas, but there is no comma after the last column in the list. The columns are returned in the order they are listed. So in our example:

```
SELECT StudentLastName, StudentFirstname, Studentemail
FROM Student
```

Sharon also used a variation of this syntax:

```
SELECT * FROM Tutor
```

The asterisk (*) is a wildcard character that tells the RDBMS to return all the columns in the table. The advantage of this is obvious—you don't have to key in all the columns. But there are disadvantages. For one, you have no say in the order in which the columns are returned. They will simply be returned in the order they have in the table. Also, the wildcard method is less efficient. The database must first query the system table to identify the columns, and then query the data table to access the data. And, finally, in SQL code, which is embedded in an application (such as a Web page), there is no guarantee that the columns returned will always be the same. If someone modified the database, the query may return unexpected columns and cause errors in the program. In general, it is better to specify the columns you wish returned, though the wildcard method can be useful during testing and development.

### Distinct

Sometimes you only want to return one instance of each value. For instance, suppose you want to run a query on the session table to see all the tutors that have scheduled sessions. If you run

```
SELECT tutorkey
FROM Session
```

You will get these results:

| TutorKey |
| --- |
| 980010003 |
| 980010001 |
| 980010001 |
| 980010004 |
| 980010001 |
| 980010001 |
| 980010002 |
| 980010004 |
| 980010004 |
| 980010002 |
| 980010004 |
| 980010004 |
| 980010002 |
| 980010002 |

**FIGURE 7-6**   Result Table

Each tutor key repeats for as many sessions as the tutor is scheduled for. If you wanted to see only one instance of each TutorKey, you can use the DISTINCT keyword:

```
SELECT DISTINCT tutorkey
FROM Session
```

This results in the following:

| TutorKey |
| --- |
| 980010001 |
| 980010002 |
| 980010003 |
| 980010004 |

**FIGURE 7-7**   Distinct Results

DISTINCT operates on the whole row, not on individual columns. The whole row must be identical to be excluded.

## Calculations

You can perform calculations in a SELECT clause. For instance, you can calculate how many hours are there in a typical year with a statement such as:

```
SELECT 365 * 24
```

The query will return a column labeled "No column Name" with the value "8760." To name the column, you can alias it—see the following SELECT statement. More useful calculations, perhaps, can be made by using the math operators with values in table columns. Assume, for instance, that you had a table that stored the item number, the price of an item, and the quantity ordered. You could calculate the total due with a query like the following:

```
SELECT ItemNumber, ItemPrice, Quantity, ItemPrice * Quantity
FROM CustomerOrder
```

Following is a table of the arithmetic operators:

| Table 7-1 | Arithmetic Operators |
|---|---|
| **Operator** | **Description** |
| * | Multiplication |
| / | Division |
| + | Addition |
| − | Subtraction |
| % | Modulus (returns the remainder in integer division) |

Some of the operators serve more than one purpose. The *, for instance, serves as both a wildcard and the multiplication symbol. The % serves both as the modulus operator and a wildcard in a WHERE clause, using the LIKE keyword. SQL determines the appropriate function by context. If there are numeric values on both sides of the *, or columns containing numeric values, SQL knows the * is the operator for multiplication. If the % is in the SELECT clause, it knows it is a modulus operator; if it is in a WHERE clause, with the LIKE keyword, it knows that it is a wildcard. The + operator behaves similarly. If the values on both sides of the operator are numbers, the + performs addition. If the values on both sides are of a character type, then it concatenates the character strings. If the values are mixed, one character, one numeric, SQL throws an error.

The division operator also behaves differently depending on whether the values around it are of an integer type (no decimal parts) or float (have decimal parts). If the dividend and divisor are both integers, the division will result in an integer value. This means that any decimal part will be discarded. If even one of the values is of a float type, then the result will default to a float value, and the result will contain any decimal amount. The modulus operator % returns the remainder of an integer division. Here are some examples:

| Table 7-2 | Integer Division |
|---|---|
| **Equation** | **Result** |
| SELECT 10/3 | 3 (integer division) |
| SELECT 10/3.0 | 3.33333 (float division) |
| SELECT 10%3 | 1 (modulus) |

### Order of Operations

SQL follows the same order of operations as algebra. That is, all multiplications and divisions are solved first moving left to right, and then all additions and subtractions are also performed left to right. In the following statement, 3 * 5 is evaluated first for 15; then 4/2 for 2; third, 1 is added to the 15 for 16; and finally, 2 is subtracted from 16 for a result of 14.

```
SELECT 1 + 3 * 5 - 4/2
```

You can control the order by using parenthesis (). Whatever is in the parenthesis is calculated first. If parentheses are nested, SQL works from the innermost parenthesis outward. For instance,

```
SELECT (((1 + 3) * 5) - 4)/2
```

results not in 14, but in 8.

## Aliasing

**ALIAS**

A substitute name for a column or table.

When you design your database tables, the column names should be descriptive and conform to naming conventions, but good column names do not necessarily make for good labels in a query or report. You can change the label for the result instance by "aliasing" the column. The basic way to do this is by using the **AS** keyword. Thus, in Sharon's query the column "StudentLastName" is aliased as "Last Name" in the results.

```
StudentFirstName AS "First Name"
```

As mentioned earlier, SQL Server distinguishes between single quotes and double quotes. Single quotes are reserved for character or date values, and double quotes are reserved for column names. You can also use square brackets.

```
StudentFirstName AS [First Name]
```

Additionally, you can leave out the **AS** keyword. It is optional.

```
StudentFirstName [First Name]
```

If the alias consists of a single word with no spaces, you do not even have to include the brackets or quotes. All of the following are equivalent:

```
StudentGender AS "Gender"
StudentGender AS [Gender]
StudentGender "Gender"
StudentGender [Gender]
StudentGender Gender
```

Although optional, it is recommended to use the **AS** keyword and quotes or brackets to identify the alias for readability and clarity.

---

Sharon thinks the query results would be better if they were sorted by last name. She adds the keywords ORDER BY. The query now looks like this:

```
SELECT StudentLastName, StudentFirstname, Studentemail
FROM Student
ORDER BY StudentLastName
```

She executes the query and gets the following results:

| StudentLastName | StudentFirstName | StudentEmail |
|---|---|---|
| Bradbury | Ron | rbradbury@mars.org |
| Carlos | Juan | Carlos23@hotmail.com |
| Carter | Shannon | shannon@carter.org |
| Martinez | Sandy | sandym@gmail.com |
| Min | Ly | lymin@hotmail.com |
| Nguyen | Lu | lstar@yahoo.com |
| Peterson | Laura | NULL |
| Taylor | Patty | p147@marketplace.com |
| Thomas | Lawrence | NULL |
| Zukof | Mark | NULL |

**FIGURE 7-8** Student Email Result

Next, Sharon decides to list the records from the Session table. She wants to sort them by the Session date, showing the more recent dates first. She writes the following query:

```
SELECT * FROM Session
ORDER BY SessionDate DESC
```

The DESC keyword causes the records to be sorted in descending order—z to a, 10 to 1, and so on. She executes the query and gets this result.

| SessionDateKey | SessionTimeKey | TutorKey | CourseKey | StudentKey | SessionStatus | SessionMaterialCovered |
|---|---|---|---|---|---|---|
| 2010-02-14 | 11:00:00.0000000 | 980010002 | ENG211 | NULL | NULL | NULL |
| 2010-02-13 | 10:00:00.0000000 | 980010002 | ITC255 | NULL | NULL | NULL |
| 2010-02-10 | 14:00:00.0000000 | 980010004 | MAT107 | NULL | NULL | NULL |
| 2010-02-10 | 13:30:00.0000000 | 980010004 | MAT107 | NULL | NULL | NULL |
| 2010-02-05 | 10:30:00.0000000 | 980010002 | ITC255 | 990001000 | C | Feasibility |
| 2010-01-22 | 14:00:00.0000000 | 980010004 | MAT107 | 990001005 | NS | NULL |
| 2010-01-20 | 11:00:00.0000000 | 980010004 | ENG211 | 990001003 | C | Document Structure |
| 2010-01-15 | 09:30:00.0000000 | 980010002 | ITC255 | 990001000 | C | Use Cases |
| 2009-11-20 | 10:30:00.0000000 | 980010001 | ITC220 | 990001002 | C | Relations |
| 2009-11-10 | 14:00:00.0000000 | 980010001 | WEB110 | 990001000 | C | Web Forms |
| 2009-11-10 | 13:00:00.0000000 | 980010004 | MAT107 | 990001004 | C | Binary Numbers |
| 2009-11-05 | 10:00:00.0000000 | 980010001 | ITC220 | NULL | NS | NULL |
| 2009-10-20 | 14:00:00.0000000 | 980010001 | WEB110 | 990001000 | C | CSS |
| 2009-10-20 | 13:00:00.0000000 | 980010003 | ITC110 | 990001000 | C | For next loops |

**FIGURE 7-9** Session Ordered by SessionDate DESC

Looking at this result, Sharon thinks it could be made even better by adding a second sort on the tutor. She modifies the query to add the second sort.

```
SELECT FROM Session
ORDER BY SessionDateKey DESC, tutorkey
```

The result set looks like this:

| SessionDateKey | SessionTimeKey | TutorKey | CourseKey | CourseStatus |
|---|---|---|---|---|
| 2010-02-14 | 11:00:00.0000000 | 980010002 | ENG211 | NULL |
| 2010-02-13 | 10:00:00.0000000 | 980010002 | ITC255 | NULL |
| 2010-02-10 | 13:30:00.0000000 | 980010004 | MAT107 | NULL |
| 2010-02-10 | 14:00:00.0000000 | 980010004 | MAT107 | NULL |
| 2010-02-05 | 10:30:00.0000000 | 980010002 | ITC255 | C |
| 2010-01-22 | 14:00:00.0000000 | 980010004 | MAT107 | NS |
| 2010-01-20 | 11:00:00.0000000 | 980010004 | ENG211 | C |
| 2010-01-15 | 09:30:00.0000000 | 980010002 | ITC255 | C |
| 2009-11-20 | 10:30:00.0000000 | 980010001 | ITC220 | C |
| 2009-11-10 | 14:00:00.0000000 | 980010001 | WEB110 | C |
| 2009-11-10 | 13:00:00.0000000 | 980010004 | MAT107 | C |
| 2009-11-05 | 10:00:00.0000000 | 980010001 | ITC220 | NS |
| 2009-10-20 | 14:00:00.0000000 | 980010001 | WEB110 | C |
| 2009-10-20 | 13:00:00.0000000 | 980010003 | ITC110 | C |

**FIGURE 7-10** Session Ordered by SessionDate and TutorKey

For this result, the primary sort is the Session date. It is in a descending order. The secondary sort is by tutor key, and it is ordered in an ascending order. The tutor keys "dfoster" and "glewis," for instance, both have the same Session date, but they are ordered alphabetically in ascending order (A to Z) for that date.

## TESTING THE DATABASE

Now Sharon is ready to start testing the database to see if it supports the business rules that she and Terry had identified. She decides to keep it simple at first and concentrate on making sure that Terry can get the kinds of demographic information she needs. For each case, she writes down what test she is conducting, the SQL she uses, and the results in a notebook. For her first query, she will simply test for gender and return all the male students.

```
SELECT StudentLastName, StudentFirstName, StudentGender
FROM Student
WHERE StudentGender = 'M'
```

This returns the following results:

| StudentLastName | StudentFirstName | StudentGender |
|---|---|---|
| Bradbury | Ron | M |
| Carlos | Juan | M |
| Nguyen | Lu | M |
| Thomas | Lawrence | M |

**FIGURE 7-11**  Male Students

## Things You Should Know

### The WHERE Clause

The WHERE keyword is used to set the criteria for filtering rows. (You filter columns by listing those you wish to see in the SELECT clause.) The basic syntax of a WHERE clause is

```
WHERE [column] [=< > LIKE IN BETWEEN IS] [value]
```

This probably looks confusing. Let's look at some examples. Say you had a database with an Inventory table that contains data about equipment sold by a Sporting goods store.

| InventoryKey | InventoryName | InventoryUnit | InventoryPrice | InventoryQuantity | InventoryDescription |
|---|---|---|---|---|---|
| 1001 | Tennis Balls | 1 tube | 2.3400 | 40 | One tube contains 4 balls. |
| 1002 | Basketball | 1 ball | 34.5900 | 20 | NULL |
| 1003 | Baseball | 1 ball | 4.5000 | 100 | NULL |
| 1004 | Baseball Bat | 1 bat | 18.7500 | 30 | NULL |
| 1005 | Lawn Darts | 1 box | 25.8800 | 20 | Box contains 2 hoops 6 darts. |
| 1006 | T-Ball Kit | I box | 32.0000 | 15 | Box contains tee, bat, and ball. |
| 1007 | T-Ball Tee | 1 Tee | 12.0000 | 18 | Individual tee. |
| 1008 | Bike Helmet | 1 Helmet | 12.9500 | 14 | NULL |

**FIGURE 7-12**  Inventory Table

You only want to see the record for tennis balls:

```
SELECT *
FROM Inventory
WHERE InventoryName = 'Tennis Balls'
```

This would return only the data for "Tennis Balls" as shown:

| InventoryKey | InventoryName | InventoryUnit | InventoryPrice | InventoryQuantity | InventoryDescription |
|---|---|---|---|---|---|
| 1001 | Tennis Balls | 1 tube | 2.3400 | 40 | One tube contains 4 balls. |

**FIGURE 7-13**   Results for Tennis Balls

When you are specifying criteria in a **WHERE** clause, Character, varchar, nchar, nvarchar, Text, XML, and DateTime values are enclosed in single quotes. The ANSI standard doesn't distinguish between single and double quotes, but SQL Server does. Values must be quoted in single quotes. If you use double quotes, you will receive an error. Here is the error generated by the preceding query with double quotes around "Tennis Balls."

```
Msg 207, Level 16, State 1, Line 2
Invalid column name 'Tennis Balls'
```

Number values are not quoted. Here is a query that returns all the items from the inventory that have a price of $12.95.

```
SELECT ItemName, ItemPrice
FROM Inventory
WHERE ItemPrice = 12.95
```

This returns:

| InventoryName | InventoryPrice |
|---|---|
| Bike Helmet | 12.9500 |

**FIGURE 7-14**   Results for 12.95

With numbers and dates, you can also use the comparative values for greater than and less than.

```
SELECT ItemName, Price
FROM Inventory
WHERE Price > 25
```

This returns:

| InventoryName | InventoryPrice |
|---|---|
| Basketball | 34.5900 |
| Lawn Darts | 25.8800 |
| T-Ball Kit | 32.0000 |

**FIGURE 7-15**   Results for > 25

The **LIKE** keyword lets you search for patterns in char, nchar, varchar, and nvarchar columns. You use the wildcard character %. The % wildcard character searches for any number of characters to replace. For instance, if you wanted to find every customer whose last name began with "S," you could write a query like this:

```
SELECT ItemName, ItemPrice
FROM Inventory
WHERE ItemName LIKE 'T%'
```

| InventoryName | InventoryPrice |
|---|---|
| Tennis Balls | 2.3400 |
| T-Ball Kit | 32.0000 |
| T-Ball Tee | 12.0000 |

**FIGURE 7-16**   Results for LIKE 'T%'

**LIKE** is considered an "expensive" operator. That means it takes a lot of processing and CPU time. Why do you think that would be the case? When do you think it would be appropriate to use the **LIKE** operator? When would it not be appropriate?

You can use more than one % in an expression. For instance, if you wanted to return customer last names that had the character string **and** in them:

```
SELECT ItemName, ItemPrice, ItemQuantity
FROM Inventory
WHERE InventoryName LIKE '%ball%'
```

This returns:

| ItemName | ItemPrice | ItemQuantity |
|----------|-----------|--------------|
| Tennis Balls | 2.3400 | 40 |
| Basketball | 34.5900 | 20 |
| Baseball | 4.5000 | 100 |
| Baseball Bat | 18.7500 | 30 |
| T-Ball Kit | 32.0000 | 15 |
| T-Ball Tee | 12.0000 | 18 |

**FIGURE 7-17**   Results for LIKE '%Ball%'

The **BETWEEN** keyword returns values between two stated ends. **BETWEEN** is *inclusive* of the ends. That means if you query values **BETWEEN 3 AND 10**, the query would return 3, 4, 5, 6, 7, 8, 9, and 10. You can get the same results by using >= and <= operators: **WHERE Number >= 3 AND Number <= 10**. (We will discuss **AND**, **OR**, and **NOT** in a later section.) **BETWEEN** is especially useful for returning a range of dates.

```
SELECT tutorkey, courseKey, SessionDate, StudentKey
FROM Session
WHERE SessionDate BETWEEN '11/1/2008' AND '11/15/2008'
```

This returns the following results from our Session table:

| TutorKey | CourseKey | SessionDate | StudentKey |
|----------|-----------|-------------|------------|
| nanderson | ITC110 | 2008-11-12 14:00:00.000 | lpeterson |
| nanderson | ITC110 | 2008-11-12 15:00:00.000 | scarter |
| nanderson | ITC110 | 2008-11-13 13:00:00.000 | lpeterson |
| sbrown | ITC220 | 2008-11-13 14:00:00.000 | scarter |

**FIGURE 7-18**   BETWEEN Results

Next, we will look at the keyword **IS**. **IS** is used instead of "=" with the keyword **NULL**. A null is an unknown value. Since it is unknown, it can't be equal to anything. It is often, however, useful to search for nulls. Say, you wanted to get a list of all the sessions that are not reserved by students. You can search for Sessions where the student key **IS NULL**:

```
SELECT tutorkey, courseKey, SessionDate, StudentKey
FROM Session
WHERE StudentKey IS NULL
```

This results in:

| TutorKey | CourseKey | SessionDate | StudentKey |
|----------|-----------|-------------|------------|
| dfoster | ENG211 | 2009-03-02 10:00:00.000 | NULL |
| dfoster | ENG211 | 2009-03-02 11:00:00.000 | NULL |
| glewis | MAT107 | 2009-03-02 11:00:00.000 | NULL |

**FIGURE 7-19**   NULL Results

## And, Or, Not

All of these different kinds of conditions can be combined by using the keywords **AND** and **OR**. When two conditions are combined with the **AND** keyword, both must be true to return a result set. If you were to have a condition, for instance, such as **WHERE** City = 'Seattle' **AND** City = 'Portland', it would never return any results because both can't be true at the same time. **OR**, on the other hand, returns results if either of the conditions are true. **WHERE** City = 'Seattle' **OR** City = 'Portland' returns results for either Seattle or Portland.

The **NOT** keyword allows you to negate a condition. For example, if you wanted to select all the customers who were not in Seattle, you could write a query like:

```
SELECT LastName, FirstName, Phone, City
FROM Customer
WHERE NOT City = 'Seattle'
```

Equally, if you wanted to find all those sessions that did have a student scheduled, you could use the **NOT** with the **IS NULL**:

```
SELECT tutorkey, courseKey, SessionDateKey, StudentKey
FROM Session
WHERE StudentKey IS NOT NULL
```

This returns:

| TutorKey | CourseKey | SessionDateKey | StudentKey |
|----------|-----------|----------------|------------|
| 980010003 | ITC110 | 2009-10-20 | 990001000 |
| 980010001 | WEB110 | 2009-10-20 | 990001000 |
| 980010004 | MAT107 | 2009-11-10 | 990001004 |
| 980010001 | WEB110 | 2009-11-10 | 990001000 |
| 980010001 | ITC220 | 2009-11-20 | 990001002 |
| 980010002 | ITC255 | 2010-01-15 | 990001000 |
| 980010004 | ENG211 | 2010-01-20 | 990001003 |
| 980010004 | MAT107 | 2010-01-22 | 990001005 |
| 980010002 | ITC255 | 2010-02-05 | 990001000 |

**FIGURE 7-20** NOT NULL Results

Sharon decides to clean up the results a little. To do this, she will use aliases for the column names and order the results by the last name:

```
SELECT StudentLastName AS "Last Name",
StudentFirstName AS "First Name",
StudentGender AS "Gender"
FROM Student
WHERE StudentGender = 'M'
ORDER BY StudentLastName
```

When she executes it, the results now look like this:

| Last Name | First Name | Gender |
|-----------|-----------|--------|
| Bradbury | Ron | M |
| Carlos | Jaun | M |
| Hayden | Patrick | M |
| Nguyen | Lou | M |
| Thomas | Lawrence | M |

**FIGURE 7-21** Results with Aliases

Returning all the males was a start, but what Terry would really need is aggregated data, data that is summarized and processed in various ways. For her first try, she decides to get the count of all students over 25. She enters this query into the editor:

```
SELECT COUNT(*) as "Total Over 25"
FROM Student
WHERE StudentAge > 25
```

| Total over 25 |
|---------------|
| 5 |

**FIGURE 7-22** Count over 25

It uses the aggregate function "COUNT." As its name suggests, COUNT returns the count of values returned. In this case, it is 5>

## Things You Should Know

### Functions

SQL Server and most DBMSs include a variety of functions. Some functions operate on individual rows, one at a time. These are called **scalar** functions. Other functions operate on sets of rows or whole tables of rows at a time. These are called **aggregate** functions.

Every function has a similar syntax that consists of the function name and a set of parenthesis. In the parenthesis are listed any parameters the function requires, separated by commas.

*SCALAR FUNCTIONS*

These operate only on a single row.

*AGGREGATE FUNCTIONS*

These operate on sets of rows.

```
<Function Name>(parameter1, parameter2, ...)
```

The function ROUND, for instance, which will round a number, takes two parameters: the number to be rounded, which can be a numeric column or a literal number, and the number of decimal places to round at.

```
SELECT ROUND(23.4567893,2) as Rounded
```

This results in 23.4600000.

### Scalar Functions

Scalar functions operate on the individual rows of a table. There are several dozen built-in scalar functions in SQL Server. In SQL Server Management Studio, you can see lists of both scalar and aggregate functions if you look at the programmability\functions\system functions for a database. This chapter uses only a small number of functions, mostly related to dates. Following is a table of those functions:

**Table 7-3** Scalar Functions Used in This Chapter

| Function Name | Description |
| --- | --- |
| GETDATE() | Returns current date and time |
| MONTH | Returns the month as in integer (1–12) from a Date value |
| YEAR | Returns the Year as a four-digit integer from a Date value |

### Aggregate Functions

As mentioned earlier, aggregate functions are functions that operate on several rows at a time. They are extremely useful for analysing data in tables. Following is a table of the most common aggregate functions.

**Table 7-4** Common Aggregate Functions

| Aggregate Function | Description |
| --- | --- |
| COUNT | Counts the number of values: **COUNT**(*) counts all the rows. **COUNT**(columnName) counts all the values in the column but ignores nulls |
| SUM | Sums or totals numeric values: **SUM** (InStock) |
| AVG | Returns the mean average of a set of numeric values: **AVG**(price). By default nulls are ignored. |
| MAX | Returns the highest value in a set of numeric or datetime values: **MAX**(price) |
| MIN | Returns the smallest value in a set of numeric or datetime value: **MIN**(price) |

### DISTINCT With Aggregate Functions

One of Terry's reporting needs is to return unduplicated student counts. It is possible to use the word **DISTINCT** with a function to do that. The COUNT function by itself will count all instances of a value. So, for instance, if we do a count of all StudentKeys from Session with the following SQL, we will get the total number of students who signed up for sessions, but each student will be counted as many times as the session they signed up for.

```
SELECT COUNT(studentKey) AS [Total] FROM Session
```

For this query, the total is 9.

Running the query with the **DISTINCT** keyword returns an unduplicated count. It only counts unique values. The following query returns 5. There are only 5 individual students who have signed up for sessions.

```
SELECT COUNT(DISTINCT studentKey) AS [Unduplicated] FROM Session
```

### Group By

Because aggregate functions operate on several rows at a time, there is a conflict when you use column names and scalar functions that only operate on one row at a time. To resolve this conflict, SQL has a **GROUP BY** clause. *Any column or scalar function that is not a part of the aggregate function must be included in a* **GROUP BY** *clause.* Suppose, for instance, Sharon wanted to count how many sessions each tutor had scheduled. She could write a query like the following:

```
SELECT TutorKey, COUNT(SessionTimeKey) AS [Total Sessions]
FROM Session
```

Running this query would throw the following error:

```
Msg 8120, Level 16, State 1, Line 1
Column 'Session.TutorKey' is invalid in the select list because it is not
contained in either an aggregate function or the GROUP BY clause.
```

The problem is that the query mixes scalar, single-row values, with aggregate, multiple-row values. TutorKey is returned for each row, while COUNT (SessionTimeKey) returns a value generated by looking at all the row. To solve this, TutorKey needs to be contained in a **GROUP BY** clause. It means that the COUNT will be grouped by TutorKey. This actually returns the information Sharon wants:

| TutorKey | Total Sessions |
|---|---|
| 980010001 | 4 |
| 980010002 | 4 |
| 980010003 | 1 |
| 980010004 | 5 |

**FIGURE 7-23** Count Grouped by Tutor

### Having

Another keyword associated with aggregate functions is the **HAVING** keyword. **HAVING** is used for criteria that involve an aggregate function. Let's say that Sharon only wants to see the tutors who have less than four sessions scheduled. To do this, she needs a **HAVING** clause:

```
SELECT TutorKey, COUNT(SessionTimeKey) AS [Total Sessions]
FROM Session
GROUP BY TutorKey
HAVING COUNT(SessionTimeKey)<4
```

This returns only

| TutorKey | Total Sessions |
|---|---|
| 980010003 | 1 |

**FIGURE 7-24** HAVING Results

Sharon writes a query to get the average age of students:

```
SELECT AVG(StudentAge) AS "Average Age"
FROM Student
```

| Average Age |
|:---:|
| 29 |

**FIGURE 7-25**  Average Age

Just for good measure, she decides to get the maximum and minimum ages for the students:

```
Select MAX(StudentAge) AS "Oldest"
FROM Student
```

| Oldest |
|:---:|
| 53 |

**FIGURE 7-26**  Maximum Age

```
Select MIN(StudentAge) AS "Youngest"
FROM Student
```

| Youngest |
|:---:|
| 18 |

**FIGURE 7-27**  Minimum Age

Now she is ready to try something more sophisticated. Sharon knows that Terry needs a count of how many students are of each ethnicity. Sharon tries this statement:

```
SELECT EthnicityKey, COUNT(EthnicityKey) AS "Total"
FROM Student
```

When she runs this query, she gets an error message:

```
Column 'Session.TutorKey' is invalid in the select list because it is not
contained in either an aggregate function or the GROUP BY clause.
```

This reminds her that she must add a GROUP BY clause whenever she has a column in the SELECT clause that is not a part of the aggregate function. She rewrites the function to include the GROUP BY clause and gets these results:

```
SELECT EthnicityKey, COUNT(EthnicityKey) AS "Total"
FROM Student
GROUP BY EthnicityKey
```

| EthnicityKey | Total |
|---|---|
| NULL | 0 |
| AfrAmer | 1 |
| Asian | 2 |
| Caucasian | 4 |
| Hispanic | 2 |

**FIGURE 7-28**  GROUP BY Ethnicity

It is time to look at some of the other business rules. The first rule was just a statement of the nature of tutors.

• A tutor can be a student but is not necessarily one.

The real issue there was not to assume that a tutor had a student key. Sharon had designed the tables so that tutors have their own key. She looked at the second rule:

• Tutors cannot work for more than 60 hours a month.

To really enforce this, Sharon would need to create a trigger or stored procedure. This is a more complicated matter, and she decides to leave it until later. She makes a note so she doesn't forget it. She can, though, make sure that the information needed for this rule can be returned from the database. First, she will get all the sessions for a particular tutor. She looks up the table and chooses Ginger Lewis. She writes this SQL statement:

```
SELECT TutorKey,
CourseKey,
SessionDateKey,
SessionTimeKey,
```

```
StudentKey,
SessionStatus
FROM Session
WHERE Tutorkey = '980010004'
```

Here are her results:

| TutorKey | CourseKey | SessionDateKey | SessionTimeKey | StudentKey | SessionStatus |
|----------|-----------|----------------|----------------|------------|---------------|
| 980010004 | MAT107 | 2009-11-10 | 13:00:00.0000000 | 990001004 | C |
| 980010004 | ENG211 | 2010-01-20 | 11:00:00.0000000 | 990001003 | C |
| 980010004 | MAT107 | 2010-01-22 | 14:00:00.0000000 | 990001005 | NS |
| 980010004 | MAT107 | 2010-02-10 | 13:30:00.0000000 | NULL | NULL |
| 980010004 | MAT107 | 2010-02-10 | 14:00:00.0000000 | NULL | NULL |

**FIGURE 7-29** Ginger Lewis Sessions

Sharon has returned all the sessions for a tutor, but she still needs to figure out how many hours that student has worked in a month. Sharon knows that there are some built-in functions that can help her extract different parts from the date and time columns. She decides to click Help. She selects Search, and in the Search text box types "Date functions." The first selection that comes up is "Date and Time Functions (Transact SQL)." "Transact SQL," she knows, is Microsoft SQL Server's specific flavor of SQL. She clicks on this to open the Help file. From the table of functions, she clicks on the Month function and looks at the example:

*TRANSACT SQL*

Microsoft SQL Server's brand of SQL.

The following example returns the number of the month from the date 03/12/1998.

```
SELECT "Month Number" = MONTH('03/12/1998')
GO
```

Here is the result set.

```
Month Number
------------
3
```

She also looks up the YEAR function, then tries the following query:

```
SELECT TutorKey,
CourseKey,
Month(SessionDateKey) AS "Month",
Year(SessionDateKey) AS "Year",
SessionTimeKey,
StudentKey,
SessionStatus
FROM Session
WHERE Tutorkey = '980010004'
```

This returns the following results:

| TutorKey | CourseKey | Month | Year | SessionTimeKey | StudentKey | SessionStatus |
|----------|-----------|-------|------|----------------|------------|---------------|
| 980010004 | MAT107 | 11 | 2009 | 13:00:00.0000000 | 990001004 | C |
| 980010004 | ENG211 | 1 | 2010 | 11:00:00.0000000 | 990001003 | C |
| 980010004 | MAT107 | 1 | 2010 | 14:00:00.0000000 | 990001005 | NS |
| 980010004 | MAT107 | 2 | 2010 | 13:30:00.0000000 | NULL | NULL |
| 980010004 | MAT107 | 2 | 2010 | 14:00:00.0000000 | NULL | NULL |

**FIGURE 7-30** Month and Year Results

Now that Sharon has a list of all the sessions for a tutor, she needs to get the count of how many hours he or she has tutored in a month. She decides to try the COUNT function.

```
SELECT Tutorkey,
MONTH(SessionDateKey) AS [Month],
YEAR(SessionDateKey) AS [Year],
COUNT (SessionTimeKey) AS [Total]
FROM Session
GROUP BY TutorKey, MONTH(SessionDateKey), YEAR(SessionDateKey)
ORDER BY YEAR(SessionDateKey), MONTH(SessionDateKey)
```

This returns the following results:

| TutorKey | Month | Year | Total |
|----------|-------|------|-------|
| 980010001 | 10 | 2009 | 1 |
| 980010003 | 10 | 2009 | 1 |
| 980010001 | 11 | 2009 | 3 |
| 980010004 | 11 | 2009 | 1 |
| 980010002 | 1 | 2010 | 1 |
| 980010004 | 1 | 2010 | 2 |
| 980010002 | 2 | 2010 | 3 |
| 980010004 | 2 | 2010 | 2 |

**FIGURE 7-31**  Count by Tutors, Month, and Year

This shows the count of sessions that each tutor had per month, and Terry could use it to calculate the number of hours, but Sharon is sure she can improve it. Each session is 30 minutes in length. Sharon knows she can multiply the number of sessions by 30 to get the number of minutes. Then she can divide the total minutes to get the number of hours. She will also alias the calculated column. After some work, she produces the following query:

```
SELECT Tutorkey,
MONTH(SessionDateKey) AS [Month],
YEAR(SessionDateKey) AS [Year],
((COUNT (SessionTimeKey)) * 30.0)/60.0 AS [Hours]
FROM Session
GROUP BY TutorKey, MONTH(SessionDateKey), YEAR(SessionDateKey)
ORDER BY YEAR(SessionDateKey), MONTH(SessionDateKey)
```

| TutorKey | Month | Year | Hours |
|----------|-------|------|-------|
| 980010001 | 10 | 2009 | 0.500000 |
| 980010003 | 10 | 2009 | 0.500000 |
| 980010001 | 11 | 2009 | 1.500000 |
| 980010004 | 11 | 2009 | 0.500000 |
| 980010002 | 1 | 2010 | 0.500000 |
| 980010004 | 1 | 2010 | 1.000000 |
| 980010002 | 2 | 2010 | 1.500000 |
| 980010004 | 2 | 2010 | 1.000000 |

**FIGURE 7-32**  Hours Grouped by Tutor, Month, and Year

As is, the query results show the number of hours for each tutor. It would be better if she could select a particular month and year. Sharon tries putting a WHERE clause after the GROUP BY, but that generates an error. Finally, she puts the WHERE clause after the FROM clause and the query runs successfully.

```
SELECT Tutorkey,
MONTH(SessionDateKey) AS [Month],
YEAR(SessionDateKey) AS [Year],
((COUNT (SessionTimeKey)) * 30.0)/60.0 AS [Hours]
FROM Session
WHERE MONTH(SessionDateKey) = 2 AND YEAR(SessionDateKey) = 2010
GROUP BY TutorKey, MONTH(SessionDateKey), YEAR(SessionDateKey)
ORDER BY YEAR(SessionDateKey), MONTH(SessionDateKey)
```

| TutorKey | Month | Year | Hours |
|----------|-------|------|-------|
| 980010002 | 2 | 2010 | 1.500000 |
| 980010004 | 2 | 2010 | 1.000000 |

**FIGURE 7-33**   Tutor Hours for February

Sharon decides to add one more thing to the query. It would be useful if Terry had a query that could flag anyone in a given time period who was scheduled for more than 60 hours. This will require a HAVING clause.

```
SELECT Tutorkey,
MONTH(SessionDateKey) AS [Month],
YEAR(SessionDateKey) AS [Year],
((COUNT (SessionTimeKey)) * 30.0)/60.0 As [Hours]
FROM Session
WHERE MONTH(SessionDateKey) = 2 AND YEAR(SessionDateKey) = 2010
GROUP BY TutorKey, MONTH(SessionDateKey), YEAR(SessionDateKey)
HAVING (((COUNT (SessionTimeKey)) * 30.0)/60.0) > 60
ORDER BY YEAR(SessionDateKey), MONTH (SessionDateKey)
```

In the current database, this will return nothing, because no one has worked for over 60 hours in the monthly period. But it would serve to check to make sure no tutor is exceeding his or her hours.

## JOINS

Sharon knows these queries would be more readable if they contained the names of the tutors rather than just the tutor key. To do this, she would need to use joins. She starts with a simple join that combines the Tutor table with the Session table. Here is her SQL and results:

```
SELECT TutorLastName,
TutorFirstName,
SessionDateKey,
SessionTimeKey,
StudentKey
SessionStatus
FROM Tutor
INNER JOIN Session
ON Tutor.TutorKey = Session.TutorKey
```

| TutorLastName | TutorFirstname | SessionDateKey | SessionTimeKey | StudentKey |
|---------------|----------------|----------------|----------------|------------|
| Anderson | Nathan | 2009-10-20 | 13:00:00.0000000 | 990001000 |
| Brown | Susan | 2009-10-20 | 14:00:00.0000000 | 990001000 |
| Brown | Susan | 2009-11-05 | 10:00:00.0000000 | NULL |
| Lewis | Ginger | 2009-11-10 | 13:00:00.0000000 | 990001004 |
| Brown | Susan | 2009-11-10 | 14:00:00.0000000 | 990001000 |
| Brown | Susan | 2009-11-20 | 10:30:00.0000000 | 990001002 |
| Foster | Daniel | 2010-01-15 | 09:30:00.0000000 | 990001000 |
| Lewis | Ginger | 2010-01-20 | 11:00:00.0000000 | 990001003 |
| Lewis | Ginger | 2010-01-22 | 14:00:00.0000000 | 990001005 |
| Foster | Daniel | 2010-02-05 | 10:30:00.0000000 | 990001000 |
| Lewis | Ginger | 2010-02-10 | 13:30:00.0000000 | NULL |
| Lewis | Ginger | 2010-02-10 | 14:00:00.0000000 | NULL |
| Foster | Daniel | 2010-02-13 | 10:00:00.0000000 | NULL |
| Foster | Daniel | 2010-02-14 | 11:00:00.0000000 | NULL |

**FIGURE 7-34**   Session Tutor Inner Join

## Joins

The process of normalization breaks tables into smaller and more focused tables. This makes for more effective database processing, but it separates things that seem to belong together. Joins allow the user to reunite or "join" elements that have been split into a single result set.

### Inner Join

An inner join returns the selected columns for all the rows in chosen tables that have a related row in the joined table. What this means is that the join returns all the tutors that have sessions in the Session table. If there are any tutors in the Tutor table who don't have sessions, they will not be included in the results. Conversely, if there are any sessions that don't have an assigned tutor, they will also not be returned.

Take a look at Sharon's query to get an overview of how an inner join works. All the columns are listed in the **SELECT** clause in the order you want to see them returned regardless of what table they may come from.

```
SELECT TutorLastName,
TutorFirstName,
SessionDateKey,
SessionTimeKey,
StudentKey
SessionStatus
```

One of the tables—it doesn't really matter which one, though usually it's the table containing the first columns—is used in the **FROM** clause.

```
FROM Tutor
```

Next, the keywords **INNER JOIN** are used to add the second table.

```
INNER JOIN Session
```

JOIN can be used by itself without the modifier **INNER**, since the default type of **JOIN** is an **INNER JOIN**. But it is better to use the INNER for clarity.

Finally, an ON clause defines how the tables relate.

```
ON Tutor.TutorKey = Session.TutorKey
```

It is necessary to show the relation even though you have defined the relational constraints in the database management system. Notice also, the dot notation. The column TutorKey, because it is both a primary key and a foreign key, exists in both tables. In order to clarify which one belongs to which table, we use the following notation to clarify which column we are referring to:

```
<TABLENAME>.<COLUMNNAME>
```

This is called a "qualified" name. A *fully* qualified name includes the following:

```
<SERVERNAME>.<DATABASENAME>.<SCHEMANAME>.<TABLENAME>. <COLUMNNAME>
```

**QUALIFIED NAME**

A name that includes a chain of ownership separated by dot notation.

The schema name is the name of the owner of the object. In most cases in SQL Server, the schema is "dbo," which is short for "Database Owner." It is possible to assign tables and other database objects to different schemas as owners of the object. This will be covered in the next chapter on security.

Any column, that is ambiguous, that exits in more than one table, whether it is in the **SELECT** clause, the **ON** clause, or the criteria, must be disambiguated or clarified by including its table name. To make this a little less tedious, you can alias the table names and use the alias instead of the table names.

```
SELECT t.TutorKey
TutorLastName,
TutorFirstName,
SessionDateKey,
SessionTimeKey,
StudentKey
SessionStatus
FROM Tutor t
INNER JOIN Session s
ON t.TutorKey = s.TutorKey
```

Notice that the alias is used in the **SELECT** clause as well, even though you don't declare the aliases until the **FROM** and **INNER JOIN** clauses.

After adding the ON clause, you can, of course, add a **WHERE** clause and **ORDER BY** as needed.

### Equi Joins

An equi join is an older form of join that doesn't use the **INNER JOIN** syntax. In some older versions of database management systems such as ORACLE (versions before 9i), equi joins were the only way to join tables. In an equi join, you list all the columns in the **SELECT** just as in the **INNER JOIN**, but in the **FROM**, instead of just listing one table, you list them all, separated by commas. There is no **ON** clause, but you still define the relationships with the = sign (thus the name "equi join") in the **WHERE** clause. The following example is equivalent to Sharon's **INNER JOIN** except for the addition of a search criterion in the **WHERE** clause to show how that would work with the definition of the relationship.

```
SELECT t.TutorKey,
TutorLastName,
TutorFirstName,
SessionDateKey,
SessionTimeKey,
StudentKey
FROM Tutor t,
Session s
WHERE t.TutorKey = s.TutorKey
AND TutorLastName = 'Brown'
```

*EQUI JOINS*

A join using the = sign to specify relations, an older alternative to the INNER JOIN syntax.

The equi join syntax may seem simpler to some people, but the **INNER JOIN** syntax should be used where possible. The **INNER JOIN** is clearer about what is going on in the query, whereas the equi join syntax mixes the join information with query criteria. Also, the **INNER JOIN** syntax protects you from a common error in the equi join syntax. In the equi join syntax, when you are joining multiple tables, it is easy to forget to specify a relationship. A query with such a mistake does not throw an error, instead it produces a CROSS JOIN with the result set before it. A CROSS JOIN (sometimes called a Cartesian JOIN) combines each row in the result set or first table with each row in the second table. You can end up with thousands of unexpected rows in your final query result. The **INNER JOIN** syntax makes this particular error virtually impossible.

*CROSS JOIN*

A join in which each row in one table is matched to every row in a second table.

---

## THINGS TO THINK ABOUT

*Why do you think cross joins are allowed as a legitimate join? What uses can you see for such joins?*

---

### Joins with Several Tables

Both inner joins and equi joins can be uses to join more than two tables. Following is an example of both forms which bring together the Student table, the Request table, and the Course table.

```
SELECT s.StudentKey,
StudentLastName,
StudentFirstName,
c.CourseKey,
CourseName,
RequestDate,
RequestStatus
FROM Student s
INNER JOIN Request r
ON s.StudentKey = r.StudentKey
INNER JOIN Course c
ON c.CourseKey = r.CourseKey
WHERE RequestStatus = 'Active'

SELECT s.StudentKey,
StudentLastName,
StudentFirstName,
```

```
c.CourseKey,
CourseName,
RequestDate,
RequestStatus
FROM, Student s, Course c, Request r
WHERE s.StudentKey = r.StudentKey
AND c.CourseKey = r.CourseKey
AND RequestStatus = 'Open'
```

In both cases, the result is the same:

| StudentKey | StudentLastName | StudentFirstName | CouseKey | CourseName | RequestDate | RequestStatus |
|---|---|---|---|---|---|---|
| 009001010 | Min | Ly | ITC226 | DatabaseAdministration | 2010-01-05 | Active |

**FIGURE 7-35** Multitable Join Results

Notice, that in the INNER JOIN syntax, you just add another INNER JOIN and ON clauses for each table. In the equi join, you list all the tables in the FROM clause and add an AND clause for each additional relationship.

### Outer Joins

An INNER JOIN returns only related rows from the joined tables. That means if there were a tutor in the tutoring table who had not entered any tutoring session, that tutor would not be returned by an INNER JOIN query with the Session table. Only those tutors who had a related row in the Session table would be returned. An outer join returns all the rows in one table and only the related rows in the second table. There are two kinds of outer joins, a left outer join and a right outer join. The only difference between the two is which table in the join you want to return all the records from. Left is the first table listed and Right is the second table. To find any tutors who were without sessions, you could write a query such as the following:

```
SELECT t.TutorKey,
TutorLastName,
SessionDateKey
FROM Tutor t
LEFT OUTER JOIN Session s
ON t.TutorKey = s.TutorKey
WHERE SessionDateKey IS Null
```

This results is:

| TutorKey | TutorLastName | SessionDateKey |
|---|---|---|
| 980010000 | Roberts | NULL |

**FIGURE 7-36** Outer Join Results

"Roberts" exists in the Tutor table, but has no sessions recorded in the Session table.

Sharon decides to expand her query to include not only the tutor's name but also the student's and course name. Now her query looks like this:

```
SELECT TutorLastName,
TutorFirstName,
c.CourseKey,
CourseName,
SessionDateKey,
SessionTimeKey,
StudentLastName,
StudentFirstName,
SessionStatus
FROM Tutor t
INNER JOIN Session s
ON t.TutorKey = s.TutorKey
INNER JOIN Course c
ON c.CourseKey = s.CourseKey
INNER JOIN Student st
ON st.StudentKey = s.StudentKey
```

The results of this query look like this:

| Tutor LastName | Tutor FirstName | CourseKey | CourseName | Session DateKey | Session TimeKey | Student LastName | Student FirstName | Session Status |
|---|---|---|---|---|---|---|---|---|
| Anderson | Nathan | ITC110 | Beginning Programming | 2009-10-20 | 13:00:00.0000000 | Peterson | Laura | C |
| Brown | Susan | WEB110 | Beginning Web Page Design | 2009-10-20 | 14:00:00.0000000 | Peterson | Laura | C |
| Lewis | Ginger | MAT107 | Applied Math | 2009-11-10 | 13:00:00.0000000 | Nguyen | Lu | C |
| Brown | Susan | WEB110 | Beginning Web Page Design | 2009-11-10 | 14:00:00.0000000 | Peterson | Laura | C |
| Brown | Susan | ITC220 | Introduction to Database | 2009-11-20 | 10:30:00.0000000 | Carter | Shannon | C |
| Foster | Daniel | ITC255 | Systems Analysis | 2010-01-15 | 09:30:00.0000000 | Peterson | Laura | C |
| Lewis | Ginger | ENG211 | Technical Writing | 2010-01-20 | 11:00:00.0000000 | Martinez | Sandy | C |
| Lewis | Ginger | MAT107 | Applied Math | 2010-01-22 | 14:00:00.0000000 | Zukof | Mark | NS |
| Foster | Daniel | ITC255 | Systems Analysis | 2010-02-05 | 10:30:00.0000000 | Peterson | Laura | C |

**FIGURE 7-37** Multiple Join Session, Tutor, and Student

## INSERTS, UPDATES, AND DELETES

Sharon looks back at her list of business rules. She looks particularly at the first three she has listed:

- Students must register for tutoring (a new rule with the database).
- Students must enter current courses.
- Students are encouraged but not required to enter demographic data.

Ultimately, the students will enter this data through a form of some kind, but it will still require inserting statements underneath. Referential integrity requires that data be entered into the Student table before data can be entered into the StudentCourse table. It also requires that the course exists in the course table prior to its being entered in the StudentCourse table. The same holds true of the EthnicityKey. Sharon writes the Student insert statement first.

```
INSERT INTO Student(
StudentKey,
StudentLastName,
StudentFirstName,
StudentEmail,
StudentPhone,
StudentGender,
StudentAge,
StudentCitizen,
StudentWorkerRetraining,
EthnicityKey)
VALUES(
'99001008',
'Steve',
'Norton',
'steve_norton@gmail.com',
'2065554002',
'M',
'32',
1,
0,
'Caucasion')
```

**Things You Should Know**

### INSERT Statements

The basic syntax for an INSERT statement is

```
INSERT INTO <tablename>(<ColumnName>, <columnName>, ...)
VALUES(<value1>, <value2>, ...)
```

You do not have to list all the column names, but you do have to enter all the required columns. The values match the columns in sequence and in data type. If you list a column that is not required and you don't want to put data in it, you can use the NULL keyword.

You must have a separate `INSERT` statement for each row you wish to insert. In a form, the same `INSERT` statement can be used every time by substituting variables for the values in the list, and there are ways to bulk insert or to insert values from another table with a `SELECT` statement instead of a value list, but these are topics for more advanced SQL.

---

When she runs the query, Sharon receives the following result, which indicates that the `INSERT` statement was successful.

```
(1 row(s) affected)
```

Next, Sharon decides she should test whether the `INSERT` statement runs successfully for a second student who is less willing to enter demographic information.

```
INSERT INTO Student(
StudentKey,
StudentLastName,
StudentFirstName,
StudentEmail,
StudentPhone,
StudentGender,
StudentAge,
StudentCitizen,
StudentWorkerRetraining,
EthnicityKey)
VALUES(
'99001009',
'Jill',
'Miller',
'jmiller92@gmail.com',
'2065551103',
'F',
NULL,
NULL,
0,
NULL)
```

This also inserts correctly.

Now it is time to test whether each student can enter what courses they are enrolled in. First, she tries for "Steve Norton." She creates a separate `INSERT` statement for each course Norton is taking.

```
INSERT INTO StudentCourse(StudentKey, CourseKey, Quarter)
Values('99001008', 'ITC220', 'Spring09')
INSERT INTO StudentCourse(StudentKey, CourseKey, Quarter)
Values('99001008', 'ITC110', 'Spring09')
INSERT INTO StudentCourse(StudentKey, CourseKey, Quarter)
Values('99001008', 'ENG211', 'Spring09')
```

She does the same for Jill Miller:

```
INSERT INTO StudentCourse(StudentKey, CourseKey, Quarter)
Values('99001009', 'ITC220', 'Spring09')
INSERT INTO StudentCourse(StudentKey, CourseKey, Quarter)
Values('99001009', 'MAT107', 'Spring09')
```

Sharon looks at the next business rule:

• Students sign up for sessions.

This involves a different action than entering the student information. The tutor will enter the session data, and the students will update it to add their StudentKey information to the row. First, Sharon inserts a new Session.

```
INSERT INTO Session (TutorKey,
CourseKey,
SessionDateKey,
SessionTimeKey,
StudentKey,
```

```
SessionStatus)
VALUES( '980010004',
'ITC220',
'2/10/2010',
'10:00 AM',
NULL,
NULL)
```

Next, she creates the SQL UPDATE statement that would let a student sign up for this session.

```
UPDATE Session
SET StudentKey = '980001009'
WHERE TutorKey = '980010004'
AND CourseKey = 'ITC220'
AND SessionDateKey = '2/10/2010'
AND SessionTimeKey = '10:00'
```

## Things You Should Know

### Updates and Deletes

Updates change existing data, and deletes remove it. Both can act on one or many rows at a time. The basic syntax of an UPDATE statement is

```
UPDATE <TableName>
SET <ColumnName> = <New Value>
WHERE <ColumnName> = <criteria>
```

You can update more than one column at a time by listing the columns you wish to update in the SET clause with their new values. Each value pair is separated from the others by commas.

```
UPDATE Student
SET StudentPhone = '2965557000',
StudentEmail = 'juancarlos23@gmail.com'
WHERE StudentKey = '980001009'
```

The DELETE statement syntax is

```
DELETE FROM <TableName>
WHERE <columnName> = <criteria>
```

For instance, if the tutor Susan Brown needed to delete all her sessions for a day, she could use the following SQL:

```
DELETE FROM Session
WHERE SessionDateKey = '4/10/2009'
AND TutorKey = '980010001'
```

*Caution*

*If you use an UPDATE or a DELETE without a WHERE clause, or if the WHERE clause isn't specific enough, you can change or DELETE all the rows in a table. For instance, the following UPDATE statement*

```
UPDATE Session
SET StudentKey =
'99001008'
```

*would set every session in the entire table to have the StudentKey "snorton." Worse, there is no easy undo. Once an UPDATE is committed, the only way to undo it would be to restore the tables from backup files and the logs. This is a tricky task and usually requires the database be offline while the files are restored. The same danger holds for the DELETE command.*

```
DELETE FROM Session
```

*This DELETE statement without a WHERE clause will delete every row in the Session table. Sometimes referential integrity can save you from this mistake, but in a table like Session that is on the child side of all of its relationships, the command will empty the table.*

## CREATING A TRIGGER

Now Sharon feels ready to try a trigger. She wants to see if she can enforce the rule that no tutor should work more than 60 hours in a month. Sharon has done one or two triggers before, but she is very uncertain about where to start from. She decides to look up triggers in SQL Server's Help files.

## Things You Should Know

### Triggers

Triggers are scripts of SQL code that are triggered by an event. The most common events are on INSERT, UPDATE, or DELETE. These triggers are specific to a given table. A trigger for INSERT into the student table, for instance, will fire every time that an INSERT into that table occurs. Triggers can respond to more than one event at a time. You could, for instance, have a trigger that responds to both the UPDATE and DELETE events.

Triggers are used to enforce business rules that can't be enforced by normal database constraints. In the Tutor database, there is a rule that no tutor can work more than 60 hours in a month. This is impossible to enforce just by referential integrity and constraints. But it can be enforced by a trigger. The rule that a student must be enrolled in a class to sign up for tutoring in that subject would be another candidate for a trigger.

SQL Server supports three kinds of triggers on tables. `FOR` and `AFTER` triggers let the `INSERT`, `UPDATE`, or `DELETE` occur and then run their SQL. `INSTEAD OF` triggers intercept the event and execute their code instead of the `INSERT`, `UPDATE`, or `DELETE`.

The basic syntax for a trigger is

```
CREATE TRIGGER <trigger_name> ON <table_name>
[FOR, AFTER, INSTEAD OF] [INSERT, UPDATE, DELETE]
AS
{SQL Code}
```

Sharon decides to use an INSTEAD OF trigger on `INSERT`. She is not going to let the tutor enter a session if it brings the total hours to more than 60. Sharon knows it is important to list out the logical steps before trying to actually write the trigger. It is easy to get confused if you don't have a clear recipe to follow. She lists these steps:

1. Get the date from the INSERTED table.
2. Extract the month.
3. Create a variable for the total hours.
4. Assign to total the sum of each session for that month (assuming 30 minutes each).
5. Check to see if the sum >60.
6. Check if it is output a message.
7. Otherwise complete the insert into the Session table.

## Things You Should Know

### INSERTED and DELETED Tables

Whenever you insert a record, SQL Server creates an INSERTED table in the Temp database. The table only exists for the duration of the transaction, but within a trigger, you can use this table to access the data that was inserted. Updates and deletes are stored in a DELETED table.

First, Sharon defined the trigger and the internal variables she was going to use.

```
CREATE TRIGGER tr_SessionHours ON [Session]
INSTEAD OF INSERT
AS
DECLARE @month INT
DECLARE @Year INT
DECLARE @tutorID NCHAR(10)
DECLARE @total FLOAT
DECLARE @Maximum INT
```

The `DECLARE` keyword is used to declare internal variables. All variables in SQL Server must start with the "@" symbol. Next, she uses the `SET` keyword to assign a value to the @Maximum variable. The sessions are in minutes, so she multiplies 60 hours by 60 minutes per hour to get 3600.

```
SET @Maximum = 3600
```

Next, she uses `SELECT` statement to assign values from the INSERTED TABLE to the variables @month and @tutorID.

```
SELECT @month = month(SessionDateKey) FROM Inserted
SELECT @Year = Year(SessionDateKey) FROM Inserted
SELECT @tutorID = TutorKey FROM Inserted
```

Now that she has these values, Sharon writes the equation to test the number of total hours. She counts the sessions and multiplies by 30 minutes, then she adds 30 for the session being inserted. In the **WHERE** clause, she makes sure that the count is only for the month, year, and tutor in question.

```
SELECT @Total = (Count(*) * 30) + 30 FROM Session
WHERE TutorKey = @tutorID
AND Month(SessionDateKey) = @Month
AND Year(SessionDateKey) = @Year
```

Finally, she tests the @total to see if it is less than @Maximum. If it is not, she performs the insert that the trigger aborted. She uses a **SELECT** to fill in the values for the **INSERT**.

```
IF @total <= @Maximum
BEGIN
INSERT INTO Session(SessionDateKey, SessionTimeKey, TutorKey, CourseKey)
(SELECT SessionDateKey, SessionTimeKey, TutorKey, CourseKey FROM Inserted)
END
ELSE
BEGIN
Print 'Too many hours for this month'
END
```

Here is the whole trigger:

```
CREATE TRIGGER tr_SessionHours ON [Session]
INSTEAD OF INSERT
AS
DECLARE @month INT
DECLARE @Year INT
DECLARE @tutorID NCHAR(10)
DECLARE @total FLOAT
DECLARE @Maximum INT
SET @Maximum = 3600
SELECT @month = month(SessionDateKey) FROM Inserted
SELECT @Year = Year(SessionDateKey) FROM Inserted
SELECT @tutorID = TutorKey FROM Inserted
SELECT @Total = (Count(*) * 30) + 30 FROM Session
WHERE TutorKey = @tutorID
AND Month(SessionDateKey) = @Month
AND Year(SessionDateKey) = @Year
IF @total <= @Maximum
BEGIN
INSERT INTO Session(SessionDateKey, SessionTimeKey, TutorKey, CourseKey)
(SELECT SessionDateKey, SessionTimeKey, TutorKey, CourseKey FROM Inserted)
END
ELSE
BEGIN
Print 'Too many hours for this month'
END
```

To test this, Sharon must insert enough session data to get one of the tutors up to 3,600 minutes, then add one more session. She does this and sees the message in the Query window.

## DOCUMENTATION

Testing a database is critical to its success. You should thoroughly test every database before committing real data to it. And, as with everything else, it is essential to document your testing. Before you begin, you should develop a testing plan. The plan should consist of each business rule or requirement you need to test. It should explain how you intend to test it and what the expected outcome should be.

Next, you should conduct each test and record its results. If the result of the test is different than the expected result, you should determine where the error lies, either in the test or in the database. After correcting the error, you should run the test again to make sure the results conform to expectations. Here is a fragment of the testing plan for the Tutor Management database:

| Table 7-5 | Testing Plan and Tests | | |
|---|---|---|---|
| **Rule to Test** | **Means of Testing** | **Expected Result** | **Result** |
| Return all students by Gender | `SELECT StudentLastName, StudentFirstName, StudentGender`<br>`FROM Student`<br>`WHERE StudentGender = 'M'` | Return all male students | Returns all male students |
| Return unduplicated count of students from tutoring sessions | `SELECT Count(StudentID) FROM Session`<br><br>`SELECT Count(DISTINCT StudentID) FROM Session` | Return unduplicated students from session | Returns duplicated students<br><br>Returns unduplicated student Count |
| Return hours for student per month | `SELECT Tutorkey,`<br>`   MONTH(SessionDateKey) AS [Month],`<br>`   YEAR(SessionDateKey) AS [Year],`<br>`   ((COUNT (SessionTimeKey)) * 30.0)/60.0`<br>`AS [Hours]`<br>`FROM Session`<br>`GROUP BY TutorKey, MONTH(SessionDateKey),`<br>`YEAR(SessionDateKey)`<br>`ORDER BY YEAR(SessionDateKey),`<br>`MONTH(SessionDateKey)` | Hours grouped by student and month | Returns hours grouped by student and month |

## Things We Have Done

*In this chapter we have*

- looked at business requirements using SQL
- selected data from the table using various criteria
- joined tables in the database for queries
- performed an outer join
- inserted data
- updated data

### SQL KEYWORDS

Following is a table of the SQL terms used in this chapter. The descriptions do not contain all the uses of the term in SQL, only the ones relevant to the examples are presented.

| Table 7-6 | SQL Keywords |
|---|---|
| **Key Word** | **Description** |
| AND | Boolean argument used in SQL criteria for the result to be counted both conditions must be true. |
| AS | Prefaces an alias for a column. |
| BETWEEN | Used in criteria with **AND**. |
| DELETE | Removes a row or rows from a database table. |
| DESC | Reverses the order of a Sort on a specific column in an **ORDER BY** clause. |
| DISTINCT | Returns only unique rows when used with **SELECT**. When used with an aggregate function, it applies function only to unique values. |
| FROM | Precedes the table name in a **SELECT** clause. |
| GROUP BY | Groups rows in a query that contain one or more aggregate functions by columns not contained in those functions. |
| HAVING | Used for query criteria that contain aggregate functions. |
| INNER JOIN | Joins two tables returning only matching records. |
| INSERT | Used to add rows to a table. |
| INTO | Precedes the table name in an INSERT statement. |
| IS NULL | Used in a query criteria to find NULL values (rather than = NULL). |
| LIKE | Used in query criteria with wildcards % _ to search for patterns in character based columns. |

*(continued)*

| Key Word | Description |
|---|---|
| NOT | Boolean argument used to exclude an option. |
| ON | Used with INNER JOIN, introduces the clause that specifies how two tables are related. |
| OR | Boolean argument used in criteria to specify an alternative value. Only one side of the OR clause must be true for the expression to be true. |
| ORDER BY | Sorts a result set by a value or a set of values. When there is more than one sort criteria listed, the primary sort is on the leftmost value, the secondary sort on the next value, etc. |
| OUTER LEFT JOIN | A join that returns all the rows in the first table listed (left) and only matching records in the second (right) table. Good for finding unmatched data such as a tutor who has no tutoring sessions or a customer who has no purchases. |
| SELECT | The first word of all queries that return data from the database. |
| SET | In an UPDATE statement used to set the initial value to be modified, additional values just have the column name = new value and are separated by commas. |
| UPDATE | First word of a command to modify existing data in a table. |
| VALUES | In an INSERT statement, this word prefaces the list of values to insert into the table. |
| WHERE | In a SELECT statement, this word introduces the criteria by which to select which rows to return. |

## Vocabulary

Match the definitions to the vocabulary words:

1. Aggregate function
2. Alias
3. Cross join
4. DDL
5. Declarative language
6. DML
7. Equi Joins
8. Procedural language
9. Qualified name
10. Scalar function
11. SQL
12. Transact SQL

— a. Data Manipulation Language
— b. A function that operates on a single row at a time
— c. A substitute name for a column or table
— d. Programming language that defines how to accomplish a task
— e. A join that uses the WHERE clause and the equal sign to specify relationships
— f. The language of RDBMS
— g. Data Definition Language
— h. A function that operates on multiple rows at a time
— i. A database name that shows a hierarchy of ownership with dot notation
— j. Microsoft SQL Server's brand of SQL
— k. A programming language in which a programmer defines what to do, not how to do
— l. A join in which each row of the first table is joined with every row in a second table

## Things to Look Up

1. Look up ANSI and ISO. Explain briefly what each is and does.
2. How many ANSI standards have been set for SQL?
3. What is the most recent ANSI standard, and what does it add to the previous SQL standards?
4. Look up a good online tutorial for SQL. What is the URL?

## Practices

Use the Pizza database created in the last chapter's practices, and write SQL to answer these questions:

1. List all last names, phone numbers, and zip of the customers
2. List only those from Zip code 98002.
3. List all the customers that have no first address entered in the database.
4. List all the products that are priced higher than $10.
5. List all the products priced between $5 and $7.
6. List all the customers whose last name starts with L.
7. What is the average price of a product?
8. What is the highest price of a product?
9. What is the total due for order 1003?
10. Join the product and the OrderDetail table so that the result contains the product name, product unit size, and product unit price as well as the charged price. Do it for order 1000.
11. List all the order and order details for each order made by the customer with the phone number 2065556623.
12. Change the price of breadsticks to 3.00.
13. Process a pizza order for a new customer (this will involve 3 INSERT statements).

# Scenarios

## WILD WOOD APARTMENTS

Now that the basic database is in place, the Wild Wood Apartments managers are eager to see the database in action and see if it meets all their needs and requirements. It is time to look at the business rules and test them with some SQL. Look at the business rules you developed previously, and design some SQL queries to test them. **Documentation**: Set up a test plan. List the rule, the SQL you wrote, and the results. Also note whether the database passes or fails the test. Your queries should include the following:

1. Two or three simple SELECTs with various WHERE criteria
2. Two or three queries using aggregate functions
3. At least two queries that use joins
4. Two or three INSERT statements
5. One or two UPDATEs and/or a DELETE

## VINCE'S VINYL

It is time to test Vince's database to see if it truly meets his needs. It is time to look back at the business rules and test them with some SQL. Look at the business rules you developed previously, and design some SQL queries to test them. **Documentation**: Set up a test plan. List the rule, the SQL you wrote, and the results. Also note whether the database passes or fails the test. Your queries should include the following:

1. Two or three simple SELECTs with various WHERE criteria
2. Two or three queries using aggregate functions
3. At least two queries that use joins
4. Two or three INSERT statements
5. One or two UPDATEs and/or a DELETE

## GRANDFIELD COLLEGE

The college is feeling pressurized to get the new system in place. There could be an inspection of their IT services any time now, and they want to be ready. It is time to look at the business rules and test them with some SQL. **Documentation**: Set up a test plan. Look at the business rules you developed previously, and design some SQL queries to test them. List the rule, the SQL you wrote, and the results. Also note whether the database passes or fails the test. Your queries should include the following:

1. Two or three simple SELECTs with various WHERE criteria
2. Two or three queries using aggregate functions

3. At least two queries that use joins
4. Two or three INSERT statements
5. One or two UPDATEs and/or a DELETE

## WESTLAKE RESEARCH HOSPITAL

The research program is almost ready to begin. Westlake is in the process of interviewing potential patients and doctors. It is important that the database be ready soon. It is also important that it does what it is supposed to do. It is time to look at the business rules and test them with some SQL. Look at the business rules you developed previously, and design some SQL queries to test them. **Documentation**: Set up a test plan. List the rule, the SQL you wrote, and the results. Also note whether the database passes or fails the test. Your queries should include the following:

1. Two or three simple SELECTs with various WHERE criteria
2. Two or three queries using aggregate functions
3. At least two queries that use joins
4. Two or three INSERT statements
5. One or two UPDATEs and/or a DELETE

## SUGGESTION FOR SCENARIOS

Review your business rules. Many are probably simple to test, requiring only SELECT statements. Others may be harder. Try the simple ones first.

You may also find that you need to adjust your sample data. It may be necessary to insert some data that shows a violation of a rule, or you may need to insert data in order to compare different dates or times.

Most SQL mistakes are syntax errors. Missing commas or extra commas are common suspects. The error messages in the query analyzer do not always pinpoint the exact error. If you double click the error message, it will place your cursor in the vicinity of the error. Look all around the region. A missing comma above or a misspelled word may be causing an error later in the code.

Another common error with joins is the ambiguous column. This usually involves a key column that occurs in other tables as a foreign key. Since it occurs in more than one table, SQL Server cannot determine which table it is from. These columns should always be qualified with the table name or table alias.

# Is It Secure?

In this chapter, Sharon looks at the security needs of the database. It is important to give everyone the access that they require to do the things they need to do. But it is also important to protect the database objects and data from either accidental or intentional damage. Sharon discovers that security is a complex issue and requires careful planning.

## CHAPTER OUTCOMES

**By the end of this chapter you will be able to:**

- Analyze security needs and restrictions for users of the database
- Analyze threats to database integrity
- Understand the concepts of authentication and authorization
- Create logins and users
- Create roles

## THE ISSUE

Sharon has set up a meeting with Terry to show her the queries she has written and to discuss the next steps in the process. Terry is impressed but a little worried. "How will tutors and students access the database?"

"We will create an application, either with Windows or on the Web that they can use to access the data. They won't have direct access to the database, of course."

"Yes, I know that, and I have talked with several people and we have agreed that we would prefer a Web application. It would be nice if students could register for sessions from anywhere. What I really mean though is how do you differentiate between a tutor and student? How do you keep a student from acting as a tutor, if you know what I mean?"

Sharon thinks for a minute. "I do know what you mean. They would have different logins, I think, with different permissions. And, if it is on the Web, that means anyone can potentially access the site. Security will be important."

Sharon pauses, "Security is a weak point in my knowledge. I think I will have to make an appointment with Professor Collins. I will let you know what results from that."

"Thanks, I do think the security will be critical."

## WHERE TO START

Professor Collins agrees to meet with her. Sharon explains briefly that what she needs is a way to approach securing the database and that she doesn't really understand the process.

He nods, "It's understandable. Security is always something we get to at the end of our database design classes or not at all, but it is crucial for a database that is actually going to be put in production and used by hundreds of users. It's not easy. Perhaps the best place to begin is to think of security in the context of two terms: 'Authentication' and 'Authorization'. Authentication is about verifying the credentials of a potential user. Are they

*AUTHORIZATION*

*AUTHORIZATION*

This is granting the authenticated user permissions on database objects.

*AUTHENTICATION*

The process of determining the user is, in fact, who he or she claims to be.

who they say they are? Are they legitimate users? Usually this is done by matching a username and a password. But it can be done in other ways too, such as by using a certificate or biometric authentication tools such as fingerprint readers. Authorization is about assigning permissions to users. Once users have been authenticated, they can be assigned permission to access a certain database and certain database objects. If they fail to authenticate, then they should have no permissions on anything, of course."

### Things You Should Know

All database management systems have ways to authenticate users and then authorize them to do what they need to do within particular databases. How they set it up and the levels of "granularity"—that is, how finely detailed the permission structure is—vary a great deal. Most database management systems use a combination of server logins mapped to database users. Most have ways of assigning roles or group permissions. Because this book is using SQL Server Express, we will look at how it handles authentication and authorization.

#### Authentication in SQL Server

Authentication is the process of verifying if a user is who he or she claims to be. With SQL Server, this authentication can be done in a variety of ways. The default method of authorization is "Windows authentication." In this method, SQL Server lets Windows authenticate the user, then that Window's account is mapped to an SQL Server login.

In SQL Server, a login is a server-level account. By itself, a login only allows a connection to the server. It doesn't contain any other permissions. A database administrator can assign additional permissions, such as the ability to back up a database, but in itself, it doesn't even have any permission to access databases on the server.

### THINGS TO THINK ABOUT

*Why do you think SQL Server uses a two-step process: first, a login to the server, and then a mapping of that login to a user account? Do you think it makes things more or less secure?*

Using Windows authentication works well on network where every user has a Windows or an active directory account but doesn't work in a mixed environment or when users, who require different permissions, are accessing the database from the Internet. For these situations, SQL Server provides SQL Server logins. These logins require a user to enter a user name and a password.

A third method is to use a certificate. A certificate can be purchased from various companies and institutions. It functions as an identifier saying this request is coming from a known source. The database administrator can map the certificate to a login.

For a login to have access to a database, it must be mapped to a specific database user. Database permissions are then assigned to the user.

*PERMISSION*

An action granted to a user.

#### Authorization in SQL Server

Authorization is the process of assigning permissions to access database objects to an authenticated login or user. Permissions differ with different objects. A user of a table, for instance, can be granted permission to `SELECT` data from that table, `UPDATE`, `INSERT`, or `DELETE`. He or she could also be granted the permission to `ALTER` or `DROP` the table. A user of a stored procedure must be granted the `EXEC` (execute) permission and could also be granted the `ALTER` or `DROP` permissions. Authorization is the set of permissions that a particular user is "authorized" to do in the database.

It is important to note that in SQL Server, users do not have any permission that is not explicitly granted them. You cannot assume, for instance, that because someone has permission to `UPDATE` a table that they also have permission to `SELECT` data from that table. Each permission is distinct and must be specifically granted.

Sharon listens carefully and then asks, "How do you set it up so that one user can do one set of things in the database, and another user can do a different set of things? For example, a tutor can set up his or her schedule. A student should be able to see the schedule but not add to it or change it, except to sign up for a session."

"Different logins can be assigned to different sets of permissions. You could do this user by user, but I would suggest creating roles, a student role, a tutor role, and so on, and assigning users to those roles. The role can contain all the permissions. Doing it user by user is too hard to maintain."

## Things You Should Know

### Roles

Roles are collections of permissions. Rather than assign the same set of permissions multiple times to multiple users, you can create a role. Then you can make individual users members of that role. As members, they inherit all the permissions associated with the role. This greatly simplifies managing permissions.

*ROLE*

It is a collection of related permissions.

### THINGS TO THINK ABOUT

*In what situations does it make more sense to use roles to control permissions? Can you think of a situation where it makes more sense to just assign permissions to individual users?*

A user can belong to more than one role. If there is a conflict in permissions between roles, SQL Server always applies the more restrictive permission. So, for instance, if you assigned a user to db_denydatawriter, but also assigned the user to a role that permits updating a table, the user would unable to update the table. The db_denydatawriter would override the other role.

SQL Server has several built-in database roles that can be used where appropriate.

**Table 8-1** Database Roles

| Database Role | Description |
|---|---|
| db_accessadmin | Can **ALTER** any user and create schema. |
| db_backupoperator | Grants the user permission to back up and restore the particular database. |
| db_datareader | Grants the user **SELECT** permission on all tables and views in the database. |
| db_datawriter | Grants the user **INSERT**, **UPDATE**, and **DELETE** permissions on all tables and views. |
| db_ddladmin | Grants the ability to **CREATE** or **ALTER** any database object. |
| db_denydatareader | Denies **SELECT** on all tables and views. |
| db_denydatawriter | Denies **INSERT**,**UPDATE**, and **DELETE** on all tables and views. |
| db_owner | Grants ownership and full permissions on all database objects. |
| db_securityadmin | Grants the ability to **ALTER** roles and **CREATE** schema. |
| public | Grants access to database but by default has no permissions on any objects. Every user is a member of public as well as any other roles. The public role cannot be removed. |

### Schema

*Schema* is a bit of an overused word in the database world. On one hand, schema refers to the meta-information about database objects. For instance, the schema of a table consists of the column names, data types, and constraints of the table. Schema also refers to a type of XML file that describes the structure of another XML file. Another use of the word involves object ownership in a database. In Oracle, for instance, an objects schema is tied to the user who created it. If a user were logged in under a Login "HR," the table would belong to the schema "HR."

In SQL Server, schemas have been cut free from logins and user names. Everything has a schema. Every database object must be owned by someone. The default schema in SQL Server is

*SCHEMA*

Object ownership in a database.

"dbo," which stands for "database owner." You can create schema that are independent of a given user and then create sets of objects that belong to that schema. Users can then be assigned to the schema and given access to those objects. A user who is a member of a schema can be limited to accessing only the objects in that schema.

In practice, SQL Server schemas behave a lot like roles. You can use them to accomplish the same tasks. There is a subtle, but important, difference, however. A role is a collection of permissions; a schema is a collection of objects owned by a schema. A student schema, for instance, would own any stored procedures or views (see the following section) needed for student access to the database. A student user would be assigned to the schema and then granted permissions on the schema objects. To make matters more complex, a role can assign permissions to a schema, and a schema can own roles. For more information on schemas, you can go to Microsoft Help at http://msdn.microsoft.com/en-us/library/ms190387.aspx.

---

Sharon continues, "Do I really want each student to have an individual login?"

"It is possible, especially if you can automate getting the student information. But it might be better to have the application map all students to a single more generic or group login. You could create a stored procedure to capture their IDs and use it to limit their access to only their own data."

"So where do I start?"

Bill thinks for a moment. "I believe first I would look at all the tables from the point of view of each user. What permissions do they need to do the things they must do?"

Sharon remembers, "I wrote down some of those things when I was planning the database."

"Good. Next, after looking at the permissions that are required, I would try to analyze the threats. What could go wrong, both by accident and by intention. It is important to remember that threats are not only things that delete data or damage objects. Bad data are a threat. If you can't trust the data in the database, it is essentially useless. Maintaining data integrity is about making sure you have good data properly organized and related. Finally, I would design a strategy for providing the access that is needed while minimizing any threats. I suspect that could mean designing roles and maybe a set of stored procedures and views, but we can look at that later. Do you feel you have enough to start?"

Sharon nods hesitantly. "Yes, I think so. Thanks."

## ANALYZING SECURITY NEEDS

First, she thinks about authentication. Terry should have her own login, of course, as program administrator. Tutors could each have an individual login, or they should be mapped to a group. A group would be easier to administer. Students should definitely have a group login.

Back at her apartment, Sharon sits down to begin analyzing the security for the tutor database. The first thing she does is review her early notes. Back when she was working on the rules for the database, she had outlined some of the requirements for Terry.

- The database administrator should have select access to all the data. That means he or she can view all the data in the tables.
- The database administrator needs to be able to add, edit, and remove records for tutors and courses.
- The database administrator should be able to create queries as needed.
- The database administrator should not be able to create or remove tables or other database objects.

As Sharon looks at this, she realizes she should change the name of the role. It shouldn't be "Database Administrator," but rather "Program Administrator." The "Database Administrator" will be someone other than Terry, who will have responsibility to maintain the database and its objects and who can add, alter, or drop objects as needed. Nobody else would have those permissions.

**THINGS TO THINK ABOUT**

A true database administrator has all rights and permissions on a database. How many people should be given full database administrator rights over a database? What are the drawbacks of having just one administrator? What are the drawbacks of having several?

So, given her earlier notes, Sharon creates a table of the permissions required for the program administrator:

| Table 8-2 Program Administrator Permissions | | | | | |
| --- | --- | --- | --- | --- | --- |
| Table name | SELECT | INSERT | UPDATE | DELETE | Constraints |
| Student | X | X | X | X | |
| Tutor | X | X | X | X | |
| Course | X | X | X | X | |
| StudentCourse | X | X | X | X | |
| Ethnicity | X | X | X | X | |
| Session | X | X | X | X | |
| Request | X | X | X | X | |
| RequestNote | X | X | X | X | |

The program administrator would have total control over the data. Sharon is not entirely sure of this, but it seems the best solution. Students, for the most part, will enter their own information. Requests too should come from students. Sessions are set up by the tutors and then signed up for by students. But Sharon can easily imagine Terry being requested to enter a tutor's schedule for them, or a student's information. She decides to leave it this way for now but makes a note to revisit it.

Next she looks at the tutors. Previously, she had made these notes:

- A tutor needs to be able to enter and edit his or her own schedules but no one else's.
- A tutor needs to be able to enter a session report.
- A tutor needs to be able to cancel one of his or her own sessions, but no one else's.
- A tutor should not be able to see student information.

| Table 8-3 Tutor Permissions | | | | | |
| --- | --- | --- | --- | --- | --- |
| Table name | SELECT | INSERT | UPDATE | DELETE | Constraints |
| Student | | | | | |
| Tutor | X | | | | A public subset of tutor info |
| Course | X | | | | |
| StudentCourse | | | | | |
| Ethnicity | | | | | |
| Session | X | X* | X* | | *Only for own sessions |
| Request | X | | | | |
| RequestNote | X | | | | |

These permissions assume that the tutor's information will be entered by the program administrator. Tutors can select courses to see what is being offered. They can also look at what is requested. Their main area of permissions though is the Session. They can insert into the sessions table and update sessions, but only their own sessions. They should not be able to update other tutors' sessions. Canceling a session means changing its status, not deleting it from the table.

She reviews her notes for students:

- A student must be able to view all available sessions.
- A student must be able to enter his or her own demographic information.
- A student must be able to enter the courses in which he or she is currently enrolled.
- A student should be able to cancel one of his or her own sessions, but no one else's.

| Table 8-4 | Student Permissions | | | | |
|-----------|--------|--------|--------|--------|-------------|
| Table name | SELECT | INSERT | UPDATE | DELETE | Constraints |
| Student | X | X | X | | Only their own records |
| Tutor | X | | | | A public subset of tutor info |
| Course | X | | | | |
| StudentCourse | X | X | X | X | Only their own records |
| Ethnicity | | | | | |
| Session | X | | X* | | *Only for empty sessions in courses in which they are enrolled |
| Request | X | X | | | |
| RequestNote | X | | | | |

Students need to enter, edit, and view their own data in the database, but they should not be able to view other students' data. This includes entering and editing what courses they are taking. Sharon includes the ability to delete a course since students often drop courses. They need to update sessions in order to sign up for tutoring but should only be able to do it for courses in which they are enrolled. They also need the ability to enter and view requests.

There is one final set of users she must consider. These are people who are just viewing the site. They may be students who have not registered for tutoring yet, or they may be people interested in becoming tutors, or they may be simply curious about the school's tutoring program. The usual name for this role, she realizes, is "public."

| Table 8-5 | Public Permissions | | | | |
|-----------|--------|--------|--------|--------|-------------|
| Table name | SELECT | INSERT | UPDATE | DELETE | Constraints |
| Student | | | | | |
| Tutor | X | | | | A public subset of tutor information |
| Course | X | | | | |
| StudentCourse | | | | | |
| Ethnicity | | | | | |
| Session | X | | | | |
| Request | X | | | | |
| RequestNote | X | | | | |

The public should have SELECT permissions on basic, nonprivate data, but nothing else.

# THREATS

Professor Collins had said that after analyzing permissions, Sharon should look at possible threats. He had also said that threats could be either accidental or intentional. Sharon decides that the best way to consider threats is to once again look at them in terms of each user.

## Things You Should Know

### Threat Analysis

Threat analysis involves identifying all the ways a program or system can be harmed and then identifying strategies for mitigating that threat. Usually threat analysis focuses on intentional attacks. With a database, for instance, an attacker could attempt to insert bad data, change existing data, delete data, add or drop database objects, or even attempt to drop the database itself. Through the network, an attacker could attempt to compromise the database files themselves. Viruses and malware are constant threats. A database administrator needs to keep up with all patches and updates as well as maintain antivirus and antimalware programs.

The database can also be damaged by accidental actions. An UPDATE statement without the proper criteria, for instance, could change more data than the user intended.

Identifying threats is a complex and ongoing task. The nature and number of threats constantly changing. Vigilance and a touch of paranoia are necessary attributes of any database or systems administrator.

### Disaster Recovery

Disaster recovery consists in planning for the worst. What happens if a hacker manages to compromise the data? Or what happens if the hard disk holding the database dies? What happens if the building is destroyed in a fire or an earthquake? When thinking about these and other disasters, you also have to determine the answers to other questions such as the following: How much data can the business afford to lose? How long can the business afford for the database to be off-line?

The answers to these questions vary, depending on the business. Some business can afford to lose a day's data; others can't afford to lose any data at all. Some can afford to be off-line for a period of a time; others cannot afford any down time.

A disaster recovery plan is a set of policies and procedures designed to mitigate the damage of a disaster. Policies are rules about how to do things. Procedures are step-by-step instructions for implementing a policy or completing a task. Typically, it includes policies of creating and storing backups, log shipping, and failover. Log shipping involves periodically shipping a copy of the transaction log from one server to another. Failover involves transferring the data connection from one server to a second server in the case of a database or server failure.

For a small company, with a single database and server, the policies and procedures could look something like the following ones:

*POLICY*

Rules for how to do things.

*PROCEDURES*

Step-by-step instructions for accomplishing a task.

*DISASTER RECOVERY PLAN*

A plan for how to recover data and its availability after various possible disasters.

#### Policies

The database server machine will have at least two separate physical drives.

Log files will be stored on a separate drive from the database files.

Backups of the database and the log files will be done twice daily.

Drives will be stored off-site in a secure site.

Each drive will be stored 24 hours or longer before reuse.

Each drive will be labeled with the backup date.

#### Backup Procedure

1. We will maintain four portable hard drives.
2. Each morning retrieve the two drives with the oldest backup date.
3. Perform a full database backup to one of the drives at 11:00 AM.
4. Backup the log files to the hard drive.
5. Record the current date and time of the backup on the hard disk.
6. Send an employee to deposit the hard drive in a safety deposit box at Westlake Security Co.
7. At closing, around 5:00 PM, do a full backup to the second hard disk.

8. Back up the log files to the hard disk.
9. Record the date and time on the hard disk.
10. Send an employee to deposit the hard drive in a safety deposit box at Westlake Security Co. (Westlake is open until 7:00 PM.)
11. If Westlake is closed, the employee is to take the disk home and deposit it when he or she picks up the drives the next workday.

### Recovery Procedure

1. Rebuild the computer as necessary.
2. Retrieve the hard disk with the most recent backup date.
3. Restore the database from backup.
4. Restore remaining transactions from the most recent logs.
5. Attempt to recover any lost data by reviewing paper receipts and invoices.
6. When the database is rebuilt, begin the backup procedure.

When she looks at the permissions tables, Sharon is surprised to realize that the most dangerous user, aside from the database administrator who can do anything, is surely the program administrator. Because the administrator has complete UPDATE and DELETE permissions, he or she could accidently delete records that should not be deleted or create updates that change records that should not be changed. The administrator could also do the most damage intentionally, though Sharon considers it unlikely that a program administrator would maliciously attack the database.

Once again Sharon makes a table, this time to list the threats.

**Table 8-6** Program Administrator Threats

| Role | Program Administrator |
|---|---|
| **Threat** | **Description** |
| SELECT | – |
| INSERT | Data entry mistakes can make the data and the reports based on the data unreliable and inaccurate |
| UPDATE | Updating more records than intended by overly broad or missing WHERE criteria; bad data in the update |
| DELETE | Accidental deletion of records |

Next, Sharon considers the tutor role. The primary area of concern with tutors is the Session table. Tutors will have permission to insert and update this table. She could imagine a tutor trying to get access to private student information. She can also imagine a tutor trying to falsify the tutoring schedule by adding student IDs to open sessions to look like they were filled when they weren't. The policy that says that a tutor's sessions can be reduced or eliminated if the tutor's services are not used provides sufficient motivation for such activities. It is also possible that a tutor whose hours have been reduced or eliminated could attempt to attack the database by changing other tutor's schedules or entering false schedules.

**Table 8-7** Tutor Threats

| Role | Tutor |
|---|---|
| **Threat** | **Description** |
| SELECT | Select private student information |
| INSERT | Accidental or malicious schedule entry |
| UPDATE | Accidental or malicious changes to one's own or other's schedule |
| DELETE | – |

Students will be able to enter their own information. There is always the chance of false or malicious entry there. They will also enter what classes they are taking that quarter. This also could be falsified and hard to verify for every student. There are dangers that a student could view another student's data. It would not be too difficult for one student to get another student's ID number. This also applies to the Session table, where a student can register for a session by entering his or her ID. A student could enter some other student's ID as a joke or a way to get back at a tutor.

**Table 8-8**   Student Threats

| Role | Student |
| --- | --- |
| **Threat** | **Description** |
| SELECT | See private information of other students |
| INSERT | False or inaccurate information in Student table |
| UPDATE | False or inaccurate information in the Session table, removing other students from scheduled sessions |
| DELETE | |

The public should only be able to view a few pieces of the database. They should be able to see what courses are listed and view the Session table. They should not be able to insert or update anything in those tables. The public will have only limited Select permissions. It is possible, if the permissions are not set up properly, that some public member could select more than they are allowed to. They might, for instance, find a way to view sensitive student data. The more likely threat is that some members would try to gain additional permissions, perhaps by attempting to impersonate someone assigned to a different role, as a student or a tutor, or even as the program or database administrators. As a member of the public role, they present little threat:

**Table 8-9**   Public Threats

| Role | Public |
| --- | --- |
| **Threat** | **Description** |
| SELECT | See private information of students, false login |
| INSERT | – |
| UPDATE | – |
| DELETE | – |

As an impersonator, a user would inherit all the potential threats of whatever role he or she managed to impersonate. Sharon realizes that authentication process will be crucial to protecting the database.

Sharon sits and thinks for a long while, trying to imagine other threats. The database could be attracted on the network level, she realizes. Someone could delete or corrupt the files themselves. She would have to talk to the network people to see how they would secure the physical files. There were also a whole set of threats that are not directly related to the users of the database. She makes a list of some of them:

- The software could fail—database could become corrupt and unusable.
- The hardware could fail—the hard disk could crash.
- There could be fire or some kind of disaster on campus that would damage the server.
- A hacker might gain access and destroy database objects or data integrity.

## FINDING SOLUTIONS

Sharon schedules another meeting with Professor Collins. She presents her assessment of permissions and threats so far. Professor Collins is impressed. "That is a good assessment, overall."

"The question I have," says Sharon, "is what do I do next? How do I handle the permissions and threats?"

"Let's start with authentication. I admit it is a bit complicated for this database. You could create a separate login for each tutor and student and then assign them to their roles. That approach has several problems, though. It is hard to maintain. You would have to manage hundreds of logins and keep them up to date. Both students and tutors come and go with some frequency."

"Even if you assign a student to a role, how do you keep them from seeing other students' information?"

"Yes, that is a problem, but it does bring up a possible solution. In your application, you have a general student login and a tutor login. When they login, they are instantly directed to a stored procedure which retrieves their student or tutor ID. Then you can use this ID as a parameter for other stored procedures which restrict what the individual user can do."

"What happens if someone doesn't have an ID?"

"Then your application would either tell them they have no permissions or direct them to a form where they could register."

"It sounds like most of the security lies in the application then. You have to make sure that things happen in the right order."

"That's true to some extent. One overall strategy is to create an access layer in the database that consists of stored procedures and views. This layer controls all access to the underlying data."

"Could you show me how to do the login procedures for a student?"

"Sure. Let's open up the Query window."

Professor Collins opens the management studio and starts a New Query window. "The first thing we are going to do is create the student login. This will be an SQL Server login. It is important to check that the server is set up to accept mixed logins. You can right click on the properties of the server and then click on 'Security' in the dialog's Object window. If it says 'SQL Server and Windows Authentication Mode,' you are set to go. If not, you will need to change the mode. Click OK, and then restart the server for the changes to take place. You can do that by right clicking on the server again and choosing 'Restart' from the menu."

"So first we make sure we are in master. Logins are stored in the master database. You can do this with the graphical interface, but I pefer to use just SQL. It is more efficient."

```
USE master
GO
```

Sharon asks "What is the 'GO?' I don't recognize it."

"The 'GO' is unique to SQL Server. It means, basically, finish this command completely before moving on to the next. Now we will create the student login."

```
CREATE LOGIN StudentLogIn WITH PASSWORD='p@ssw0rd1',
DEFAULT_DATABASE=TutorManagement
GO
```

"Now we will switch to the Tutor database and create a student role. A role is basically a set of permissions on database objects. Right now the role has no permissions."

```
USE TutorManagement
Go
CREATE ROLE StudentRole
GO
```

---

*STORED PROCEDURES*

One or more SQL statements grouped to be executed together.

*Caution*

*When you change the server to mixed mode so that it processes both Windows and SQL Server accounts, you expose a built-in system administrator's account called "sa." Because "sa" is built into the server, it is a common target for hackers to attack. In SQL Server 2008, the account is disabled by default. You should only enable it if you have to for some application. If you do enable it, make sure you give it a strong password.*

**FIGURE 8-1** SQL Server Authentication Options

"Now we are going to create the actual procedure. To do that, we give the procedure a name. I usually prefix them with 'usp' to signify that it is a 'user stored procedure' rather than a system stored procedure which usually begins with 'sp.' After the name, you list all the parameters for the procedure. Parameters are values the user must enter when they execute the procedure. In our case, I think we will just need the StudentKey. After the parameters, the 'AS' keyword signals the start of the content of the procedure. The first thing we are going to do is see if a record exists for the user in the student table. The BEGIN and END keywords mark the beginning and ending of the true block. If it does, it will return the student's last name. If it doesn't exist, we won't do anything. The application can test to see whether the name is returned. If it is not, the user can be directed to a registration form."

```
CREATE PROCEDURE usp_StudentLogIn
@studentKey nchar(10)
AS
IF EXISTS
 (SELECT *
 FROM student
 WHERE studentKey=@studentKey)
BEGIN
SELECT studentLastName
FROM Student
WHERE Studentkey=@studentKey
END
```

## Things You Should Know

### Stored Procedures

Most database management systems support stored procedures. SQL Server provides Transact SQL for procedures, and Oracle provides Procedural SQL or PSQL. MySql 5.0 and better allow the users to create procedures if they choose the InnetDB file system. Microsoft Access does not support stored procedures although it does allow parameterized queries. The syntax for creating and modifying stored procedures varies with the platform.

Stored procedures consist of one or more SQL commands. They allow all the commands to be executed as a unit. So if you have to insert into several tables in sequence, for instance, you can encapsulate all the insert commands into a single stored procedure and guarantee that they are run in the correct order.

Stored procedures can accept parameters, values that are passed to the procedure by the user. In the preceding example, for instance, all the values to be inserted into the tables can be passed to the procedure as parameters. Internal variables can be declared with the `DECLARE` keyword. In SQL Server, all parameters and variables start with the @ symbol.

Stored procedures also allow some of the features of procedural programming languages such as C# or JAVA. You can add branching with IF statements and looping structures using `WHILE`. You can also add error checking and transactions. (See the following discussion with Professor Collins.)

"Now that we have an object, we will assign execute permission on the object to the Student role."

```
GO
GRANT EXEC ON usp_StudentLogIn TO StudentRole
GO
```

"Now we are going to create a database user based on our login."

```
CREATE USER StudentUser FOR LOGIN StudentLogin
```

"Finally, I am going to use one of the system-stored procedures to add the user to the Student role."

```
EXEC sys.sp_addrolemember StudentRole, StudentUser
```

"OK, now let's test our procedure. First, I need to get a valid student key."

```
SELECT * FROM Student
```

"Now let's test it."

```
usp_StudentLogin '980001008'
```

**Caution**

*It is a common practice to develop databases and database-driven applications with the administrator's permissions. It guarantees that the developer has access to all the system and application tools that he or she needs. Many things that work perfectly in Admin mode may not work at all in a restricted user's environment. The solution is not to give users administrative rights. That opens up too many possibilities for attack and error. The solution is to test the database and any database objects or applications in the user's security context.*

"So we see that it returns the lastname 'Bradbury.' That is not the end of testing though. We need to check what happens when you enter a key that isn't in the database. We also need to log in as a student and test it in that permissions context."

"How do you log in as a student?"

"There are several ways. One way is to right click on the Query window. Choose 'Connection' and then 'Disconnect.' Then right click again, choose 'Connection/Connect' in the login dialog box. Change the authentication mode to SQL Server and enter the login name and password."

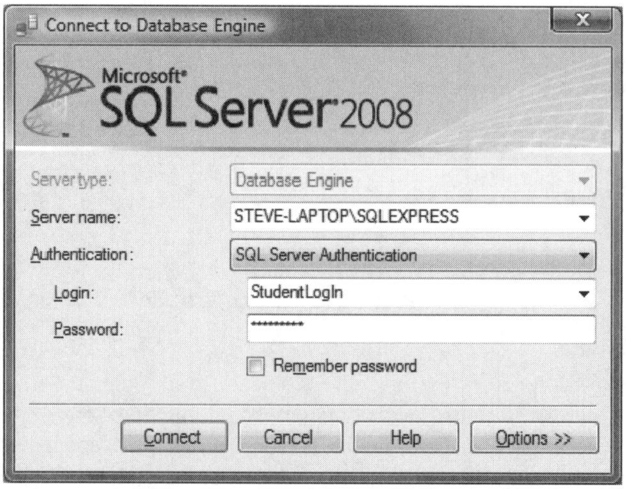

**FIGURE 8-2** Logging in with SQL Server Authentication

"Click Connect. Notice that at the tray at the bottom of the Query window, it now says 'StudentLogin.' Try the SELECT statement again. Notice the results this time."

```
Msg 229, Level 14, State 5, Line 1
The SELECT permission was denied on the object 'Student', database
'TutorManagement', schema 'dbo'.
```

"The StudentUser doesn't have permission to look at this or any of the other tables directly. Now let's try the stored procedure."

Professor Collins runs the stored procedure. It returns the name "Bradbury."

Sharon says, "You also mentioned views?"

"Yes, views are, as their name suggests, ways to view data. The big difference between views and stored procedures is that views don't accept parameters. Each role would have distinct views associated with it. Let's create a view for the students to look at the tutoring sessions. First, we need to log in again as administrator."

After logging in, he types the following code.

*VIEW*

A stored query or filter that represents a user's "view" of the date.

```
CREATE VIEW vw_Sessions
AS
SELECT TutorLastName AS [Tutor],
StudentKey AS [Student],
SessionDateKey AS [Date],
SessionTimeKey AS [Time],
CourseKey AS [Course]
FROM Tutor t
INNER JOIN [Session] s
ON t.TutorKey=s.TutorKey
WHERE SessionDateKey >=GetDate()
```

"You can see," he says, "that a view is really just a stored query. It doesn't actually hold the data, it just filters the data from the tables. It has some other advantages though. Notice how I aliased the columns? As far as the user is concerned, those aliases are the column names. A view can be used to hide the true database names and structures from the user. The user never needs to know or see how the tables are structured or what the actual names of the columns are. Also, like a procedure, you can give permissions to SELECT against a view without giving any permissions on the underlying tables. That GetDate() at the end is a function that returns the current date according to the computer's internal clock, so the user should only see current or future session times."

He turns back to the screen. "OK, let's add permission to select from this view to the StudentRole."

```
Grant SELECT on vw_Sessions TO StudentRole
```

"Now let's try it. You can treat a view just like a table. You can select everything in it, or just some columns or rows."

```
SELECT * FROM vw_Sessions
```

This results in:

"Now let's try to select against the underlying column names. We will try to get a distinct list of tutors."

```
SELECT DISTINCT tutorLastName
FROM vw_Sessions
```

"Notice, the result is an error":

```
Msg 207, Level 16, State 1, Line 1
Invalid column name 'tutorLastName'.
```

"So let's try it again with the column alias":

```
SELECT DISTINCT [Tutor]
FROM vw_Sessions
```

| Tutor | Student | Date | Time | Course |
|---|---|---|---|---|
| Anderson | 990001000 | 2009-10-20 | 13:00:00.0000000 | ITC110 |
| Brown | 990001000 | 2009-10-20 | 14:00:00.0000000 | WEB110 |
| Brown | NULL | 2009-11-05 | 10:00:00.0000000 | ITC220 |
| Lewis | 990001004 | 2009-11-10 | 13:00:00.0000000 | MAT107 |
| Brown | 990001000 | 2009-11-10 | 14:00:00.0000000 | WEB110 |
| Brown | 990001002 | 2009-11-20 | 10:30:00.0000000 | ITC220 |
| Foster | 990001000 | 2010-01-15 | 09:30:00.0000000 | ITC255 |
| Lewis | 990001003 | 2010-01-20 | 11:00:00.0000000 | ENG211 |
| Lewis | 990001005 | 2010-01-22 | 14:00:00.0000000 | MAT107 |
| Foster | 990001000 | 2010-02-05 | 10:30:00.0000000 | ITC255 |
| Lewis | NULL | 2010-02-10 | 13:30:00.0000000 | MAT107 |
| Lewis | NULL | 2010-02-10 | 14:00:00.0000000 | MAT107 |
| Foster | NULL | 2010-02-13 | 10:00:00.0000000 | ITC255 |
| Foster | NULL | 2010-02-14 | 11:00:00.0000000 | ENG211 |

**FIGURE 8-3** Results of SELECT * from View

"This time the results are what you would expect":

| Tutor |
|---|
| Anderson |
| Brown |
| Foster |
| Lewis |

**FIGURE 8-4** SELECT DISTINCT Results

Sharon looks at the screen for a moment and then asks, "What about letting people insert or update data?"

Professor Collins nods. "That is a bit more complex. Since we are on the Student role, let's make a procedure that processes a student signing up for a session. First, we need the parameters. I am assuming that the student has already been authenticated and that the courses have been validated. We could add the course validation here, but it would make the whole thing more complicated."

"I would like to see it anyway."

"OK, the first thing we need to do is to make sure we are logged in as administrator again. Then we need to get the parameters. We basically need to know what the session is and who the student is."

```
CREATE PROCEDURE usp_SessionSignUp
@StudentKey NCHAR(10),
@SessionDateKey DATE,
@SessionTimeKey TIME
```

"Now, since you want to include a check on whether the student can sign up for the course or not, I am going to introduce an internal variable. Variables are different from parameters in that they don't have to be provided by the user. They are declared and consumed inside the procedure itself. So here I declare the variable to store the CourseKey and then assign a value to it using a SELECT statement."

```
AS
DECLARE @CourseKey NCHAR(10)
SELECT @CourseKey=CourseKey
FROM [Session]
  WHERE SessionDateKey=@SessionDateKey
  AND SessionTimeKey=@SessionTimeKey
```

"Next, we test to see if the student has listed this as one of his or her courses. We use the EXIST keyword to do this. It returns a Boolean, true or false. Either the student has the course listed or not":

```
IF EXISTS
 (SELECT *
 FROM StudentCourse
 WHERE StudentKey=@StudentKey
 AND CourseKey=@CourseKey)
```

"Now we are going to tell the procedure what to do if the EXISTS query returns true. We use the keyword BEGIN to mark the beginning of the true block. The first thing we are going to do in the true block is another Exists test. This one is to make sure the student isn't trying to sign up for a session that is already taken."

```
BEGIN
 IF EXISTS
 (SELECT *
 FROM [Session]
 WHERE SessionDateKey=@SessionDateKey
 AND SessionTimeKey=@SessionTimeKey
 AND StudentKey IS NULL)
```

"So next we need a second true block to tell what we do if the session is, in fact, available. If it is, we can update the record to add the StudentKey. I will put it in a TRANSACTION with a TRY CATCH to make sure that any update errors are handled."

```
BEGIN
        BEGIN TRAN
        BEGIN TRY
            UPDATE [Session]
            SET StudentKey=@StudentKey
            WHERE SessionDateKey=@SessionDateKey
            AND SessionTimeKey=@SessionTimeKey
        COMMIT TRAN
        END TRY
        BEGIN CATCH
            ROLLBACK TRAN
        END CATCH
        END
END
```

"Could you explain the TRANSACTION and the TRY CATCH a little bit more?"

"Sure, technically every action the database executes is a transaction. But you can use the BEGIN TRAN or BEGIN TRANSACTION to control the processing of a transaction. Once you declare a TRANSACTION, you have two choices about how to complete it. You can either COMMIT it, which causes the SQL to be fully processed. In our case, the update will occur. Or you can ROLLBACK, which causes the SQL to undo any actions within the TRANSACTION. That is where the TRY CATCH comes in. The TRY tests the code for errors. If any errors occur, the processing immediately jumps from the line of code where the error occurred to the CATCH block. If no errors occur, the Transaction commits; if it jumps to the CATCH, the transaction is rolled back. So here's the whole procedure."

```
CREATE PROCEDURE usp_SessionSignUp
@StudentKey NCHAR(10),
@SessionDateKey DATE,
@SessionTimeKey TIME
AS
DECLARE @CourseKey NCHAR(10)
SELECT @CourseKey=CourseKey
FROM [Session]
 WHERE SessionDateKey=@SessionDateKey
 AND SessionTimeKey=@SessionTimeKey
IF EXISTS
        (SELECT *
        FROM StudentCourse
```

```
                              WHERE StudentKey=@StudentKey
                              AND CourseKey=@CourseKey)
               BEGIN
                              IF EXISTS
                              (SELECT *
                              FROM [Session]
                              WHERE SessionDateKey=@SessionDateKey
                              AND SessionTimeKey=@SessionTimeKey
                              AND StudentKey IS NULL)
                              BEGIN
                                      BEGIN TRAN
                                      BEGIN TRY
                                              UPDATE [Session]
                                              SET StudentKey=@StudentKey
                                              WHERE SessionDateKey=@SessionDateKey
                                              AND SessionTimeKey=@SessionTimeKey
                                      COMMIT TRAN
                                      END TRY
                                      BEGIN CATCH
                                              ROLLBACK TRAN
                                      END CATCH
                              END
               END
```

"The logic of it goes like this: If the student has the Session course listed as one he or she is registered for, and if the session has no other student signed up for it, update the session record to add the student key. If either test returns false, nothing happens. We should grant EXEC permission to the Student role and test the procedure, of course, to make sure it behaves as it is expected. But, I think you can see the advantage of using procedures. You control how the update occurs. There is no chance of accidentally or purposely updating unintended records."

Sharon looks at the code, thoughtfully. "OK, she says, but how do you know what views or procedures to make?"

Professor Collins replies, "It is not easy. It takes time and testing. The first thing I would do is go through each of your roles and make a list of all the ways users need to access the data. Then I would make a procedure or view to match that need. It is a lot of work, and it is essential that your set of procedures and views is complete enough for your users to successfully interact with the database, but it is the most secure way to channel that access."

Sharon thinks a bit more. "How do you control which procedures are used when?"

"That's a good question. You really have to depend on the application to control that. You can also set up certain policies and procedures."

"Policies and procedures?"

"Yes. There are a lot of things you can't enforce directly in the database management system. For instance, removing users who should no longer have access to the database. You need to make a policy that says something like 'Inactive users should be removed from the database within *x* number of hours after becoming inactive.' Policies are rules about how things should be done. Procedures are step-by-step descriptions of how a particular task should be performed. For instance, with the policy I just mentioned, you might have a procedure that tells, step by step, how to inform the database administrator that a particular login is no longer valid. The same thing holds true, by the way, for your disaster recovery plan. It is really a matter of identifying the correct policies and then the procedures to implement them."

"Could you explain a little more about what a disaster recovery plan would look like?"

"Sure. The first thing to do is really determine how much data the business can afford to lose."

"Can a business really afford to lose any data?"

"Most of the time, no. But many businesses, particularly small ones, can afford some data loss. They can often recover some bits of information from paper receipts or invoices. The tutor database can, I think, tolerate some loss. Regular backups should

> ✋ *Caution*
> *Whether you use stored procedures or assign permissions directly on the tables, it is essential that your users have all the rights and permissions to do their job. If the permissions are too inflexible, or if something important is left out, it can make the database essentially useless. On the other hand, giving too many rights and permissions—ones not necessary for a user's work—can lead to accidents and data integrity errors. It is a delicate balance and requires a strong sense of the business needs of each user as each relates to the database.*

probably be sufficient. This is something you will have to talk to the IT people about. I am sure they have some backup policies already in place."

"Thank you. Looks like I still have a lot of work to do."

"Security is work. But if you don't do the work, I'm afraid, it wouldn't be long before your database is compromised. Cleaning up after mistakes or deliberate attacks is even more work."

## DOCUMENTATION

As with every aspect of the database, it is crucial to document the security set up. Security, especially for a large organization, can be extremely complex. Attempting to maintain or troubleshoot it without clear documentation can be difficult or impossible. Also, without proper documentation, it is difficult to assess threats and also to assess whether they have been properly addressed.

Authentication types and policies should be spelled out. It might be policy, for instance, that only users with active directory accounts can have access and perhaps among them only members of certain groups. Additionally, policies should be in place that describe how to remove a login or user who is no longer with the company or who no longer requires access to the database. Each role should be described along with a list of all the permissions associated with it. Each view and stored procedure should be described, and all parameters and their types listed. A complete catalogue of these views and procedures can be given to developers who are designing applications to work with the database.

Backup and recovery, including disaster recovery policies and procedures, should be clearly spelled out and reviewed on a regular basis. Good disaster management can make the difference between a business surviving a crisis or going under.

## Things We Have Done

*In this chapter we have*

- looked at authentication and authorization
- mapped the permissions needed by each user
- created new SQL logins and users
- created a role to contain the permissions for the student user
- created stored procedures and a view
- granted permissions on the procedures and view to the role
- done a preliminary threats assessment
- looked at basic disaster recovery

## Vocabulary

*Match the definitions to the vocabulary words:*

1. Authentication
2. Authorization
3. Disaster recovery plan
4. Permission
5. Policies
6. Procedures
7. Roles
8. Schema
9. Stored procedures
10. Views

— a. An action that a user has been granted the right to do in a database
— b. A stored query or filter that reflects a user's view of the data
— c. The process of confirming a user is who he or she claims to be
— d. A set of related permissions
— e. A rule for how to do some activity
— f. One or more SQL statements grouped to be executed together
— g. The processes of assigning permissions to authenticated users
— h. A plan to recover data and maintain availability after any kind of disaster
— i. Step-by-step plan for accomplishing a task
— j. Object ownership in a database

## Things to Look Up

1. Find some best practices for creating strong passwords.
2. Find out how MySQL manages basic authentication and authorization.
3. Find out how Microsoft Access manages basic authentication and authorization.
4. Look up some best practices for Disaster recovery.
5. Find a tutorial on stored procedures in SQL Server.
6. Find some best practices for securing SQL Server.

## TABLE OF ADDITIONAL SQL KEY WORDS

**Table 8-10**  Additional Keywords

| Term | Description |
|------|-------------|
| AS | Used with stored procedures and views to mark the beginning of the body of the procedure or view. |
| BEGIN | Marks the beginning of a block. Often used with other keywords such as BEGIN TRAN and BEGIN TRY. |
| CATCH | With BEGIN and END, it marks a block to catch and handle any errors cast from code in a TRY block. |
| COMMIT | With TRAN, it completes all the SQL statements in the current transaction and where necessary writes them to the database. |
| CREATE | Used with an object type to create an instance of that object. For example, CREATE PROC, CREATE TABLE, and CREATE VIEW. (Once an object is created, it can be edited by using the keyword ALTER instead of CREATE.) |
| DECLARE | Declares a variable. All SQL Server variables begin with @ and must be given a data type. For example, DECLARE @ StudentKey NCHAR(10). |
| DEFAULT_DATABASE | Sets the default database for a login. |
| END | Ends a block. Often used with other keywords such as END TRAN, END TRY, and END CATCH. |
| EXISTS | Used with a subquery, it returns a Boolean. True if the query returns any values, false if not. |
| GRANT | With ON and an object name, grants a permission to a user or role. |
| IF | Tests an expression to see if it is true or false (Any expression must return a Boolean.) If it is true, one branch of code can be executed, if it is false, another branch. |
| LOGIN | With CREATE, it adds a login to the Server. |
| PASSWORD | Sets the password for an SQL Server login. |
| PROCEDURE (PROC) | An object that stores a set of related SQL code that is meant to be executed as one process. It can be used to safely handle user input and output. A user can be granted permissions to execute a stored procedure without being given permissions on the underlying tables. |
| ROLE | With CREATE, it adds a role to the database. |
| ROLLBACK | Used with TRANSACTION, it undoes any statements contained within that TRANSACTION. |
| TRANSACTION (TRAN) | Used with BEGIN, a TRANSACTION keeps all the SQL statements within; the TRANSACTION is suspense until they are all committed to the database or rolled back. |
| TRY | With BEGIN and CATCH, starts a block of code to be run. If any command generates an error, the execution will immediately jump to the CATCH block for processing. |
| USER | With CREATE, adds a User to a particular database. |
| VIEW | A VIEW is a stored query or filter. A VIEW doesn't contain any data, but filters it. The idea is to create "views" of the data that correspond to how particular sets of users interact with the data in the database. |
| WITH | Sets Properties on an object such as a LOGIN. |

## Practices

1. Review the pizza database we built in Chapter 6 and queried in Chapter 7. Identify the users of the database, and determine what kind of access to the tables each of them needs.
2. Develop a threat analysis for the pizza company database.
3. Create roles for the various types of users in the pizza database.
4. Create a SQL Server login for a user, and assign the user to a role.
5. Create a view for one of the roles and grant permission to select from the view to one or more users.
6. Assume you are working for a small bookstore. It has a database that keeps track of all the inventory and all the sales and trades with customers. This bookstore also maintains an online presence with a Web site, where users can browse the catalog and purchase books using second-party software to process the payment. There is only one store and they are located in the downtown area of a city known for occasional severe earthquakes. Create a disaster recovery plan for this company.

6–11 Look at this stored procedure and answer the following questions:

```
CREATE PROCEDURE usp_AddRequest
@CourseKey NCHAR(10),
@StudentKey NCHAR(10),
@RequestKey NCHAR(10)
AS
DECLARE @Date DATE
DECLARE @Status NCHAR(10)
SET @Date=GETDATE()
SET @Status = 'Active'
```

```
BEGIN TRAN
    BEGIN TRY
        INSERT INTO REQUEST(
        RequestKey,
        CourseKey,
        RequestDate,
        RequestStatus,
        StudentKey)
        Values(
        @RequestKey,
        @CourseKey,
        @Date,
        @Status,
        @StudentKey)
    COMMIT TRAN
    END TRY
    BEGIN CATCH
        ROLLBACK TRAN
    END CATCH
```

7. What are the names of parameters in the procedure?
8. What are the names of the variables?
9. What happens to the transaction if there is no error?
10. What happens to the transaction if there is an error?
11. Why do you need a TRY CATCH with a TRANSACTION?

## Scenarios

### WILD WOOD APARTMENTS

The apartment managers at Wild Wood like what you have done so far, but as the database takes shape, they have begun to worry about security. The tenant information should not be accessible to just anyone. And they would like to keep the financial information internal, and not let outsiders or other companies see the details of their operation.

1. Create tables of the data access needs of your users.
2. Create a security plan that includes authentication and authorization and general policies and procedures. Consider the use of roles, stored procedures, views, and other tools.
3. **Documentation:** Document and define all the aspects of your plan.
4. Create a preliminary threat analysis.
5. Make a preliminary disaster management plan.
6. Create a view of the data that is tailored to the needs of one of your uses.
7. For extra-credit, create a stored procedure that executes one of the basic activities for your database (making a rent payment, for instance, or a maintenance request).

### VINCE'S VINYL

Having shown Vince your work so far, you broach the topic of security. At first, Vince doesn't see much need for security measures, but you point out a few areas where that should be considered. For one thing, Vince probably doesn't want to share his list of interested customers. That is valuable information in itself, and his customers will have an expectation of privacy. Additionally, the day-to-day financial information concerning sales and purchases is probably best not available for general public perusal. You also point out that it is important that Vince be able to trust his data. He needs to know that no one has accidentally, or on purpose, messed up his inventory or sales data.

1. Create tables of the data access needs of Vince's users.
2. Create a security plan that includes authentication and authorization and general policies and procedures. Consider the use of roles, stored procedures, views, and other tools.

3. **Documentation:** Document and define all the aspects of your plan.
4. Create a preliminary threat analysis.
5. Make a preliminary disaster management plan.
6. Create a view of the data that is tailored to the needs of one of your uses.
7. For extra-credit, create a stored procedure that executes one of the basic activities for your database (purchasing an album, for instance, or recording a customer request).

### GRANDFIELD COLLEGE

As with any database, data integrity is important to the software database at Granfield College. If the data are audited, they have to show that they know what software they have, how it is licensed, and on which machines it is installed. Accident and error are the most likely threats to their data integrity, but it is always possible that someone might try to purposely disrupt their data.

1. Create tables of the data access needs of your users.
2. Create a security plan that includes authentication and authorization and general policies and procedures. Consider the use of roles, stored procedures, views, and other tools.
3. **Documentation:** Document and define all the aspects of your plan.
4. Create a preliminary threat analysis.
5. Make a preliminary disaster management plan.
6. Create a view of the data that is tailored to the needs of one of your uses.
7. For extra-credit, create a stored procedure that executes one of the basic activities for your database (installing a piece of software, for instance, or processing a software request).

### WESTLAKE RESEARCH HOSPITAL

Security has always been a part of the WestLake Hospital's database. In a double-blind study, it is absolutely essential that no one tampers with the data. Also, patient confidentiality and the sensitive nature of the study require that the patients' records and the records of their sessions with the doctors be kept absolutely private and secure. The researchers are anxious to see your plan for securing the data.

1. Create tables of the data access needs of your users.
2. Create a security plan that includes authentication and authorization and general policies and procedures. Consider the use of roles, stored procedures, views, and other tools.
3. **Documentation:** Document and define all the aspects of your plan.
4. Create a preliminary threat analysis.
5. Make a preliminary disaster management plan.
6. Create a view of the data that is tailored to the needs of one of your uses.
7. For extra-credit, create a stored procedure that executes one of the basic activities for your database (making an appointment, for instance, or letting patients see some of their doctors' session notes on them.)

## SUGGESTIONS FOR SCENARIOS

Security is difficult, and each of these scenarios has very different security needs. First think about the authentication. Who is going to use the database? Are there many potential users or just a few? If there are many, you might consider whether they naturally fall into just a few roles. If there are only very few, you might just use individual logins.

Next, I would think about the different users or groups of users. What permissions do they need on the tables to do their work? Then look at the threats. Where are the potential areas for attack, but also where are the potential areas for mistakes and bad data entry? Consider whether creating stored procedures and views could lessen those areas of vulnerability.

Finally, identify the ways the data could be harmed or lost. What policies and procedures would help minimize that potential loss? These are what make up your disaster plan.

# APPENDIX A

## Using Microsoft Access with the Book

The planning and design aspects of a database are the same irrespective of the database management system you are using. Chapters 1 through 5 can be used without modification. The physical design, however, does require some variation.

### CREATING THE TUTORMANAGEMENT DATABASE IN ACCESS

Start Access. Choose Blank database and name it "TutorManagement" and click "Create."

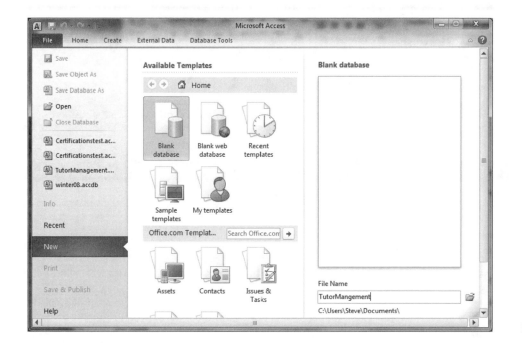

**FIGURE A-1** New Database

In the new TutorManagement database, click "Create" tab for the Create ribbon, and then click the "Table" icon. Click the triangle and ruler icon to get the table design view. In the dialog box that pops up, name the table "Tutor." Right click on the ID field, and from the context menu, choose "Delete." Say "Yes" to the dialog that pops up, explaining that this requires deleting the primary key. Now add the fields and the data types. Note the Field Properties below the table. In the "General" tab, you can set the length and other properties of the field. The "Required" property is used to set the status of nulls. Required with a value of "no" means allow nulls. Required with a value of "yes" means the field does not allow nulls.

To make "TutorKey" a key field, select the TutorKey row in the design view and click the Key icon on the ribbon. In those tables where you need to select multiple fields for a key, hold the Control key down and select each of the fields to be included in the key, then click the key icon on the ribbon.

Access data types differ somewhat from the SQL Server data types. In the following table, only the data types used in the TutorManagement database are listed.

**FIGURE A-2** Tutor Table

| Table A-1   Some Access Data Types | |
|---|---|
| **Microsoft Access Data Type** | **SQL Server Data Type** |
| Text | Varchar() |
| Yes/No | Bit |
| Numeric | Default is INT, |
| Date/Time | To make the table resemble the Date data type, choose the format "short date"; to make it match the datetime data type, choose the "General" format; to make it resemble the time data type, choose the format "Long Time" |
| Memo | Varchar(max) |

Create the remaining tables the same way, remembering to remove the ID column that Access adds.

## CREATING THE RELATIONSHIPS

Once the tables have been created, you can add the relationships. From the ribbon tabs select "Database Tools." On the Database Tools ribbon, click the "Relationship" icon. In the Show Dialog box, click on the first table, hold down the Shift key, and then click on the last table. Click the "add" button. This will load all the tables into the Relationship window. It should look something like this:

The tables can be moved around however you wish to make viewing them more convenient. To create a relationship, select the key field in the table on the one side of the relationship and drag it to the corresponding foreign key in the many side of the relationship. This will pop up the following dialog box:

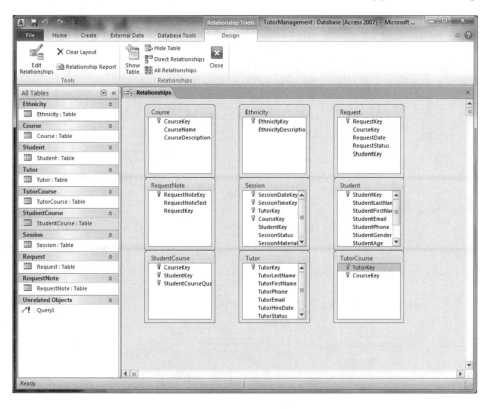

**FIGURE A-3** Relationship Window

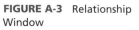

**FIGURE A-4** Edit Relationships Dialog

Make sure that the tables and the fields are correct. Check the Enforce Referential Integrity check box. Then click create.

When you are done, your relationships should look something like this. The tables have been rearranged to show more clearly.

## ADDING DATA

To add data to the tables, close the Relationship window. Double click on a table name in the All Tables list. This will open the table in the add/edit mode:

Do this for all the remaining tables. It is important that you do them in the proper order. Parent tables must be completed before child tables.

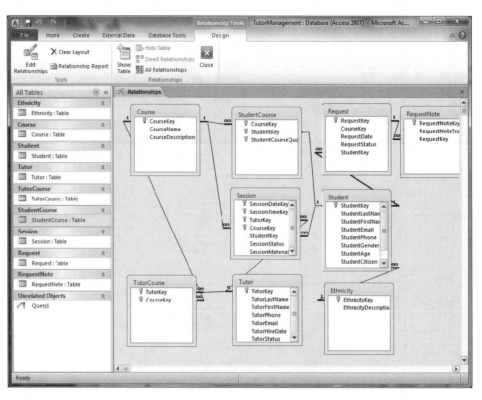

**FIGURE A-5** Relationship Window with Relationships

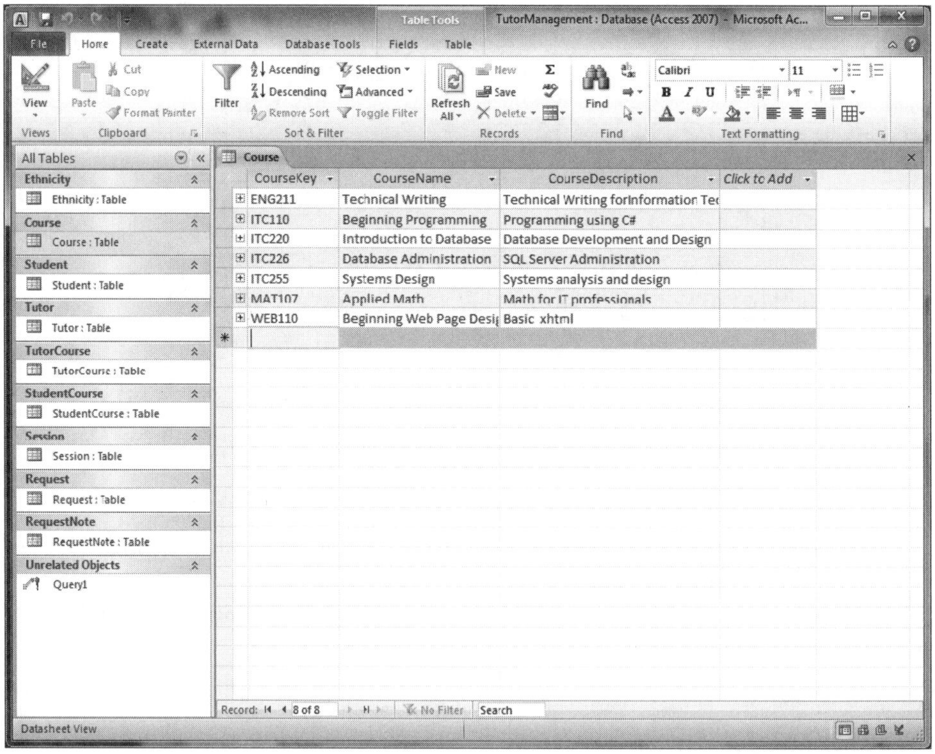

**FIGURE A-6** Editing Data

## SQL in Microsoft Access

To run an SQL statement in Microsoft Access, go to the Create Ribbon tab and create a new query in Design View. Click the x to close the Add Table dialog.

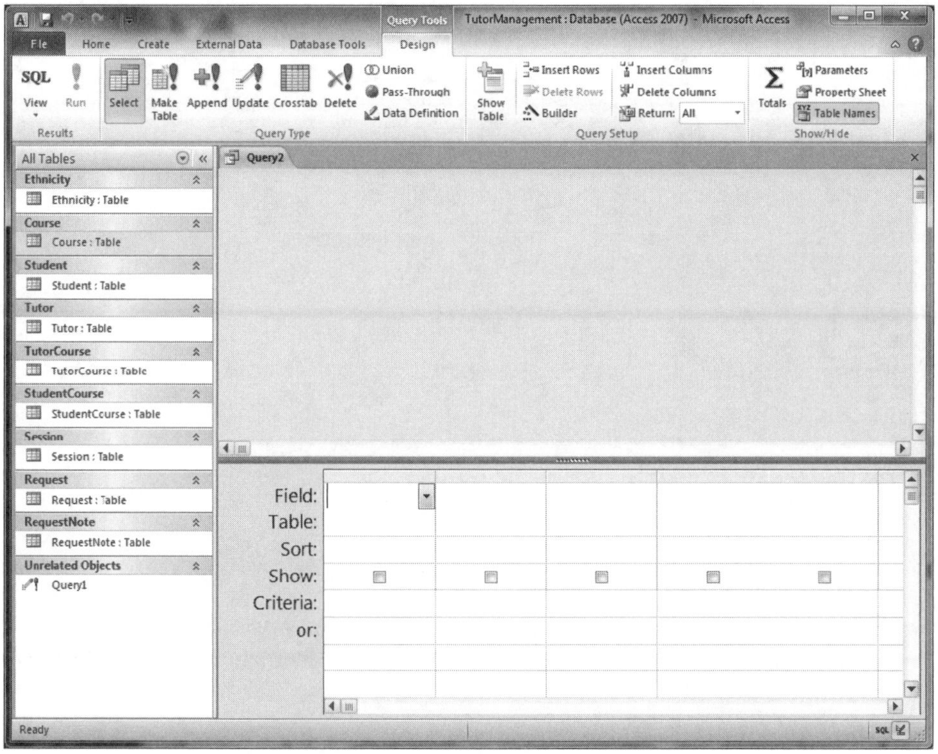

**FIGURE A-7** Query Design View

Click the SQL View on the Ribbon and enter the SQL.

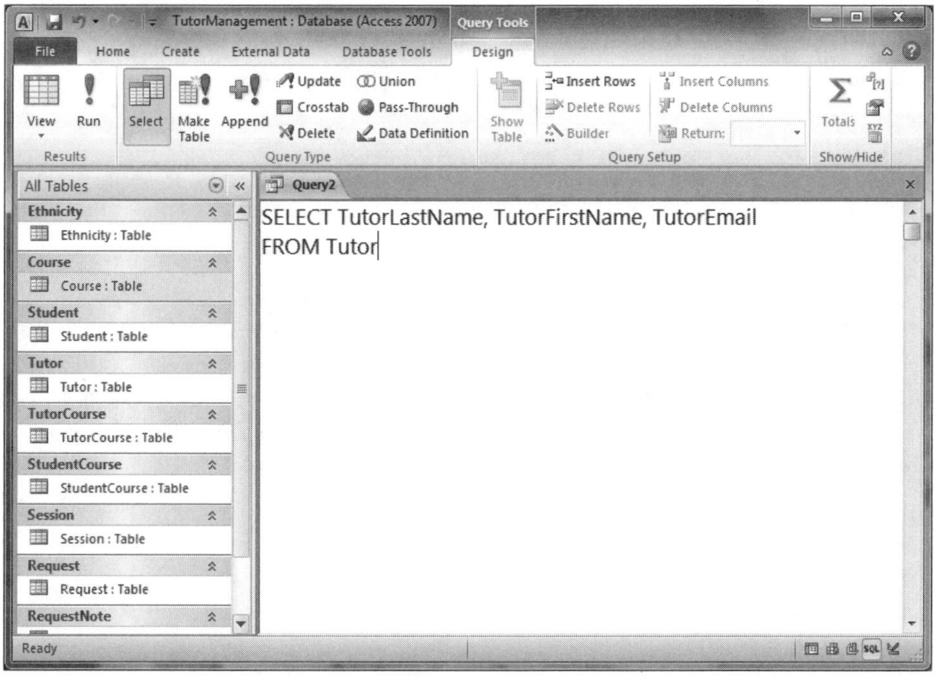

**FIGURE A-8** SQL View

Click the RUN icon to run the query.

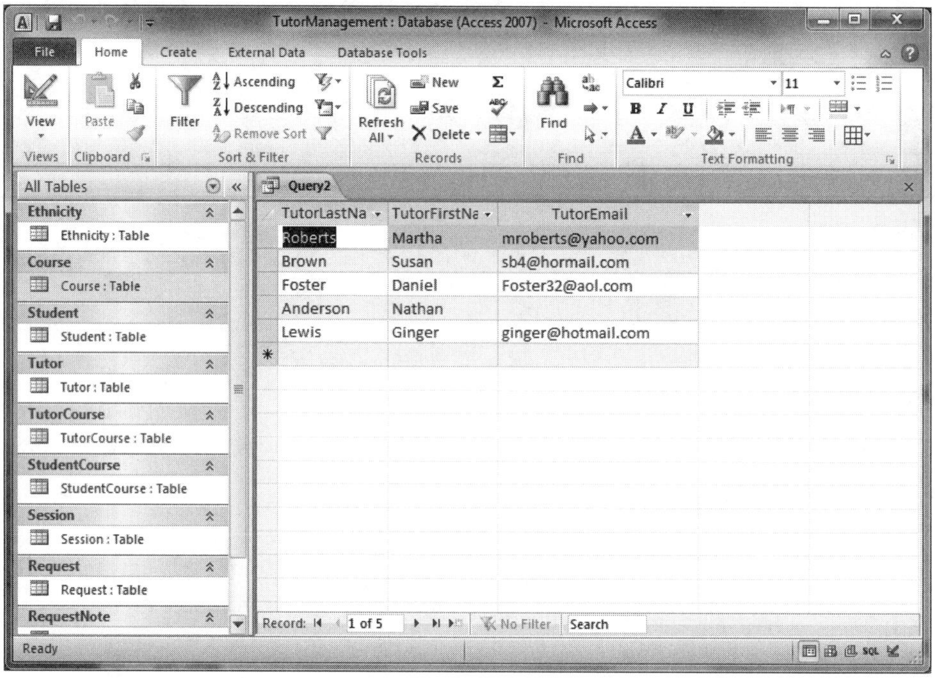

**FIGURE A-9** Query Results

The following queries need some adjustment to run in Access.

Queries with the LIKE keyword use an "*" for a wildcard rather than the percent "%" sign. So

```
SELECT ItemName, ItemPrice
FROM Inventory
WHERE ItemName LIKE 'T%'
```

would be

```
SELECT ItemName, ItemPrice
FROM Inventory
WHERE ItemName LIKE 'T*'
```

Queries with dates in the critera delineate dates with the pound "#" sign rather than single quotes.

```
SELECT tutorkey, courseKey, SessionDate, StudentKey
FROM Session
WHERE SessionDate BETWEEN '11/1/2008' AND '11/15/2008'
```

becomes

```
SELECT tutorkey, courseKey, SessionDate, StudentKey
FROM Session
WHERE SessionDate BETWEEN #11/1/2008# AND #11/15/2008#
```

Single inner joins work with the INNER JOIN keywords, but multiple INNER JOINS must be embedded. In Access, it is easier to use the equi join syntax for any query that requires more than one join. Instead of

```
SELECT s.StudentKey,
StudentLastName,
StudentFirstName,
c.CourseKey,
CourseName,
RequestDate,
RequestStatus
FROM Student s
INNER JOIN Request r
ON s.StudentKey = r.StudentKey
```

```
INNER JOIN Course c
ON c.CourseKey = r.CourseKey
WHERE RequestStatus = 'Active'
```

use the following query:

```
SELECT s.StudentKey,
StudentLastName,
StudentFirstName,
c.CourseKey,
CourseName,
RequestDate,
RequestStatus
FROM, Student s, Course c, Request r
WHERE s.StudentKey = r.StudentKey
AND c.CourseKey = r.CourseKey
AND RequestStatu s= 'Open'
```

The outer join listed in Chapter 7 also works fine.

## SECURITY IN MICROSOFT ACCESS

The security features may be where Access differs most from SQL Server. Neither Microsoft Access 2007 nor Access 2010 support user-level security. (Earlier versions do, but Microsoft does not recommend going back to these earlier versions unless you have a legacy system that requires user-level access.) You cannot create users and groups. Security access is managed by the Network or SharePoint. It is possible to encrypt the database and assign password protection to the database itself.

Further, Access does not support true Views or Stored Procedures. It does support parameterized queries which allow the user to supply criteria for the query when the query is run. There are also action queries that can be used to create tables or update or delete records. But unlike true stored procedures, each query can only do one thing, and there is no error checking. One could replicate much of the functionality of stored procedures using Visual Basic for Applications, but this would require skills that are beyond the scope of this book.

Students using Access should be able to do all the practices except 4 and 5. They should be able to do all the Scenario exercises except creating a stored procedure. The view can be emulated by creating and saving a simple query.

# APPENDIX B

## SQL Server Express

This appendix is meant to describe generally how to get and install SQL Express and how to navigate through some of the features used in the book. It is not meant to repeat all the step-by-step instructions listed in the book or provide a full description of the menus and features of SQL Express.

### WHERE TO GET SQL SERVER EXPRESS

SQL Server Express can be downloaded for free from Microsoft. Just go to *http://www.microsoft.com* and enter SQL Express in the search box. Usually, there are a couple of choices of what to download. Make sure that you download the one that is appropriate to your operating system (×86 32 bit or 64 bit). Also, if possible, choose one that has the management studio included. If not, you will have to download the management studio separately.

SQL Server is a part of the default install with any full version of Visual Studio, though the management studio is not included. It is possible to build databases, database tables, and add data from within the Visual Studio environment, but for compatibility with the book and ease of use, it is recommended that you download and install the management studio separately. It is not necessary to download and reinstall SQL Server Express itself.

### INSTALLATION

After downloading the file, double click it to run the installation program. Accept the defaults. Use Windows authentication. If prompted, add the current Windows account to the administrators group.

### THE MANAGEMENT STUDIO

When you open the management studio, you will need to connect to an instance of SQL Server. The SQL Express service is named [computer name]\sqlexpress. You can enter the relative path ".\sqlexpress." Use Windows Authentication and press Connect.

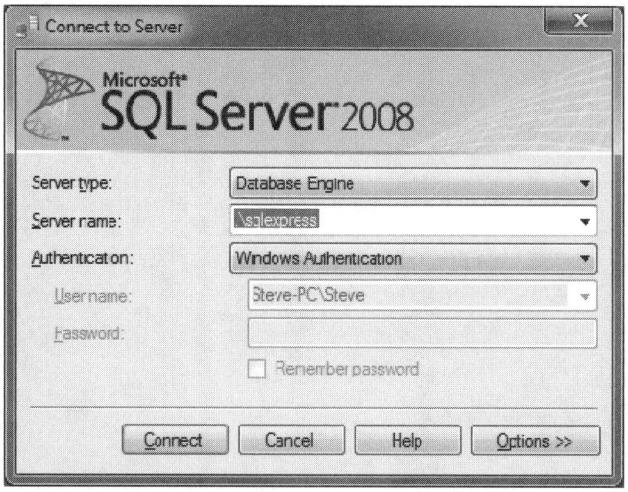

**FIGURE B-1**   Connect to Server

The first look of SQL Server can vary, but the following is a typical view.

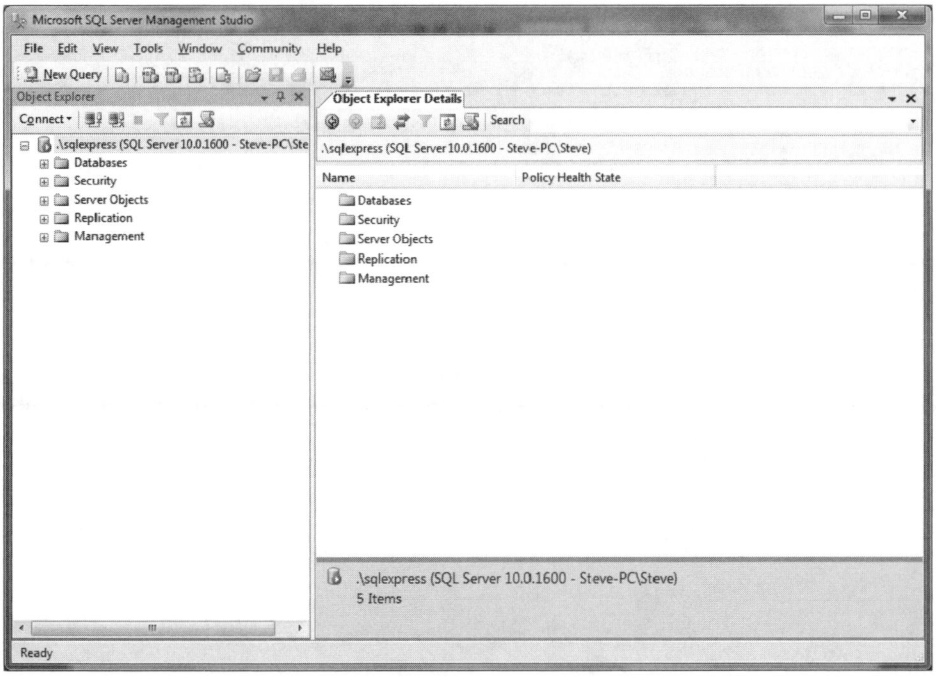


**FIGURE B-2** Typical View

The first thing to look at is the Object Explorer. The Object Explorer shows all the objects related to the server. Related objects are grouped in folders. For the purposes of the book, we will focus on the Database folder and the Security folder. Clicking the "+" beside the folder will expand a folder and show its contents. Right clicking a folder will open a context menu with all the options for that object type. Right clicking on the Database folder will provide several options including "Create Database." Once the database is created, you can click the "+" beside the database to expand its contents. Right clicking on the Tables folder opens a menu that contains "Create Table." Expanding the folder of a particular table reveals a Columns folder that can also be expanded to show the particular table's columns.

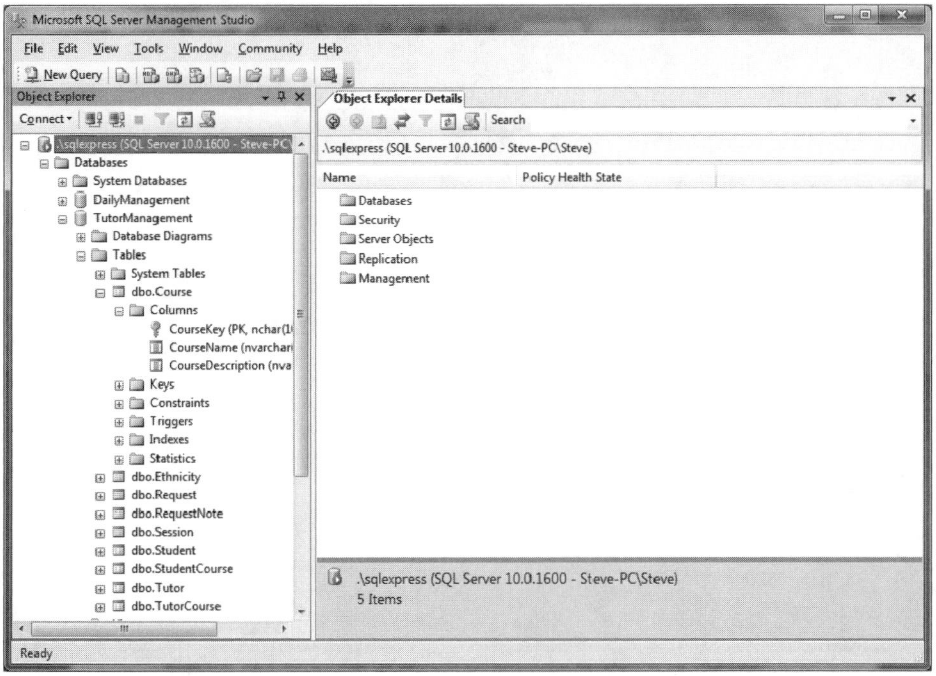


**FIGURE B-3** Expanding Table and Columns Folders

The Database Diagram folder contains database diagrams. Right clicking on this folder the first time will open a dialog.

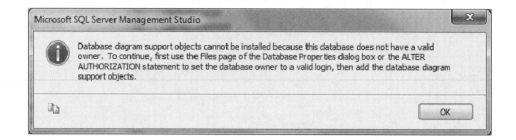

**FIGURE B-4** Database Diagram Support Materials Dialog

Saying OK will enable you to make a new database diagram.

It is important to realize security folders exist in two distinct places. Each database has its own security folder for database-specific security objects including Users. Each server also has a Security folder for server-level security, including Logins:

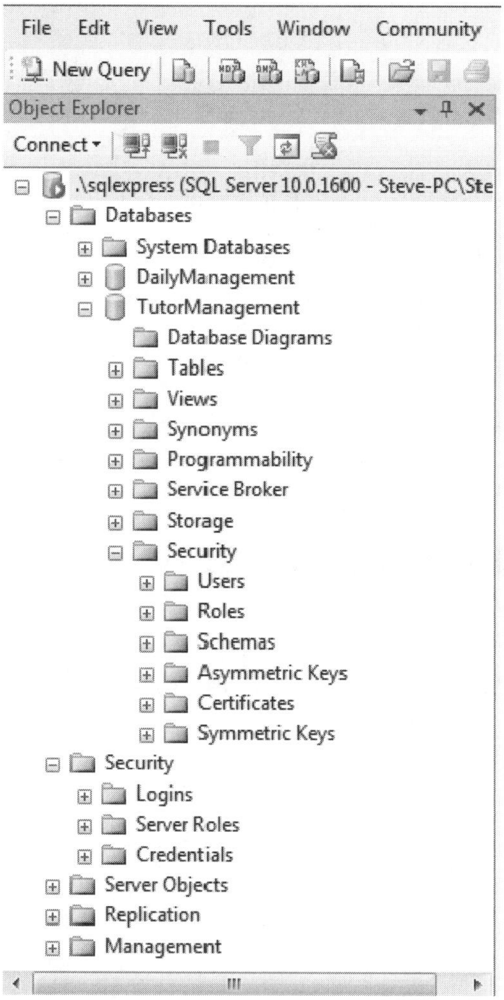

**FIGURE B-5** Security Folders

# APPENDIX C

## Visio

Microsoft's Visio Professional is a modeling and diagramming program. It is considered a Microsoft Office program but does not ship with Office. It must be purchased separately. Visio comes in different editions: Standard, Professional, and Enterprise. The standard edition does not contain the Database Model Diagram template. To get it, you need to have at least Microsoft Professional. (The Professional version is available to students at low or no cost in schools which belong to Microsoft's Academic Alliance.)

Visio has a rich set of templates for modeling everything from a household garden space to complex software components. The scope of these templates is much too rich and varied to be covered here. This appendix will only focus on the Data Modeling template used in Chapter 4.

### OPENING THE DATA MODEL TEMPLATE

When you open Visio, choose "Software and Database" under Template Categories. Then choose "Database Model Diagram." You can choose U.S. Units or Metric for a measurement unit. This only affects the background grid. If you choose U.S. Units, the grid will be arranged in inches, if metric, in centimeters.

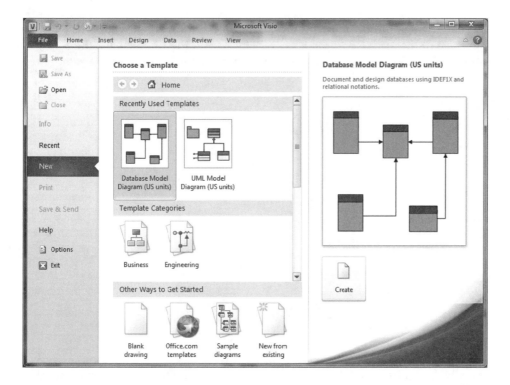

**FIGURE C-1**  New Database Model Diagram

Click the "Create" button to create a diagram.

### COMPONENTS OF THE DATABASE MODEL DIAGRAM

Following is a picture of the Database Model Diagram template when it first opens. Yours may vary depending on previous sessions and what options are selected.

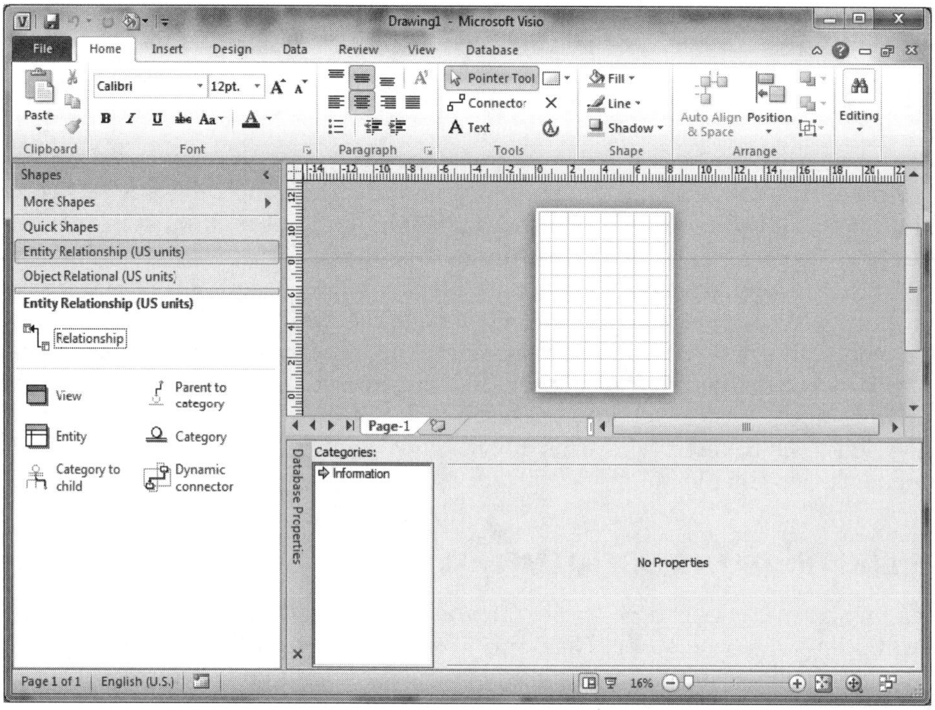

**FIGURE C-2** Database Model Diagram

You may want to do a few things before proceeding with anything else. First adjust the size of the grid. Go to the View tab, then from the ribbon, click the zoom icon. Set the zoom to 100%. This will make the grid big enough to actually be usable.

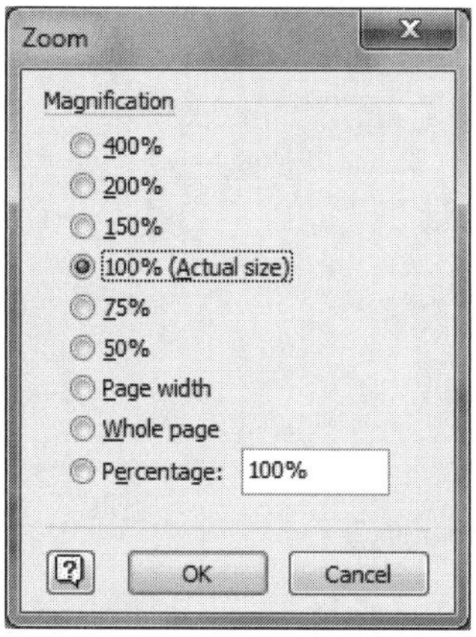

**FIGURE C-3** Zoom Dialog

Only the Entity and Relationship shapes are relevant to the diagrams in this book.

## ENTITIES

To add an entity to the diagram, drag the entity shape onto the grid. Following the grid is the Properties window. When the Entity is selected, you can see and edit the entity's properties. An entity is divided into categories. The first category is Definition. It lets you name the entity.

The second category is "Columns." Clicking on this lets you define the entity columns and data types. It also lets you define the primary key.

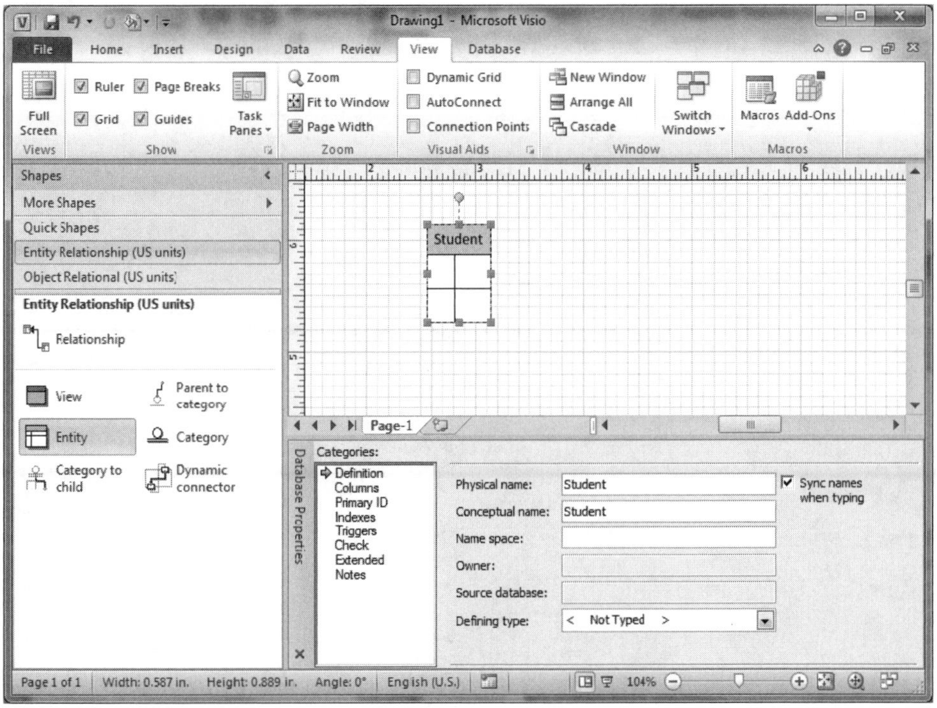

**FIGURE C-4** Entity Definition

## RELATIONSHIPS

To create a relationship, drag a relationship shape onto the grid. Take the arrow end and drag it to the center of the primary key side of the relationship. The outline of the entity will turn red when the end is connected to the entity. Take the other end of the relationship shape and drag it to the foreign key entity. It will also turn red when connected. Visio will also add the primary key column to the child entity as a foreign key.

When the Relationship is selected, you can alter its properties. In particular, if you select the "Miscellaneous" category, you can set the cardinality of the relationship.

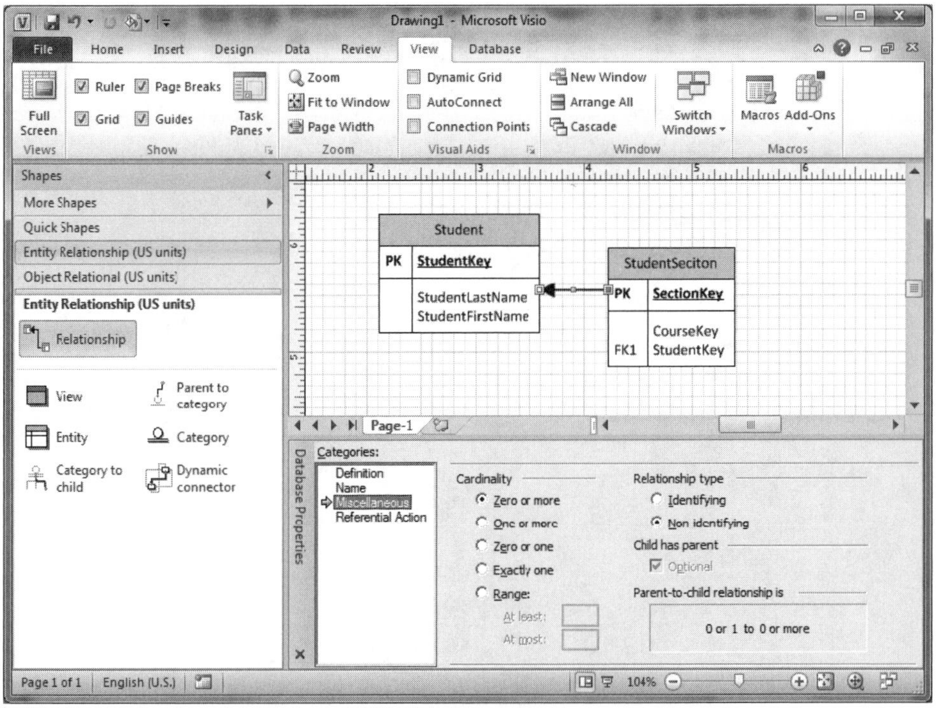

**FIGURE C-5** Relationship Properties

If you need the foreign key to be a part of a composite key in the child, select the Child entity, and under the Columns properties, check the PK checkbox for that column.

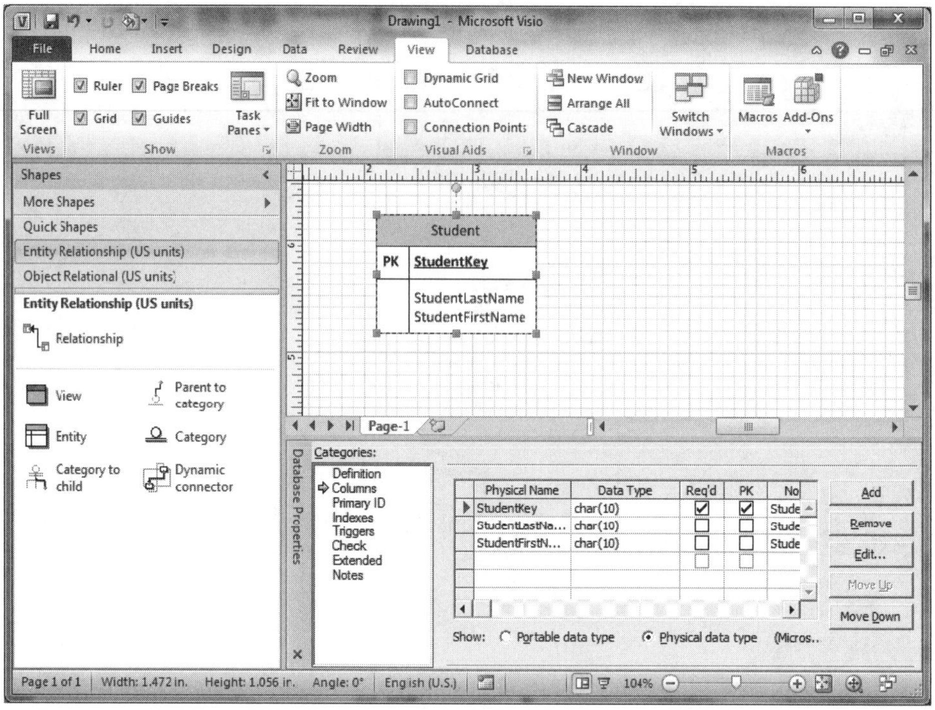

**FIGURE C-6** Column Definition

## DATABASE OPTIONS

On the Database tab are two very important dialogs for setting diagram options. The Database Drivers option lets you choose the underlying database type. You can use it, for instance, to change the type from Microsoft Access to SQL Server.

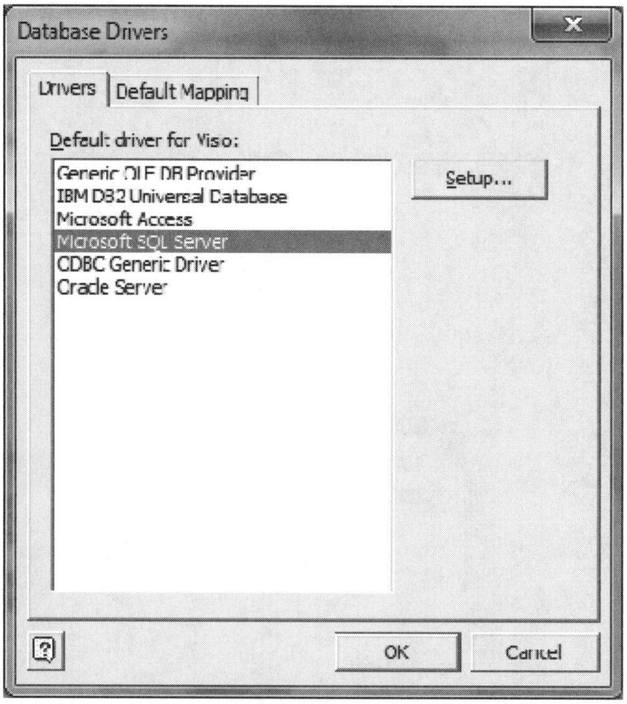

**FIGURE C-7** Database Drivers Dialog

The Display Options on the Database tab will open the Document dialog box that lets you change things about the way the model is displayed in Visio. Under the Relationship tab of this dialog, you can change from the default arrow-headed relationships to the crow's feet relationships used in the book.

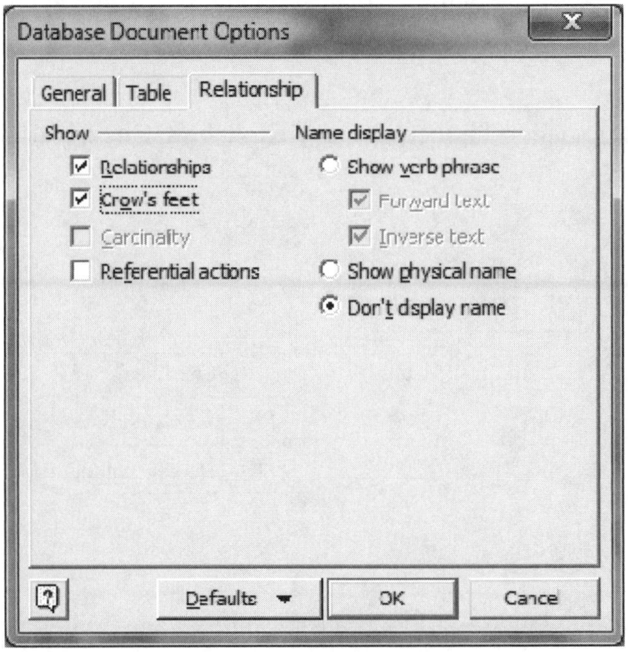

**FIGURE C-8** Database Document Options

# APPENDIX D

## Common Relational Patterns

There are many types of relations that occur over and over again in relational design.

### ONE TO MANY

This is the normal relationship between any two tables. One department can contain many employees.

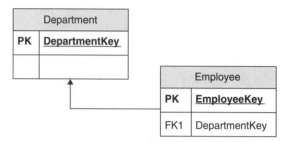

**FIGURE D-1** One to Many

### LINKING TABLE

Every man-to-many relation must be resolved into two one-to-many relationships by means of a linking table. One book can have many authors; one author can write many books. The linking table often has a composite key consisting of the foreign keys from the two tables it resolves.

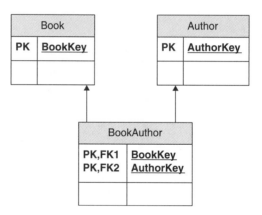

**FIGURE D-2** Linking Table

### LOOKUP TABLE

Lookup tables help maintain constancy and data integrity. The following diagram shows a table that lists the states as a lookup for an Address table.

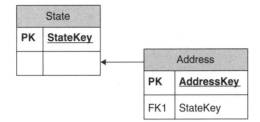

**FIGURE D-3** Lookup Table

## WEAK ENTITY

A weak entity is an entity that depends on another entity for its meaning. For instance, the doctor contacts depend on the Doctor table for their meaning. Weak entities are way of dealing with a multivalued attribute such as Contacts or Dependents.

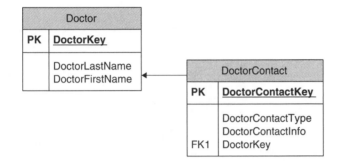

**FIGURE D-4** Weak Entity

## MASTER DETAIL

Typically, many kinds of business transactions are broken into at least two tables. One table stores the basic information of the transaction, while the other stores the line-by-line details. If you look at a receipt, you will see the general information at the top: the date, the customer number, the employee number, and so on, and then below that the line-by-line list of what has been purchased. The master table stores the general information; the detail table stores the specific item information. In the following example, the Customer table and the Employee table are not pictured, though they are represented in the Sale table as foreign keys.

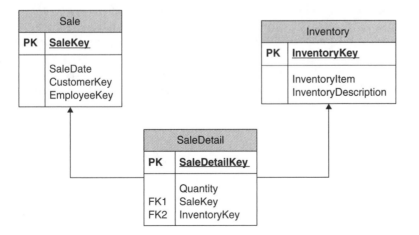

**FIGURE D-5** Master/Detail

## GENERALIZATION/SPECIALIZATION

The generalization/specialization pattern is used as a way to prevent excessive nulls in a table. Different resources have different attributes to describe them. If all were stored in the Resource table, when the resource was a book, the Article and Web attributes would be null. If the resource were an article, most of the Book and Web attributes would be null. In the generalization/specialization pattern, the General table, in this case the Resource table, stores all the common data that is shared by each kind of resource. The data that is specific to each kind is separated out into the appropriate table. The child tables have a one-to-one relationship with the parent table. (This is very similar to *inheritance* in object-oriented programming.)

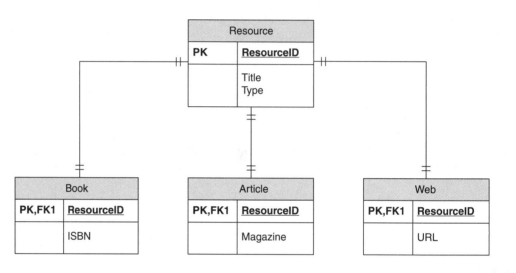

**FIGURE D-6** Generalization/Specialization

## TAKING NORMALIZATION A LITTLE FARTHER

Following the logic of normalization, it is possible to argue that Employees and Customers are both, first of all, people, and that they all have names and birthdates, and so on. So rather than create a separate Customer table and an Employee table, which means repeating those fields, one can create a single Person table. There is still an Employee table that contains information specific to employees, but it doesn't contain the Person information. The Employee table is linked through a linking table to the Person table. This has the additional advantage of making it easier to secure personal information from those who don't need to see it.

Addresses can also be seen as a distinct entity, especially since any person can have multiple addresses. The same goes with contact information. The result of this is a more complex set of tables and relations, but it is more thoroughly normalized, with even less redundancy. The following ERD shows these relations. It also includes the Master/Detail relation. It is also useful to note the product table is separate from the inventory table. This prevents a product from disappearing if it is no longer in inventory (the deletion anomaly).

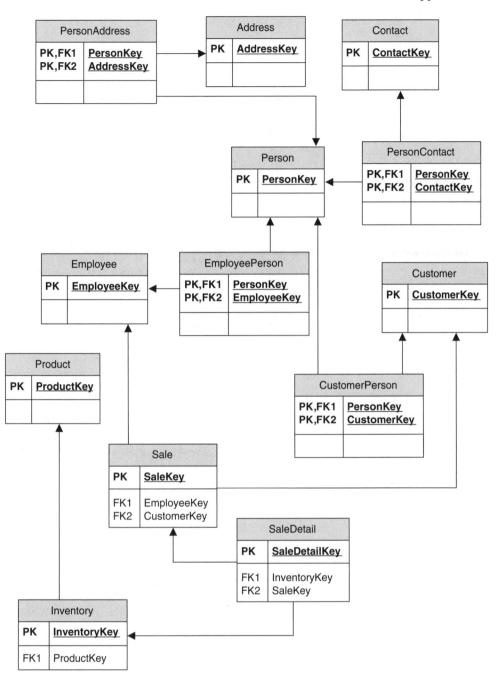

**FIGURE D-7** More Fully Normalized

# GLOSSARY

**Actor** A person or program that makes some use of the database. It is useful to look at the database requirements from each actor's point of view.

**Aggregate Function** An SQL function that operates on several rows at a time. These are functions like COUNT, AVG, and SUM.

**Alias** Providing an alternative name for a column or table in SQL to make the results more readable.

**AND** SQL Boolean operator that joins conditions in a WHERE clause. With an AND operator, both conditions must evaluate as true for the criteria to be true.

**AS** SQL keyword used to alias columns or tables.

**AS** SQL keyword used to mark the start of the body of a View, Stored Procedure, or a Trigger.

**Attribute** A quality that describes or defines some aspect of a database entity. Attributes often correspond to the columns in the table created in the physical design process.

**Authentication** Used in Security and Logins. Authentication determines if users are who they claim to be. This can be done with user name and password, with certifications, or by other means.

**Authorization** Authorization is the granting of permissions on objects in the database.

**BEGIN** SQL keyword used to begin a block of code.

**BETWEEN** SQL operator used in the WHERE clause that returns all values BETWEEN two values. It is inclusive of the ends.

**Business Intelligence** Business intelligence involves analyzing database data for valuable trends, patterns, or other information. Many database management systems include suites of tools to facilitate this kind of analysis. Business intelligence is often associated with data warehousing.

**Business Rule** A business-specific rule about how data is captured, stored, and/or processed. For instance, a valid grade point must be between 0 and 4.0.

**Cardinality** Cardinality refers to the number of allowed instances of a relationship. In the usual cardinality of one to many, for instance, each record on the one side can have zero to any number of records on the many side. Cardinality can be more specific however. Each patron at a library can have only 20 items checked out at once. This has a cardinality of 0 to 20.

**CATCH** SQL keyword used in error trapping as part of a TRY CATCH structure. CATCH catches all errors that occur in the TRY block and contains any SQL code to deal with those errors.

**Client** An application that calls on a service offered by a server. For instance, a Web browser requesting a specific Web page from an Internet server.

**Closed-Ended Question** A question with limited possible responses, such as a multiple choice or a ranking.

**COMMIT** SQL keyword used with TRANSACTION. COMMIT executes all SQL statements in the transaction and writes any changes to the database.

**Composite Key** A key that consists of more than one attribute. No entity has more than a single key, but that key can consist of multiple attributes.

**Constraints** Limits on values or actions. For instance, the Primary Key constraint limits a column to unique values; a Foreign Key constraint limits the Foreign Key column to values that exist in the Primary Key table.

**CREATE** SQL keyword for creating objects such as TABLE, VIEW, PROCEDURE, TRIGGER, and so on.

**Cross Join** An SQL join that joins each row of the first table to every row of the second table. Sometimes called a "Cartesian Dump."

**Crow's Feet Notation** A type of notation for entity relationships in entity relation diagrams that depicts the many side of a relationship with a three-pronged end called a "crows foot." This type of notation provides more information about the cardinality of a relationship than the arrow notation for relationships.

**Data integrity** Refers to the accuracy and quality of the data.

**Data Mining** Data mining is the process of querying vast quantities of disparate types of data looking for statistic trends and patterns that provide business intelligence.

**Data Types** Columns in a table are assigned a data type to help constrain the data they can contain. Data types basically fall into character type data, numerical data, date and time data, and large file data such as pictures or whole documents. Some DBMSs add other data types such as XML, geographical, or geometrical data.

**Data Warehouse** A data warehouse is a collection of data from disparate sources used in data mining.

**Database Transactions** Every action that occurs in a database is a transaction. Transactions are processed as a whole and either committed or rolled back. Transactions can be manually controlled in SQL with the BEGIN TRAN keywords.

**DDL** Data Definition Language. Refers to that part of SQL that is concerned with creating and modifying database objects.

**Declarative Language** A language like SQL where programmers declare *what* they want to do, not *how* they want to do it.

**DECLARE** SQL keyword used to declare a new SQL variable.

**DEFAULT_DATABASE** SQL keyword used to assign a default database to an SQL Login.

**DELETE** SQL keyword used to delete one or more rows of data.

**Deletion Anomalies** Where removing data in one table leaves data "orphaned" in another table. For example, deleting a customer leaves orders without a customer making the order. Also where deleting a row unintentionally deletes needed information—removing the last item in a category, for instance, removes the category as well.

**Delimited files** Text files with values separated by a delimiter such as a comma or tab.

**Denormalization** The process of combining tables that had been separated through the process of normalization in order to improve application performance.

**DESC** SQL keyword used to sort a column in descending order.

**Disaster Recovery Plan** A plan preparing for database and business recovery after any of a variety of disasters.

**DISTINCT** SQL keyword used to return only unique rows in a query.

**DML** Data Manipulation Language: The portion of SQL used for querying, inserting, updating, and deleting data from tables.

**Domain** The business problem area. In an Inventory database, for example, the domain would include things like products, suppliers, orders from suppliers, and so on.

**Domain entities** Those database entities that relate directly to the business problem under consideration.

**END** SQL keyword which terminates a block of code.

**Entity** An object of concern to a database, such as a customer or sale. Used in the logical design phase of a database.

**Entity Relation Diagrams** A diagram that shows entities, their attributes, and the relationships among them.

**Equi Joins** A join of two or more tables where the relationship between tables is expressed with the = sign. In some older DBMSs, this is the only way to perform a join. (The term is also used sometimes to describe any join that has equality as a criteria.)

**Exception** A variation from the rule. For instance, the rule is no discounts for customers, but an exception is made for one very long-term customer.

**EXISTS** SQL keyword used with subqueries to see if a value exists in the result set.

**First Normal Form** In 1NF, all multivalued attributes and all arrays or lists are separated into unique rows.

**Fixed-width files** Text files, with each column occupying a set width.

**Foreign Key** A primary key from one table repeated in a second table in order to create a relationship between the tables.

**Form** A form is used to take data entry, whether on the Web, in Windows, or on paper.

**FROM** SQL keyword used with a **SELECT** statement to specify which table or tables are being used.

**Functional Dependencies** When two or more attributes depend on each other for meaning rather than on the table key. These can be spotted by blocks of repetition. They represent separate themes and should be broken into separate tables.

**GRANT** SQL keyword used in granting permissions on objects.

**GROUP BY** SQL keyword used for sorting table by given columns.

**HAVING** SQL keyword used for criteria which include an aggregate function. For example: HAVING AVG(Price)<100.

**IF** SQL keyword used for branching conditions.

**INNER JOIN** SQL keyword used for joining two tables. Inner joins return all matching records in both tables.

**INSERT** SQL keyword beginning a statement to insert a record into a table.

**Insertion Anomalies** Anomaly where one cannot insert a record because another is required, but one cannot insert that record because it depends on the previous record and so on.

**INTO** SQL keyword used with the **INSERT** statement to specify the table where the insertion will occur.

**IS NULL** SQL keywords used in a **WHERE** clause to determine if a column value is null or not.

**LIKE** SQL keyword used in a **WHERE** clause to search for a pattern in character data. Used with wildcards "%" and "_." The wildcard "%" is used for any number of characters; "_" is used for a single character.

**Linking entity** An entity used to resolve a many-to-many relationship into two one-to-many relationships.

**Logical design** The design of a database without regard to the physical implementation of the database.

**LOGIN** SQL keyword used in creating a new login to SQL Server.

**Lookup entity** An entity used to store lookup values such as state names or zip codes.

**Management Information System** A database system designed to provide management-level information such as profit and loss statements, sale summaries, and so on.

**Maximum cardinality** The highest number of allowed relationships.

**Minimum cardinality** The least number of allowed relationships.

**Naming conventions** Conventions for naming database objects in order to maintain consistency and readability.

**Natural Key** A key that naturally occurs in the attributes of an entity, such as a student ID or a course name.

**Normal Forms** Normal forms are sets of principles and practices meant to remove data anomalies from databases. Each originated as a white paper on how to remove specific types of anomalies from data sets.

**NOT** SQL Boolean operator used in the **WHERE** clause to exclude a value from the results.

**Null** A null is an unknown value. It is not the same as a 0 or an empty string. As an unknown, it cannot be evaluated with = <> !.

**ON** SQL keyword used with an **INNER JOIN**, to introduce a clause that shows how two tables relate.

**Open-Ended Question** A question without a set number of responses.

**PASSWORD** SQL keyword, part of **CREATE LOGIN**.

**Permission** The right to do some action in the database such as **SELECT, UPDATE,** or **DELETE**.

**Physical design** The design of the database within a particular DBMS. The physical design takes account of file systems and disk locations as well as DBMS-specific data types.

**Policies** A list of rules for dealing with events or tasks.

**Primary Key** A constraint that uniquely identifies each row in a table. The primary key is repeated in other tables as a foreign key in order to make relationships between tables.

**Problem Domain** The part of the database design that deals with the specific business-related objects and concerns.

**Procedural Language** A programming language like C#, Java, or C++ in which the programmer specifies the procedure or steps to do a task. A procedural language defines *how* to do something, whereas a declarative language describes *what* to do.

**Procedure** A collection of parameters, SQL statements, and variables that are executed together as a single program to accomplish a task.

**PROCEDURE (PROC)** SQL keyword used when creating or modifying a stored procedure.

**Qualified Name** In SQL, a column can be qualified to distinguish it from other columns with the same name. A qualified column consists of the table name, a dot, and the column name. For example, Table1.Column1. A fully qualified column consists of ServerName.DatabaseName.SchemaName.TableName.ColumnName.

**Redundancy** Redundancy refers to data that is repeated in multiple places in a database.

**Referential Integrity** Referential integrity refers to enforcing the constraints of primary key–foreign key relationships. Specifically, you cannot insert a value into a child table unless it exists in the parent table. You update the foreign key column of a child table if it would change it to a value that is not in the parent table. You cannot delete a record from the parent table if it has related records in a child table, unless you first delete the records in the child table.

**Relational Database** A database that stores data related in two-dimensional tables, where unique column values from one table repeated in another table form relationships.

**Relational Design** The process of identifying the entities, attributes, and relations among elements of data related to a specific business problem.

**Report** Output of summary material from data.

**Requirement** Something a database or program must do to fulfill its function.

**ROLE** In a database, a set of permissions related to a particular use of a database.

**ROLLBACK** Used with a **TRANSACTION, ROLLBACK** undoes all SQL statements since the **BEGIN TRAN** statement.

**Scalar Function** An SQL function that operates on one table row at a time.

**Schema** Schema has several related meanings. On the one hand, it is the structure of a database and its tables; on the other, it is the structure of ownership of objects. "dbo," for instance, is the default schema for database objects. Lastly, it can be an XML document that describes the structure of another XML document.

**Second Normal Form** The removal of functional dependencies. The separation of broad themes into separate themes.

**Server** A program that offers services to a client application. For instance, a Web server offers Web pages to a browser; a database server offers data to a client requesting it.

**SQL** The language that is most commonly used in relational database to define database objects (DDL) and to manipulate data (DML).

**Stakeholder** Someone who has a "stake" in the success or contents of the database.

**Statement of work** A statement of what needs to be done often including a history of the problem, a statement of scope, objectives of the project, timelines, and deliverables.

**Stored procedures** See procedures.

**Surrogate Key** A primary key usually numerical and often automatically generated. It has no meaning but uniquely identifies each row.

**Third Normal Form** Removes transient dependencies. These occur where one column is more closely related to another column in the table than the primary key. Transient dependencies should be separated into their own table.

**Transact SQL** Microsoft's version SQL.

**Transaction Database** A database used to store data from immediate transactions such as the point of sale data or real-time activities of various types. Transaction database needs to be fast and often must be available 24x7.

**Transient Dependencies** Transient dependencies occur when one column depends on another column, not the key, for its meaning. Transient dependencies are more subtle than functional dependencies, but they also should be broken into separate entities.

**Trigger** A trigger is a collection of SQL commands that are executed when a database event occurs such as an **INSERT, UPDATE,** or **DELETE.**

**TRY** SQL keyword used with a **TRY CATCH** structure to capture errors. All the codes in a **TRY** block will be tested. If an error occurs, the execution will jump to the **CATCH** block.

**Unicode** An expanded text standard that includes definitions for most language and character groups, not just English. The first 255 characters are equivalent to the ASCII standard.

**Update Anomalies** An update anomaly occurs when a record must be updated in more than one table. Errors in entry can make it so that the records no longer agree in their values. To avoid this, a database should be normalized so that any update of a record occurs in only one place.

**USER** SQL keyword which specifies a **USER** with permissions in a particular database.

**User Access** Refers to what permissions each user should be granted in a particular database, and which database objects they will be able to see and use.

**VIEW** SQL keyword: A **VIEW** is a stored query which organizes data for a particular *view* of the database.

**Weak entities** A weak entity is an entity that depends on another entity for its meaning. For instance, a table of employee dependents which relies on an Employee table for its meaning.

**WITH** SQL keyword used to assign properties in a statement.

**Work Shadowing** The act of following someone, as he or she performs the duties of his or her job, to see what the job entails and what actions he or she typically performs during the workday.

**XML** Unicode-based markup language that conforms to a small set of rules ensuring consistency. It is used for document file formats and to transfer data between databases and applications.

# INDEX